The Journey to
Separate but Equal

MADAME DECUIR'S QUEST
FOR RACIAL JUSTICE IN THE
RECONSTRUCTION ERA

Jack M. Beermann

University Press of Kansas

Published by the University Press of Kansas (Lawrence, Kansas 66045), which was
organized by the Kansas Board of Regents and is operated and funded by Emporia
State University, Fort Hays State University, Kansas State University, Pittsburg State
University, the University of Kansas, and Wichita State University.

Library of Congress Cataloging-in-Publication Data

Names: Beermann, Jack M., author.
Title: The journey to separate but equal : Madame DeCuir's quest for racial justice in
the Reconstruction era / Jack M. Beermann.
Description: [Lawrence] : University Press of Kansas, [2021] | Includes index.
Identifiers: LCCN 2020036228
  ISBN 9780700631834 (cloth)
  ISBN 9780700631841 (ebook)
Subjects: LCSH: Race discrimination—Law and legislation—United States—History—
19th century. | Equality before the law—United States—History—19th century. | Race
discrimination—Law and legislation—Louisiana—History—19th century. | African
Americans—Civil rights—Louisiana—History—19th century. | Louisiana—Race
relations—History. | Reconstruction (U.S. history, 1865–1877) | DeCuir, Josephine.
Classification: LCC KF4757 .B343 2021 | DDC 342.7308/73—dc23
LC record available at https://lccn.loc.gov/2020036228.

British Library Cataloguing-in-Publication Data is available.

Printed in the United States of America

10 9 8 7 6 5 4 3 2 1

The paper used in this publication is recycled and contains 30 percent postconsumer
waste. It is acid free and meets the minimum requirements of the American National
Standard for Permanence of Paper for Printed Library Materials Z39.48-1992.

To the memory of my grandmothers,

Leona Beermann

and

Rose Stern

I cannot conclude without expressing the fond and sincere hope, that the time may speedily come when a fostering government may by wise laws and a mild administration, aided by an independent judiciary, venerable by its gravity, its inflexible integrity, its benign dignity, profound wisdom, and official independence and supported by a willing, patriotic people, inspired by a unity of political purposes, and striving for the general welfare, may submerge and do away with every necessity for investigations of causes like this, and when all distinctions germinating in prejudice, and unsupported by law, may be finally forgotten, and when the essential unity of American citizenship shall stand universally confessed and sincerely acquiesced in by the national family.

—*From the opinion of Judge E. North Collum,*
Fifth District Court, New Orleans, Louisiana,
in Decuir v. Benson, *June 14, 1873*

CONTENTS

PREFACE AND ACKNOWLEDGMENTS

Sometime around 2010, the title of a law review article in the *Harvard Civil Rights-Civil Liberties Law Review* caught my eye: "The Tyranny of the Minority: Jim Crow and the Counter-Majoritarian Difficulty." The central point of the article, written by Gabriel Chin, then a law professor at the University of Arizona Law School, and Randy Wagner, then a researcher at the same school, was that the violent overthrow of Reconstruction-era governments across the South raised serious questions about the legitimacy of the current governments of those states. The article cited a case I had never heard of, *Hall v. Decuir*, describing it as involving a Louisiana "non-discrimination statute, struck down by the Supreme Court in 1877." Having studied Supreme Court civil rights decisions of the era, I found it difficult to believe that such a decision existed and that I had never heard of it. Despite all I knew about the Supreme Court's dismantling of Congress's program of Radical Reconstruction, I doubted that the US Supreme Court had invalidated a *state* antidiscrimination statute. I immediately read the opinions in *Hall v. Decuir* and then, in a short while, found the complete printed record in the case. A bit more research, including a couple of trips to Louisiana to read the original state court files and visit "the scene of the crime," and I was off on a yearslong journey to document this little-known first step toward Supreme Court approval of race-based segregation in US society. The project took me longer than it should have, mainly because I had never engaged in this sort of writing before. My scholarly work until now has largely focused on legal doctrine, and my books are all in the textbook and study-aid genre. But the more I learned about *Hall v. Decuir* the more interesting I found it, and the more I realized that I would have to document its history as best as I could.

Many people helped me in various ways during the several years that I worked on this project. First and foremost, I want to thank Julie Lee, an independent historian and Decuir descendant who specializes in Louisiana, Pointe Coupée Parish, and Decuir family history from the earliest days of European exploration through the

Reconstruction era. Julie generously shared her archive about the Decuir family with me and showed me around the New Roads area, including a visit to Madame Decuir's home on the False River. New Roads historian Brian Costello was similarly generous with his time and knowledge of the history, people, and culture of the False River area and the Decuir and Dubuclet families.

I owe special thanks to two distinguished historians for help, advice, and encouragement: Rebbeca J. Scott of the University of Michigan and Mary Frances Berry of the University of Pennsylvania. Joe Singer at Harvard Law School also provided helpful input. I benefited greatly from input at faculty workshops at the Boston University School of Law, New York Law School, and the University of Washington School of Law, and from classroom presentations at the Boston University School of Law and Vermont Law School. My colleagues (current and former) at Boston University also provided help and advice, including Kristin Collins, David Seipp, Paul Gugliuzza, Gary Lawson, Keith Hylton, and David Lyons.

The research for this book was conducted in numerous libraries with the aid of incredibly helpful librarians who consistently went out of their way for me. In addition to the amazing librarians at the Fineman and Pappas Law Libraries at the Boston University School of Law, I was assisted by Florence Jumonville at the University of New Orleans Library (where Louisiana Supreme Court records are housed), and Sonnet Ireland and Irene Wainwright at the New Orleans Public Library (where New Orleans trial court records are housed). At the New Orleans Public Library, the librarians carefully placed case files that had probably not been opened in more than one hundred years into a humidifier overnight so they would not disintegrate when opened for examination. I did encounter a couple of problems with the files—Antoine Dubuclet's pledge for security for costs was glued to Madame Decuir's complaint, and because I was not allowed to detach it, I could not read the entire handwritten document. Also, some of the pages of E. K. Washington's divorce complaint had fallen to pieces, and although I was able to read the sentence in which he claimed a familial connection to George Washington, part of the document was not legible. I also did research at the Pointe Coupée Parish Library in New Roads, Louisiana; Harvard Law Library; the National Archives; the Library of Congress; and the Brown Research Library at the Maine Historical Society.

I had the benefit of excellent research assistance from a number of Boston

University law students, including Lydia Cuddeback, Alice Kuo, Jacob Shapiro, Daniel Storms, and Marissa Tripolsky, as well as Danielle Goldman, then an undergraduate student at Vanderbilt University.

I also want to thank my literary agents Lynn Chu and Glen Hartley for their support and encouragement, including help improving the manuscript. Thank you also to the University Press of Kansas and the two anonymous reviewers who provided valuable advice. And extra special thanks to Azriel Shiloh for producing the family tree.

Thanks also to the Boston University School of Law for financially supporting this project through sabbatical leave, summer research stipends, and travel funding for research trips.

Although many people helped bring this project to fruition, I alone am responsible for any errors of fact and judgment it may contain.

The Journey to
Separate but Equal

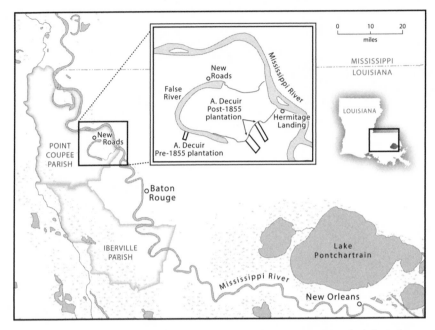

Map of route from New Orleans to Pointe Coupée Parish, with detail of the False River Area. Created by Erin Greb Cartography.

Dubuclet/Decuir Family Tree

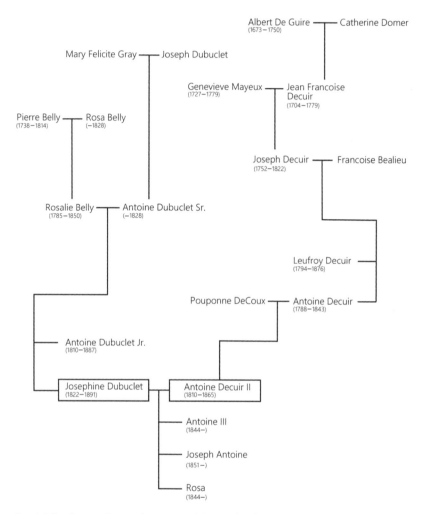

Partial family tree for Madame Josephine Dubuclet Decuir and Antoine Decuir II. Created by Azriel Shiloh.

INTRODUCTION

Plessy v. Ferguson is the iconic nineteenth-century post–Civil War US Supreme Court decision on race. *Plessy* upheld Louisiana's requirement that railroads provide "equal, but separate" passenger facilities on railroad travel within the state.[1] In what has been called a "long forgotten" decision, nearly twenty years before *Plessy*, in *Hall v. Decuir* the Supreme Court held that the Reconstruction-era Louisiana state government could not prohibit racial segregation on riverboats operating on the Mississippi River.[2] *Plessy* may have been the pinnacle of the Supreme Court's embrace of separate but equal, but *Hall* had planted important seeds two decades earlier, the first milestone in the "conventional account" of the institutionalization of racial segregation in transportation in the United States.[3] While *Plessy* is among the more studied nineteenth-century Supreme Court decisions, *Hall v. Decuir*, its history and its context, has received little attention beyond a small group of legal historians. This book aims to correct that oversight through a detailed study of the litigation record of the case as well as an examination of the lives and circumstances of the parties, attorneys, and judges in this fascinating period in Louisiana's history.[4]

This book centers around the story of Madame Josephine Decuir's complaint that she had been illegally barred from the cabin reserved for White women on the riverboat the *Governor Allen*, a steamer likely named for Civil War–era Louisiana governor Henry Watkins Allen who had risen to the rank of brigadier general in the Confederate army. It is also the story of how, after the Civil War, the US Supreme Court chose to perpetuate the subjugation of the non-White population of the United States by actively preventing a Southern state from prohibiting segregation.

The litigation in *Hall v. Decuir* spanned the pivotal period of 1872 to 1878, during which White segregationist Democrats "redeemed" the South from Republican control. When Madame Decuir refused to be seated in the "colored" section of the boat, she was asserting what Rebecca Scott and others have called a "public right"—basically, a right to human dignity that would soon be obliterated by the full force of Jim Crow.[5] The decision was a signal that the always-free colored population of Louisiana would lose its privileged status in Louisiana's culture and that Americans of African descent—its elite as well as newly freed slaves—were consigned to the bottom rung of the legal and social ladder. It was also a pivotal period for French-speaking people of color in Louisiana. The coalition between French-speaking colored aristocracy and freedmen that brought *Plessy v. Ferguson* as a test case illustrates that people of Madame Decuir's class realized that the White establishment no longer recognized them as a racial or social group distinct from former slaves.

The Case

Hall v. Decuir was an early case in the development of the judicial doctrine and social practice of "separate but equal." The dispute arose out of the refusal of Captain (and owner) John Benson of the riverboat the *Governor Allen* to provide Madame Decuir, née Dubuclet, with a stateroom in the "ladies' cabin," the area of the boat reserved for White women. At the time of Madame Decuir's July 1872 trip from New Orleans to Hermitage Landing, Louisiana's 1868 constitution and an 1869 statute prohibited racial segregation and exclusion in many public places, including all modes of transportation. Captain Benson's actions were thus clearly illegal but were just as clearly supported by the near-universal custom of racial segregation on riverboats in Louisiana. Captain Benson based his refusal on that custom, and on the potential negative effects he claimed integration would have on his business.

Madame Decuir was a French-speaking woman of color whose family, and that of her husband's, except for her maternal grandmother, had not in living memory been enslaved. She belonged to a privileged class of French-speaking mixed-race people with a long and storied history in Louisiana. When she brought the case, her brother, Antoine Dubuclet, was treasurer of the state of Louisiana, and he supported her efforts in the litigation. The purpose of Madame Decuir's trip was to accompany her new lawyers, the White ex-Northerner Eugene. K. Washington and his associate, French-speaking man-of-color Seymour R. (S. R.) Snaer, upriver to Pointe Coupée Parish to examine records related to the succession of her late husband's property. Her husband, Antoine Decuir II, a one-time wealthy plantation owner, had died in 1865. Like many in the South, Antoine's finances suffered greatly during and after the Civil War, and disputes over the remnants of his property were still ongoing in 1872 when Madame Decuir engaged Washington's services.

Madame Decuir was not simply asserting a legal right to color-blind treatment on the *Governor Allen*. Her case was an effort to assert her right, and with it the right of all people of color, to equal dignity and respect in post-slavery United States. The Louisiana Supreme Court recognized this when it characterized her treatment on the *Governor Allen* as "a gross indignity to her personally." In fact, dignity was a consistent and prominent theme in discussions about slavery and racial justice, and the post–Civil War era placed US society at a crossroads, with an open question concerning whether people of color would be provided with the full dignity of personhood and citizenship to which they were legally entitled.[6]

From the defendant's perspective, the litigation was less about Madame Decuir's treatment on the *Governor Allen*, which Captain John Benson did not dispute, than about the practice of segregation on riverboats. Benson sought to justify his practice as a universal custom and reasonable and necessary for business on the Mississippi River. And his view, and the litigation, was supported by several steamboat captains and other boat officials called as witnesses. According to the testimony for the defense, all boats operating on the Mississippi had separate (but equal) quarters for colored passengers, and if segregation was not allowed, business would suffer. Madame Decuir's witnesses testified to the contrary—that colored passengers were ill-treated and humiliated by segregation.[7] They were asserting their right, termed "public rights" at the time, to be treated in all public matters as full and equal members of society.[8] For women of color, there was the added significance of their special vulnerability to abuse and the indignity that would result from the failure to separate the sexes in the colored areas of riverboats.

Madame Decuir won her case in the state trial court. She was awarded $1,000 in damages, then successfully defended the verdict in the Louisiana Supreme Court. On Benson's appeal to the US Supreme Court (ultimately prosecuted by his widow and administratrix Eliza Jane Hall), the court reversed, holding that Louisiana lacked the power to prohibit discrimination on the *Governor Allen* because it was engaged in interstate commerce on the Mississippi River.

Pause for a moment to consider what the Supreme Court did here. Rather than use the power of federal law to advance equality and freedom for people of color, it frustrated the cause. When Republicans, including people of color, briefly controlled the government of Louisiana (as well as other Southern states) after the Civil War, Louisiana's Constitution and laws prohibited segregation in public accommodations and transportation. But White Southerners chafed at newly freed slaves and other people of color exercising political power over them. With struggles over racial justice festering all over the South, the Supreme Court prevented Louisiana from enforcing its laws against segregation. *Hall v. Decuir* was one of many blows cast in this period by the Supreme Court against civil rights enforcement but the only one in which the Court prevented a Southern state from using its *own law* to protect Black people from discrimination. That is what makes a deeper inquiry into this case, its run-up and its consequences, so worthwhile.

With hindsight we can now see that *Hall v. Decuir* was a significant milestone in the march toward Jim Crow. *Hall v. Decuir* was seen as a tragedy in the Black community—even more so as time went on. With the Compromise of 1877 in which Republicans agreed to abandon supervision of the racial practices of Southern states in exchange for victory in a disputed presidential election, people of color throughout the United States could see the writing on the wall. Slowly but surely, "redeemed" Southern governments disenfranchised Black people and relegated them to second-class status. While many enacted "equal but separate" rules for transportation, they were much better at enforcing "separate" than "equal." Had the Supreme Court thrown its weight behind racial equality in *Hall v. Decuir* and other decisions in the postwar period, the history of segregation and exclusion may have been very different.

The Supreme Court's decision in *Hall v. Decuir* was an early application of the negative, or dormant, aspect of the Commerce Clause, a doctrine under which the grant of power to Congress to regulate "commerce . . . among the several states" is viewed as implying federal exclusivity in certain matters of interstate commerce. Since the birth of the Republic, the Court had threatened states with Commerce Clause review of their laws, but not until 1872, the year that Madame Decuir traveled on the *Governor Allen*, did it actually strike down a state law for interfering with interstate commerce. *Hall v. Decuir* is therefore interesting not only for what it says about race, but because of its role in the development of Supreme Court doctrine on the Commerce Clause, which was an important step in the Court's perception that it should partner with Congress to safeguard the national economy from state interference.[9]

The litigation in *Hall v. Decuir* took place against the background of the convulsive legal changes that occurred in the aftermath of the Civil War, which historian Eric Foner has termed a "second founding." Three constitutional amendments and four civil rights statutes were enacted into law in the period from 1865 through 1875, all best understood as attempts to grant people of color in the United States legal status equal to that of Whites. The Thirteenth Amendment abolished slavery; the Fourteenth Amendment, in its most familiar provisions, established birthright citizenship, granted all citizens the privileges and immunities of citizenship, and guaranteed all persons the right to due process and equal protection; and the Fifteenth Amendment granted Black men the right to vote. Civil rights statutes enforcing these constitutional provisions were passed in 1866, 1870, 1871, and 1875. However, the "second founding" was in effect virtually dismantled by Supreme Court decisions, lax federal enforcement, and state resistance. Thus, although the case is important as an early application of the Dormant Commerce Clause, it is best understood as a step in the march toward enshrining the social practice of Jim Crow in the law of the United States.[10]

The Evidence

The complete record of testimony in *Hall v. Decuir* has been preserved, providing a rich and fascinating glimpse into racial attitudes in post–Civil War Louisiana, including those of socially and politically powerful French-speaking people of color. Because the defendant admitted that the *Governor Allen* was segregated by race, Madame Decuir's case focused on the importance of the custom of segregation and the quality (or inequality) of its facilities for non-Whites. On the latter issue, the record contains compelling testimony from mixed-race high-status men of color of Madame Decuir's social class. These men compared the colored area to a pen for animals—and certainly no place for a lady. On some boats, high-status people of color were given rooms in the area reserved for Whites, but the doors of these rooms that led to the common eating and lounging area would be locked, with the only exit from this room to the outside on what was called "the guards." This was the "equal" treatment riverboat captains claimed to provide their colored passengers. There are hints, but only hints, of how the custom of segregation was related to the ethic that segregation was necessary to safeguard White womanhood, which was viewed as the "personif[ication] of the South itself."[11] The case is thus a glimpse into the origins and early experience of the social practice of "separate but equal."

The People

Chief Justice Waite's opinion for the Court in *Hall v. Decuir* reflects none of the actual emotion of Madame Decuir's case against Captain Benson. Yet the case was potentially revolutionary, which leads one to ask, Who was she? What in her life had led her to bring such a suit? What lawyers would take on such a case? Who were the Louisiana judges who ruled in her favor? Was Captain Benson's behavior out of the ordinary, or typical, for the captain of a riverboat at that time and place? What about his lawyers? Was this a political test case for them or just routine representation of a business client?

Madame Decuir was a French-speaking mixed-race woman, born free in Iberville Parish, Louisiana, just downriver from Pointe Coupée where she later lived with her husband Antoine Decuir II. The Dubuclets were successful planters, and her brother, also named Antoine, was reputed to be one of the wealthiest men of color in Louisiana. He was the elected treasurer of the state of Louisiana at the time the litigation began. She had lived in Paris for more than ten years with her two children, returning to Louisiana after the death of her husband. She was of the higher class of French-speaking Louisianans of color, and apparently suffered greatly when it became apparent that her husband had left her with debts far exceeding the value of their property. Her trip on the *Governor Allen* was part of an effort to see if anything more could be salvaged from her husband's estate.

Little is known about the life of Captain Benson. He was born around 1824, perhaps in Ohio. He spent his professional life on riverboats, came to New Orleans after the Civil War, and had owned the *Governor Allen* for only a short time before the incident that led to the litigation. He was supported in the litigation by his competitors and associates in the riverboat industry who saw Madame Decuir's lawsuit as a threat to their businesses. Some testified on Benson's behalf at trial, and many helped post security for his appeal to the Supreme Court. Captain Benson died on November 12, 1875, while the case was pending in the Supreme Court of the United States, and the appeal was then pursued by his widow and executrix Eliza Jane Hall, who was already once a widow when she married Benson just nine days before his death.

The lives of the lawyers in *Hall v. Decuir* also enrich our understanding of the case and its times. As noted, Madame Decuir initially sought E. K. Washington's help with problems relating to the succession of her late husband's property. Washington came to New Orleans from Philadelphia sometime in the 1850s, served in the Confederate military, and married a local woman, Mary Cady, in 1864. For several years in the late 1860s and early 1870s, they were engaged in nasty divorce proceedings, with allegations that today would be worthy of tabloid coverage. Washington was with Madame Decuir on the *Governor Allen* and, together with his associate S. R. Snaer, later represented her in litigation concerning her husband's estate, as well as in her civil rights suit against Captain Benson.

How did Madame Decuir come to choose Washington and Snaer to represent her? Although the historical record is virtually silent on Washington's political leanings and activities, there are a few indications that he may have had a reputation for being friendly to the colored community, or at least willing to take on their legal causes. Perhaps most important to Madame Decuir, he practiced together with lawyer S. R. Snaer, who warned Washington that Madame Decuir would not be happy on the *Governor Allen*. Snaer was a prominent mixed-race lawyer in Reconstruction Louisiana. His brother, Louis A. Snaer, was a Civil War hero on the Union side, serving as an officer in a colored regiment mustered in New Orleans shortly after the Union captured that city in 1862. Louis also served in the Louisiana legislature and at the constitutional convention that wrote the prohibition on discrimination into Louisiana law.

Captain Benson's trial lawyer, Bentinck Egan, was a respected admiralty and commercial lawyer. He was said to have had a large practice that had made him wealthy, following a failed sojourn to California in the mid-nineteenth century. After death, he was eulogized as zealously devoted to his clients and his family. At the US Supreme Court, Benson was represented by lawyer Robert H. (R. H.) Marr. Marr later served briefly on the Supreme Court of Louisiana and then as a longtime state trial judge in criminal court. During the 1860s and 1870s, he took up the cause of restoring White rule and resisted calls for integration and racial equality. Marr died mysteriously in 1892, reportedly last seen walking on the levee in New Orleans, and was replaced on the criminal court bench by John Ferguson, the judge/defendant in *Plessy v. Ferguson.*

Who were the judges and justices who heard and decided the case? Would Louisiana state court judges appointed during the turmoil of Reconstruction all be Republican loyalists predisposed to favor Madame Decuir's claim? Little information remains about E. North Collum, the Louisiana state trial court judge who awarded Decuir $1,000 in damages (and rejected her request for punitive damages). Judge Collum was a Democrat. His father, a carpenter turned lawyer, once assisted a slave owner's efforts to regain ownership of a man of color who had lived free for a period. Judge Collum concluded his opinion in Madame Decuir's case with an eloquent and impassioned plea for racial harmony under the banner of United States citizenship, so although he was not a Republican, he may have been generally sympathetic to Madame Decuir's cause.

Chief Justice John T. Ludeling, who wrote the opinion of the Louisiana Supreme Court upholding Madame Decuir's judgment, was a well-known Republican moderate who had opposed Louisiana's secession. Despised by Louisiana Democrats, he had once been forced to hide out in his home due to death threats during a political campaign. His son Frederick was murdered in 1881 in a dispute over the employment of colored laborers on the Ludeling plantation. The killers were acquitted, a result attributed to the anti-Republican sentiment in Louisiana at the time.

Chief Justice Morrison Waite wrote the US Supreme Court's opinion overturning the state court decisions in favor of Madame Decuir. Waite was an Ohio Republican and a moderate on race. As chief justice, he apparently excelled in minimizing disagreement at the Court, maintaining good personal relations with justices with whom he often disagreed. The Court he led, however, made a number of decisions that effectively dismantled the Radical Republicans' legislative program in pursuit of racial justice, paving the way for the decision in *Plessy v. Ferguson.*

The Aftermath

Like many Louisiana plantation owners, Madame Decuir's family fortune was wiped out by the Civil War. The war halted most business in the area, and when Northern troops invaded Pointe Coupée Parish in 1863, they seized any property that could aid in the war effort, including substantial livestock and stores from the Decuir plantation. Further, a large portion of the family wealth consisted of slaves who were freed at the end of the war. She and her husband owned dozens of slaves, perhaps more than one hundred, and her brother Antoine owned a similar number, placing them among the wealthiest families of color in antebellum Louisiana. Ultimately, most if not all of her late husband's remaining property was sold to pay off the estate's debts. After losing her plantation property, Madame Decuir lived the rest of her life with her daughter Rosa on Marigny Street in the neighborhood of the same name just outside the French Quarter in New Orleans.[12]

The Supreme Court's decision in *Hall v. Decuir* initiated judicial recognition of the onset of nearly a century of official and unofficial segregation throughout the South. Once the Supreme Court decided *Plessy v. Ferguson*, which permitted official segregation, and held in another case that the federal government lacked the power to end private racial exclusion and segregation, the legal void had been filled.[13] States, through Jim Crow laws, implemented de jure segregation, while the custom of segregation in interstate transportation in the South was pursued de facto if not de jure.[14] *Hall v. Decuir* continued to mark an indefinite boundary between state and federal power well into the civil rights movement of the twentieth century.[15] It was not until 1953 that scholar Sarah M. Lemmon could safely predict that "the present trend of court decisions would indicate that segregation will soon be abolished on interstate carriers if such is a requirement of state laws."[16]

Hall v. Decuir is among the earliest of hundreds of cases brought over racial discrimination in transportation in nineteenth- and twentieth-century America. As historians have amply documented, transportation was a constant source of racial friction in the United States, long before Rosa Parks sparked the Montgomery bus boycott by refusing to relinquish her seat to a White man.[17] Black people who needed to travel had no choice but to use established rail and boat routes on which, in the South, segregation had long been the norm. After *Plessy*, transportation litigation often broke out over whether a person ought to have been treated as White, and over whether the facilities provided to Black people met the rarely enforced legal standard of equality, especially on the rails when they purchased first-class tickets and were provided inferior facilities in the smoking car.[18] As steamboat travel declined, cases about them did too, but *Hall v. Decuir* remained an important marker of segregation in transportation.

Why is the Decuir case not better known today by the general public? In its day, it received significant attention, especially among Black people, who viewed the decision as a great tragedy. For people of color who had looked to the federal government for protection and help in establishing racial justice in the South, nothing could be worse than the Supreme Court deciding that federal law would block state efforts to prohibit discrimination. It ultimately came to be overshadowed by *Plessy v. Ferguson*, so today, only those who focus their study on the Reconstruction era are familiar with it. Legal historian Barbara Welke devoted substantial attention to *Hall v. Decuir* in her 2001 book *Recasting American Liberty: Gender, Race, Law, and the Railroad Revolution, 1865–1920*, and the case has made minor appearances in several additional volumes.[19] Most recently, in "Discerning a Dignitary Offense: The Concept of 'Equal Public Rights' during Reconstruction," historian Rebecca J. Scott explores the themes of dignity and public rights inherent in the case.[20] But it appears in no legal casebooks focused on race in US law or constitutional law. Yet, the case seems to hold a key not only to the development of the Court's "separate but equal" doctrine on race, but to the growth of federal supremacy under the developing doctrine of interstate commerce. In all likelihood, it was overshadowed by decisions such as *Plessy v. Ferguson* and the *Civil Rights Cases* that were more explicitly about race, and it lacked precedential value as Commerce Clause jurisprudence matured.

A note on terminology is in order at this point. First, concerning the use of the terms *of color, colored,* and *Black,* in general, during the time period captured in this book, mixed-race people like Madame Decuir were referred to as "colored" or "of color," while darker-skinned people of African descent were referred to as "Black" or "Negro" (when not referred to by more patently offensive terms). I have often employed the terms *colored* and *of color* the way they would have been used in the nineteenth century and have used *Black* to refer to those who would have been so characterized at the time. *Negro* appears only in quotations or when reporting others' use of the term, along with, unfortunately, some even more offensive terms. At times, the term *of color* appears as a reference to non-White people in contemporary usage. By describing people in racial terms, I do not mean to suggest or endorse the existence of race as a personal characteristic separate from the social conventions of which it is a part. Race is, in my view, a socially constructed tool of stratification and subordination that does not correspond to material reality. Perhaps it would be more accurate to refer to racial strati-fication in the United States as a caste system based in large part on charac-teristics conventionally understood as signifying race.[21] The use of race as a method of categorization in this book is necessary for historical accuracy even though it may partly obscure the social roots of this story and millions of stories like it throughout the history of the United States.

The attentive reader might also notice that the term *Creole* does not ap-pear in this book except when reporting others' use of it. That is by choice. Many people take *Creole* to refer to mixed race or Black residents of Louisi-ana, perhaps only those who speak or spoke French. Others use it to refer to French-speaking Whites in Louisiana and distinguish non-Whites by call-ing them "colored Creoles." Some understand it to exclude those French-speaking Louisianans descended from the Acadians who fled to Louisiana after French Nova Scotia fell to the British in the 1750s and 1760s. By still others, the term is used to refer simply to Louisiana natives, White, Black, or colored. To avoid confusion, I have avoided the term.[22]

1

Louisiana's *Gens de Couleur* and the Decuir and Dubuclet Families

Prologue

On January 14, 1871, Charles Sauvinet—the elected civil sheriff of Orleans Parish, former city alderman, and captain in both the pro-Confederacy 1st Louisiana Native Guard and later the United States Army during the Civil War—went to one of his favorite drinking establishments in New Orleans, Walker's Saloon, also known as the Bank Coffeehouse. The Bank was located at No. 6 Royal Street along Canal Street, close to the United States Customs House building. Sauvinet was a well-known figure in New Orleans and was the Parish's first non-White elected sheriff. He had been to the Bank many times to drink, at least once at Walker's "special invitation." This time, however, Sauvinet was there on official business. The building in which the saloon was located had been seized in legal proceedings, and the sheriff was there to collect the rent. Sauvinet was told to meet the proprietor, Joseph Walker, in his upstairs office. After engaging in some friendly chitchat and handing over the rent, Walker asked Sauvinet if he would like a glass of wine. Sauvinet accepted, but when Walker reached for a bottle of champagne, Sauvinet demurred, explaining that he did not like champagne. The two of them then had a glass of whiskey or cognac instead, after which Walker said, "I have a favor to ask you."[1]

What was this favor? Walker asked Sauvinet to stop coming to his bar to drink. Walker's explanation was that he had been informed that Sauvinet was a "colored" man and that it would harm his business if it were known that he was in the habit of serving him. Sauvinet was taken aback by Walker's request. Although it was widely known that he was colored, and had been so identified in the 1870 election when he became sheriff, Sauvinet had always enjoyed the privilege of drinking "in all houses" and, as he said, "It was too late now for me to go back." Walker did not press the matter, and they parted amicably, with Sauvinet under the impression that he was still welcome at the Bank.[2]

The following week, on January 20, after conducting official business together in his office related to an injunction, Sauvinet and some White friends decided to go out for a noontime drink. Sauvinet proposed that they go to a place he frequented at the corner of Exchange Alley and Bienville Street, in the French Quarter, but his friend W. H. Finnegan objected because "in the French part of the city, there were not good liquors." They then walked by another place, possibly called the Saranac, but again Finnegan demurred, suggesting they go to the Bank where they have "better liquors." When they arrived at the Bank, Sauvinet immediately noticed a "disposition" in the bartender not to serve him. Sauvinet asked for a drink, and the bartender told him he could not serve him and his friends. When asked why not, the bartender's reply was nonsensical: "Never mind, it is all right." Sauvinet's friends were perplexed, and they pressed the bartender for a reason for not serving them, but he kept on giving them the same confusing answer. Finally, Sauvinet informed his companions that the reason was "because I am said to be a colored man."[3]

On January 26, 1871, Sauvinet sued Walker in the Eighth District Court of New Orleans for violating Louisiana's antidiscrimination laws, requesting $10,000 in damages and, as provided in the statute under which he brought suit, forfeiture of Walker and his partner's license to operate.[4] The Louisiana Constitution of 1868 and statutes passed thereunder prohibited race discrimination in transportation, businesses open to the public, and all businesses licensed by the state or local governments.[5] With a speed that present-day lawyers can barely imagine, Sauvinet's case was called to trial on March 1, 1871, less than two months after the incident. The defendant objected to the composition of the jury pool, mainly because Sauvinet, as sheriff, was in charge of assembling the jurors, and he had apparently not observed the formalities required by law for doing so. The judge decided to enlist the parish coroner to assemble a special pool of seventy-five prospective jurors, which he did, and the case came back for trial on March 16 and March 17.[6]

At trial, Sauvinet made it clear that although he had, for at least twenty-five years, been treated socially as a White person in New Orleans, it was widely known that he was colored, and he did not enjoy all of the legal rights of

White people. For example, although he was elected to public office after the war, before the war, he did not even have the right to vote, much less run for office.[7] The defendant offered no testimony, but even without any conflict in the evidence, the jury was unable to come to a unanimous verdict. The Louisiana Reconstruction legislature anticipated the likelihood that White jurors would refuse to find in favor of non-White discrimination claimants, and in February 1871, while Sauvinet's case was pending, the legislature passed a new statute, providing that in the event a jury in a race discrimination case could not agree on a decision, "the case shall be immediately submitted to the Judge upon the pleadings and evidence already on file."[8]

Rather than decide the case immediately, the judge in Sauvinet's case gave the parties ten days to file briefs, and the defendant raised numerous objections to the procedure that allowed the judge to step in for a deadlocked jury, focusing largely on due process and the right to a trial by jury. On April 27, 1871, the trial judge rejected all of the challenges, pointing out that the federal Constitution's right to a jury trial in civil cases applied only in the federal courts. The judge then rendered judgment in favor of Sauvinet. In a lengthy written decision, the judge ordered Walker to pay Sauvinet $1,000 in "exemplary damages" based on his view that "the plaintiff shows an infringement of such civil rights. His citizenship has been degraded." He did not, however, order the forfeiture of Walker's license to operate because Sauvinet had abandoned that request.[9] Walker appealed, and almost four years later, on January 1, 1875, the Louisiana Supreme Court affirmed the judgment, over the objections of two judges who, while agreeing with the verdict, felt that the damages were excessive.[10] Walker again appealed, this time to the US Supreme Court, relying primarily on his argument that depriving him of the benefit of a jury trial violated his right to due process of law. The Supreme Court rejected this appeal, concluding in a brief opinion that all that due process required was that the Louisiana courts apply the procedures specified by Louisiana law.[11]

Why, after twenty-five years of being treated socially, if not legally, as a White person was Sauvinet suddenly excluded by the owner of the Bank? The answer lies in the evolution of racial and social politics that was occurring at the time. The non-White citizens of Louisiana, both recently freed and always free and now legally recognized as citizens of the United States and the state of Louisiana, were asserting their "public right" to be treated with equal dignity and respect in all facets of public life. As mainstream conservative

Whites grew weary of radical Republican and non-White rule, their attitudes on race were hardening into strict maintenance of the segregation and exclusion that had always existed in Louisiana.[12]

The Dubuclet and Decuir Families and Free People of Color in Louisiana

Historically, the free people of color in Louisiana had been recognized both socially and legally as a distinct race from lower status and enslaved Black people, especially in the period before Louisiana became part of the United States. Socially, they enjoyed privileges and economic success that were unavailable to darker-skinned free people known as "Blacks" or "Negroes." In rural areas, they were among Louisiana's most successful planters, with land and slaveholdings rivalling those of the most successful Whites. In New Orleans, they owned valuable real estate, dominated many skilled professions, and operated grocery stores and other retail establishments. Some had brought their skills with them from Senegambia, the area of Africa from which many of Louisiana's slaves had been seized.[13] They were tailors, musicians, furniture makers, silver smiths, writers, and artists, and they made sure that their children received first-class educations, even if that meant sending them to France. Legally, they were recognized as a race distinct from darker-skinned "Negroes."[14] In census documents and legal papers, they were identified as colored or mullato rather than Negro. Early in the nineteenth century, the courts in New Orleans created a presumption that Black people were slaves and that mixed-race people of color were free.[15] After Reconstruction, when Whites regained complete dominance in the Southern states, the always-free people of color lost their special status and were viewed as racially, socially, and legally indistinct from the darker-skinned people previously known as Negroes or Blacks, whether previously free or enslaved.

Madame Josephine Dubuclet Decuir faced this changing social landscape after her return in 1865 to Louisiana from France, and she chafed at the treatment to which she was subjected as a woman of color. She claimed that in France, she had been treated as a "White lady," and even in prewar Louisiana, she was accustomed to special treatment as a member of the middle race of French-speaking lighter-skinned people of color. Madame Decuir could not accept the refusal of ship captains to provide her with accommodations in the area set aside for White ladies. Left with no alternative, she sued, hoping to succeed as Sheriff Sauvinet had succeeded against Walker. Given Sauvinet's notoriety, Madame Decuir was probably aware of his case when she was refused accommodations in the ladies' cabin of the riverboat *Governor Allen*. Her lawyers, E. K. Washington and S. R. Snaer, were also probably aware of it, and their decision to sue Captain John Benson was made much easier by Sauvinet's favorable result. Washington and Madame Decuir may have even discussed Sauvinet's case on the *Governor Allen* as they plotted their legal strategy over Madame Decuir's treatment. However, before getting to the story of Madame Decuir's case against Captain Benson, some background on Louisiana and its people is in order.

Spanish explorers first visited the area that later became Louisiana early in the sixteenth century. The territory they explored was occupied by numerous Native American tribes, including the Atakapa, Tunica, and other groups comprising the Natchez and Choctaw Nations and the Caddo Confederacy. European attempts to settle the area did not begin until the French arrived in the late seventeenth century. By 1722, France claimed a vast expanse of North American land on both sides of the Mississippi River south of the Great Lakes. In 1762, France sold Louisiana to Spain to help finance the French and Indian War but then regained the territory from Spain in 1800 only to sell it to the United States in the Louisiana Purchase of 1803.

In 1719, two events occurred that are integral to the story of Madame Decuir's journey on the *Governor Allen*. The first was the arrival of Louisiana's first African slaves, aboard two French ships from West Africa.[16] Slaves provided the labor that fueled the development of Louisiana as an important planting and commercial hub, and they contributed to the mixture of races and nationalities that made Louisiana ethnically unique in North America. Slavery in the French territories, including Louisiana, was governed by the French Code Noir of 1685 as promulgated for Louisiana in 1724. The Code Noir liberally allowed masters to free their slaves, and provided that once freed, they should enjoy "the same rights, privileges, and immunities which are enjoyed by free-born persons."[17] Masters were also required to observe the Sabbath and were not allowed to work their slaves on Sundays, when slaves would work for themselves to raise funds to purchase their freedom.[18] A significant number of African slaves were also freed by the French for fighting in the 1729 to 1730 Natchez Wars between the French and Native Americans. Many people of color also came to Louisiana as refugees and immigrants after the 1791 to 1804 overthrow of the French government of the colony of St. Domingue in present-day Haiti, either directly from St. Domingue or via Cuba. As a result, more free people of color called Louisiana home than other areas of North America.[19]

The second event of 1719 was the decision of Albert de Cuire or de Guire, of the Macon, Hainaut region of present-day Belgium, to emigrate, with his family, to the colony of Louisiana. He contracted as an indentured servant with the St. Catherine concession, one of a few concessions that had been established in the area around Natchez by the French Company of the Indies. Shortly before the family's planned departure for Louisiana, Albert's wife, Marie Catherine Domer, died, leaving the widowed Albert to travel with their four surviving children to Louisiana. For an unknown reason, when they boarded the *La Loire* at the French port of L'Orient, Albert was assigned on the ship's manifest to the St. Reyne concession, a sister concession of the Sainte Catherine, near what is now St. Francisville, West Feliciana Parish, Louisiana. That was a lucky mistake because, after repeated violent skirmishes with local natives, most of the residents of the St. Catherine concession were killed in what is known as the Natchez massacre of 1729.[20]

Albert and his family arrived at Biloxi in November 1720 and made their way to St. Reyne. Mismanagement, the harsh environment, and the 1729 massacre led the Company of the Indies to close the St. Reyne concession and dismiss their indentured workers. Albert and his children—Anne Catherine, Jean François, Etienne, and Marie Marguerite—remained in the area, settling on the bank of the Mississippi River in what is now Pointe Coupée Parish ("Cut Point" in English), just south of St. Francisville and west of Baton Rouge, Louisiana. The name has something to do with a bend in the Red River in the northern area of the Parish where early explorers found a shortcut through a creek that was in the process of becoming the main channel of the river, "cutting off" the old channel and turning it into the oxbow lake now known as the False River.[21] The most important town in the Parish is New Roads, located at the northern end of the False River, about fifteen miles southwest of St. Francisville. The name New Roads, *Chemin Neuf* in French, came from a road built by the Spanish in the 1770s to connect the False River area with the Mississippi River. The town was laid out in 1822 by Catherine Depau, a free woman of color whose plantation included the land that later became the town at the terminus of the new road.[22]

Albert became a successful planter and a prominent member of the community, helping dedicate the first St. Francis of Assisi Catholic Church, which was located on the bank of the Mississippi River in Pointe Coupée Parish. At some point, the spelling of his family name evolved to Decuir. Life in the Pointe Coupée area remained relatively calm, even through the turmoil of the 1763 transfer of Louisiana from France to Spain.

The Decuir family history took another fateful turn in its third generation in America, when Albert's two grandsons established intimate domestic relationships and fathered children with free women of color. Throughout the eighteenth century and during the early nineteenth century, there were many more White European men than White European women in Louisiana, and a gender imbalance among Black people with fewer Black men than Black women.[23] Although neither interracial marriage nor interracial sexual relationships were legal under Louisiana's Code Noir, sexual relationships between White men and women of color were common in antebellum Louisiana.[24] The social aspects of these interracial relationships was complex and worthy of separate, detailed study. Some of these relationships must have been abusive, like those between master and slave. Others, involving White men and free women of color, resembled marriages, although it was not uncommon for a White man to have a White wife in addition to his colored domestic partner.[25]

Many of these relationships are reputed to have begun in New Orleans at the quadroon balls, so-called because they were said to be frequented by women with one-quarter African blood.[26] The quadroon balls were promoted by entrepreneurs as money-making ventures, sort of the singles dances of their day, providing an opportunity for White men to meet free women of color, mixed-race women who were known for their beauty and grace.[27] There are stories, subject to dispute, of White men procuring young women of color at these balls and entering into relationships known as "plaçage."[28] Historical accounts portray these as economic transactions between White men and the mothers of young women of color, in which the men would promise to support the chosen woman, perhaps even buying a house for her to live in with the children the relationship was expected to produce.[29] Restrictions on interracial marriage and inheritance necessitated creativity in the structuring of these relationships, resulting in the need for explicit advance negotiations and written contracts, which were enforceable at least until the Louisiana Purchase brought more conservative US law to Louisiana. Although these accounts, portraying plaçage as an economic transaction, have been disputed, there is no doubt that there were many White men, married and unmarried, who carried on long-term intimate relationships with women of color for whom they provided economic and familial support. These and other relationships such as those entered into by Albert Decuir's grandsons produced a class of wealthy free people of color who formed a substantial part of Louisiana's third race.[30]

Antoine Decuir's White grandson Joseph began a long-term relationship in the 1780s with Françoise Beaulieu, a free woman of color living in New Orleans. Family lore has it that they met either while Joseph was serving in the Spanish militia or through her brother, also Joseph. She was the daughter of a wealthy and distinguished family—her great-grandfather had been treasurer of the Company of the Indies, and her grandmother and grandfather had their own concession in Tchoupitoulas. Her White father, Louis Chauvin Beaulieu II, had five children with his freed slave Marianne, including Françoise. Joseph brought Françoise to Pointe Coupée to live with him. Although Joseph was listed on his service record as "married," an actual legal marriage between Joseph, a White man, and Françoise, a free woman of color, would have been illegal, unless perhaps they traveled out of the country to be married. They had children together and, whether legally married or not, they lived together as a family, settling on land fronting on the False River in what was known as the Lower False River District, referred to currently as Oscar, that Joseph purchased in 1783 from a pair of local Native American chiefs.[31]

Joseph's brother Antoine had eight children with his domestic partner, Sophie Deslondes, also a free woman of color.[32] The family lived on River Lake Plantation, which Antoine established sometime in the 1790s. Antoine became one of the wealthiest men in Louisiana. Unlike Joseph, but like many other White men in nonmarital relationships with women of color, Antoine married a White woman, the widowed Louise Tanneret.[33] These marriages provided social legitimacy for the married couple and a legally legitimate heir to the family fortune. Antoine provided economically for his "natural children" (as children of nonmarital, interracial relationships were called) with Sophie by a gift of property to their mother in 1836, but due to the racially based marriage and inheritance laws in effect at the time, his daughter with Louise, Antoinette, was Antoine's sole legal heir when he died in 1829, and she inherited the bulk of his estate.[34]

Joseph Decuir and Françoise Beaulieu built a successful plantation on the False River in Pointe Coupée. Françoise died in 1812, and their sons Antoine and Leufroy inherited the plantation their father had given her years before, probably to circumvent the racial restrictions of the inheritance laws. Their sisters inherited personal property and slaves from their mother. After Françoise's death, Joseph fathered another natural child with Claire Quevain, also a free woman of color. When Joseph died in 1822, his natural children inherited half of his estate, which included the plantation, with its more than one hundred slaves, investments, real estate in New Orleans, and a sugar plantation in Cannes Brulée (now known as Kenner), just north of New Orleans. Joseph used part of his share to purchase additional parcels from the estate, and the extended family remained neighbors on the plantations along the False River. They were wealthy, sharing in an estate worth nearly $500,000 in 1822 dollars, which would have had the buying power of approximately $20 million in 2020.[35]

The extended Decuir family lived together as neighbors on a trio of adjoining False River plantations, along with friends and numerous slaves. When Antoine died in 1843, his son Antoine II took over as leader of his branch of the family. Sectional conflict over slavery was a growing problem in the United States at this time, and Antoine II and his uncle Leufroy were concerned about the future of the slave-based plantation system. A recession affected the agricultural economy in the late 1830s and early 1840s, but the Decuir family thrived, in part because they had introduced sugarcane to their agricultural operations in addition to, and later in place of, cotton. In 1855, they decided to sell their plantations along the False River and relocate their own families to smaller holdings in an area a bit to the east known as the *Chenal,* or Channel in English, so-called because of the local canal running from the eastern edge of the False River to the Mississippi River. It was here that Madame Decuir last lived with her husband Antoine Decuir II.[36]

Madame Decuir was born in 1822 as Josephine Dubuclet in Iberville Parish, just downriver from Pointe Coupée. Although three of her four grandparents were people of color, no record remains of enslavement in her family except for her maternal grandmother who was freed by her White owner/ husband. Her paternal grandparents were Joseph Antoine Dubuclet and Marie Felicite Gray. The historical record contains only speculation as to how her non-White ancestors came to be free. The Dubuclets were a successful planter family that originally owned a plantation in the Attakapas area of Louisiana, now St. Martin Parish, later moving east to Iberville Parish.[37] Her maternal grandparents were Pierre Belly, a White man born in France in 1738, and his non-White slave/wife, Marie Rose Belly, born in Jamaica, date unknown, identified as being of the Nago tribe.[38] Beginning in 1785, Pierre and Marie had four daughters together before Pierre freed Marie, and two more after. Pierre was "a judge and by far the wealthiest planter of Iberville Parish."[39] Pierre freed three of his slave-born daughters when they were infants, and he freed Genevieve, born in 1788, together with her mother Rose in 1802. The two born after 1802 were free from birth. Pierre remained a slave owner, reportedly owning ninety-seven slaves when he died in 1814.[40]

Pierre and Rose Belly's oldest daughter, Rosalie, married Antoine Dubuclet Sr. and lived with him on his plantation in Iberville Parish.[41] They had numerous children—one account says eleven, another says nineteen, with five dying in infancy.[42] Their daughter Josephine was one of the later to arrive, sometime around 1822.[43] Antoine Dubuclet Sr. died in 1828 with an estate valued at nearly $20,000, including part ownership of Cedar Grove Plantation. This was substantial, but would not have made his family wealthy. After his death, his eldest son Antoine Jr. remained on the plantation, but most of Antoine Jr.'s siblings, including Josephine, relocated to New Orleans with their mother. Although the plantation was successful in the early years after Antoine Sr.'s death, they were affected like everyone else by the economic downturn of the late 1830s, and Rosalie found it necessary to mortgage her property in New Orleans to provide for her children.[44]

Any financial problems Antoine Dubuclet Jr. experienced after his father's death were ameliorated by his marriage to Claire Pollard, a wealthy free woman of color, sometime in the 1830s. With their combined properties and numerous slaves, Antoine became very wealthy, identified as "not only the largest free Negro slave owner in Louisiana but the richest of his class as well."[45] According to Eric Foner, "On the eve of the Civil War, he owned land worth $100,000 and more than one hundred slaves."[46] As the patriarch of the family, Antoine must have felt some responsibility for the futures of his numerous siblings. For Josephine, he apparently found a husband, Antoine Decuir II of neighboring Pointe Coupée Parish. A marriage contract was agreed to between the two Antoines, and Josephine Dubuclet and Antoine Decuir II were married in New Orleans in 1835. Antoine Dubuclet also found a good match for his younger brother Augustin. He was married, also pursuant to a contract, to the granddaughter of Cyprien Ricard of Iberville Parish, another of the wealthiest men of color in Louisiana.[47]

Antoine Dubuclet was a singular figure in post–Civil War Louisiana. He was an active Republican after the war and was elected Louisiana State Treasurer in 1868 in the election that brought Henry Clay Warmoth, characterized derisively as a "carpetbagger," to the governorship.[48] In that position, Dubuclet fought a difficult battle against the endemic corruption in Louisiana government, even taking the governor and others to court over their attempt to steal part of the proceeds of the sale of government bonds.[49] He won the admiration of White conservatives who condemned Republican attempts to dump him from the ticket in 1874 in favor of a candidate who would be more amenable to corruption. When Democrat Francis Nicholls became governor, Dubuclet was subjected to an intensive investigation, because some Democrats could not believe that he, a colored Republican, had not participated in the corruption of the previous administration. Dubuclet was completely exonerated in this investigation, but Democrats finally replaced him in 1878 with E. A. Burke, an active member of the White League whose mission was to help "take back" the Louisiana government. Burke's corruption promptly sent the state into severe financial distress and he was forced to flee, ultimately living out his life in Honduras as a fugitive from justice.[50]

After her marriage in 1835, Antoine Dubuclet's sister Josephine went to live with her husband Antoine Decuir II on his False River plantation in Pointe Coupée Parish, which later became known as Austerlitz sometime after Antoine and Josephine sold it in 1855. There, they prospered, enjoying life as wealthy planters on their property in Pointe Coupée Parish: "Their total estate, including real property, machinery, livestock, and 112 slaves, had been worth in excess of $150,000."[51] Antoine and Josephine had three children together: Antoine III, born around 1844; Rosa, born around 1847; and Joseph Antoine, born around 1851.[52] As was common for families of French-speaking free people of color at the time, Josephine took their two youngest children to Paris to be educated and to escape the discrimination they suffered as members of Louisiana's third race, which worsened in the 1850s.[53] The family's long-term plan may have been to resettle in France, but any such plan to remain in France was indefinitely interrupted and then made impossible by the devastation of the Civil War and the death of Antoine Decuir II.

While the wealth of the Decuir and Dubuclet families made them far from representative of the free people of color in Louisiana, their relatively high social status as members of Louisiana's third race, the *gens de couleur*, was typical for their time. Because so many of them owned slaves, they participated in slave patrols, and when slaves revolted, as they did in Pointe Coupée Parish in 1795 and more broadly in Louisiana in 1811, the *gens de couleur* would be aligned with Whites in putting down the revolt.[54] At the beginning of the Civil War, many of Louisiana's free people of color supported the Confederacy and even formed a battalion in the Confederate army, although they changed sides as soon as the Union victory in New Orleans became clear.[55]

One reason why free people of color thrived in Louisiana was that many of them were not the product of master-slave or other illicit sexual relationships that would have led to them being socially ostracized or shunned by their fathers. In Louisiana, mixed-race families lived openly, and many fathers provided for their children and did not keep them in slavery as was common elsewhere in the United States. While they were not admitted into White society, and "chafed at the humiliations imposed on them" by not being recognized as full citizens of Louisiana or the United States, mixed-race Louisianans made important economic and cultural contributions that earned them the respect of Whites. They also developed parallel educational and cultural institutions that set them well apart from slaves and lower-caste Black people.[56]

That is not to say that Louisiana's free people of color were satisfied with their status in prewar Louisiana. The imposition of US law after the Louisiana Purchase resulted in more race-based restrictions than they had experienced under the French and Spanish. Numerous free people of color emigrated to France from Louisiana in the years following the transition to US law, although the number is not entirely clear. As Rodolphe Desdunes explained, with regard to the poet Pierre Declour, "It was completely natural that he should return to France, for what man, accustomed from childhood [in France] to contact with civilization, could conform himself to the degradation of slavery and racial prejudice?"[57] To some, the treatment of the *gens de couleur* was "just above the slave level" and certainly worsened in the years immediately preceding the Civil War.[58]

Social inequality became more pronounced after the Civil War. No matter how much money they had or how firmly entrenched they were in the postwar political establishment, they were not the social equals of Whites. Madame Decuir's lawyer explained it years later in his brief to the US Supreme Court: Madame Decuir "never belonged to the servile class. She was, before the war, a large owner of inherited slaves. Before that time she traveled freely both in this country and Europe. . . . It is since the rise of the question of legal equality has begun that more strict social demarcation [*sic*] has taken place on account of color alone, though she is hardly distinguished from one of the Caucasian race."[59]

As Sheriff Sauvinet's experience in the Bank Coffeehouse illustrates, any special privileges Louisiana's free people of color had enjoyed were slipping away, as White racial identity became the organizing political and social principle of the postwar South. Upon her return in 1865, Madame Decuir would discover a transformed Louisiana from the one she left in the 1850s, and for her and people like her, the overthrow of slavery and the legal establishment of racial equality would not make for positive change in the social order. It was against this background that the case of *Hall v. Decuir* arose.

2

Madame Decuir Returns from France and Hires New Lawyers

With six hundred and twenty thousand dead on the battlefield, the Civil War brought personal tragedy to many US families, Northern and Southern. For the four million men, women, and children who were freed from slavery over the course of the war and its immediate aftermath, the end of the war was a time for celebration and excitement. Slave owners, by contrast, lost a great deal of their wealth, and coupled with the physical and economic devastation of the war, many found themselves in dire economic straits at war's end. Louisiana's *gens de couleur* may have had an additional cause for concern. They must have wondered what the future would hold for them as a people. Would they enjoy equality with Whites in the new South? Would they maintain their middle position, enjoying greater privileges than the newly freed slaves and other Black people but without full equality with Whites? Or would they find themselves in a new struggle for dignity and social and legal equality, together with their darker-skinned fellow countrymen of African descent?[1]

Because she spent the war years in Paris with her children, Madame Decuir may have been unaware of her family's economic distress until her postwar return to Louisiana. When she was notified in 1865 of her husband Antoine's death, she hurried home with her children. She must have known that managing her husband's "succession," as inheritance proceedings were referred to in Louisiana, would be complicated and time consuming. Madame Decuir left for Paris as the wife of one of the wealthiest plantation owners in Louisiana and mother of three young children, and she returned as a forty-three-year-old widow to bury her husband and discover that the family finances were, along with the defeated South, in shambles.

The Succession of Antoine Decuir II's Estate

Madame Decuir was appointed administratrix of Antoine's estate on July 24, 1865, and promised in an official document to properly discharge her duties in that role on behalf of herself and her two minor children. She hired Pointe Coupée lawyers Archibald Debow Murphey Haralson and Louis Bingaman Claiborne to handle the legal aspects of the succession.[2] Haralson and Claiborne were prominent White lawyers in Pointe Coupée who often represented the parish government, known as the Police Jury, as well as private clients, including many of the wealthy colored planters.[3] Haralson was the son of a Princeton-educated lawyer and district attorney for the Eighth Judicial District in Louisiana. He served as district attorney after his father and was known as a brilliant prosecutor. He was married to a White woman but also had children with two women of color. Haralson's junior partner Claiborne was educated at Georgetown University, served as the elected parish attorney of Pointe Coupée Parish from 1869 to 1888, and was a judge thereafter.[4]

In 1880, Claiborne founded the *Pointe Coupée Banner*, which was the most important newspaper in the Parish. While at Georgetown, Claiborne had a personal relationship with president James Buchanan, but he left school shortly after the Civil War broke out to serve in the Confederate army. In fact, Claiborne was a committed Confederate. Before he left Georgetown, when he was just eighteen or nineteen years old, he delivered an eloquent defense of the Confederate cause, characterizing the Civil War as a fight for freedom and liberty against the "vile despotism that holds its seat at Washington."[5]

After the Civil War, a great deal of the work of Haralson and Claiborne involved cases arising out of the financial problems that beset the area in the wake of the war. They litigated a wide variety of commercial and family disputes in the Pointe Coupée area, including cases involving other Decuir family members. For example, in 1881, they represented the "widow Lefroy Decuir" in a pair of appeals, one that was dismissed for her failure to file a proper record of proceedings in the trial court and another in which the Louisiana Supreme Court rejected efforts to prevent the execution of a judgment seizing her property.[6]

It was not long before the succession proceedings must have made it painfully clear to Madame Decuir that she was no longer a wealthy woman. In one undated letter from the period during which the succession was pending, Madame Decuir claimed that she had paid $11,000 to her late husband's creditors since his death, and the letter leaves the impression that she was already living in modest circumstances. In late 1870, three groups of estate creditors banded together to seek Madame Decuir's removal as administratrix. These creditors alleged that Madame Decuir had not filed required accounts (likely a failing of her lawyers), that they held judgments against the estate exceeding $48,000 before interest, and that Madame Decuir's security was not sufficient to cover that amount. The creditors claimed that her brother Antoine Dubuclet's assets did not exceed $25,000, and thus his security was insufficient. Madame Decuir admitted that she had not filed required accounts of her administration, but she claimed that the estate's property and security she had provided were sufficient to ensure proper performance of her duties. She also provided a new pledge signed by her brother Antoine Dubuclet, then treasurer of the state of Louisiana, representing that his assets exceeded his liabilities by at least $75,000.[7] The trial court and Supreme Court of Louisiana both denied the creditors' efforts, mainly because there was insufficient evidence to establish that the creditors were prejudiced by the apparent maladministration of the estate. But it was clear that Madame Decuir was in serious financial trouble.

Although Haralson and Claiborne succeeded in preventing Madame Decuir's removal as administratrix, not much else about the succession proceedings went well for Madame Decuir. The Decuirs, like many Southerners, especially slaveholders, suffered severe economic distress during and after the war. What caused the family's finances to crumble during this period? The primary cause, of course, was the physical and economic devastation wrought by the Civil War. The monetary system was destroyed, with Confederate money and Confederate bonds rendered worthless. The end of slavery also had a profound economic effect, and not only due to the end of free labor. Of course, after the war, they lost the underlying value of their slaves. Antoine had borrowed money by pledging his slaves as security. Without operating income or slave property to sell or surrender, these debts became judgments, and the family balance sheet changed from black to red.

The Decuir family's assets were also affected directly by military action during the Civil War. When Northern troops overran Pointe Coupée in

March, 1863—during protracted fighting to take Port Hudson, Louisiana, on the east side of the Mississippi River—they seized supplies from local farms, including twenty-four mules, eight horses, one hundred sheep, eight cows, eight wagons, six thousand bushels of corn, five barrels of sugar, and six thousand pounds of fresh pork from the Decuir plantation. This was the usual practice during the war, and it is safe to assume that the troops left little of value behind, if only to prevent supplies from falling into the hands of Confederate troops. It was not until 1915 that the Decuir children received compensation for the seized property from the United States government, although the amount paid, $4,115, was based on the value of the goods when seized and not the 1906 valuation by the Court of Claims, which was $12,300. Compensation was available because, as the Court of Claims found, two conditions were met: Antoine Decuir II had remained loyal to the Union, and the family had made repeated attempts to procure compensation in the 1870s.[8]

In 1871, an auction was held, and all of Antoine Decuir II's remaining property, real and personal, fetched $25,762, which was insufficient to cover the estate's outstanding debts. After years of proceedings, Antoine Decuir's succession was completed in 1871 or 1872 when the parish court of Pointe Coupée, in the vernacular, "homologate[ed] her final account and tableau of distribution" of the succession. In other words, the Court approved the final accounting of the estate's assets and liabilities and the distribution of the assets according to the accounting. This left Madame Decuir with virtually no assets. It is unclear whether she retained the property in the Chenal or whether that also went to satisfy creditors. Whatever the result, Madame Decuir soon became dissatisfied with the result of the succession, and as we shall see, she sought new lawyers to investigate whether she had been treated properly in the proceedings, resulting in an unsuccessful effort to reopen the proceedings.[9]

Madame Decuir was experiencing additional challenges. She claimed to suffer from mental and physical illness after the death of her husband and her return to Louisiana. Further, she had grown accustomed to the relative lack of discrimination against persons of African descent in Paris, and she found it difficult to adjust to the treatment she received in Louisiana where, after the Civil War, discrimination seemed to increase against mixed-race French speakers like her. In fact, the emotional impact of discrimination may have contributed to her depression and her apparent general lack of a feeling of well-being.

Madame Decuir Hires New Lawyers

One day in July, in the oppressive summer heat and humidity, perhaps still in widow's weeds even seven years after the death of her husband, Madame Decuir went to the law office of New Orleans lawyer E. K. Washington on St. Charles Street.[10] She was likely preoccupied by the loss of her wealth in the succession of her husband Antoine's estate and the sense that her privileged position as a high-class French-speaking woman of color was slipping away. Her official residence was still in Pointe Coupée, and she was probably staying with relatives in New Orleans at the time, either with her brother Antoine Dubuclet, who was treasurer of the state of Louisiana, or with her daughter Rosa. Her manner was dignified, refined, and more than likely somber as she introduced herself as a prospective new client. Washington was not expecting her, and although he must have at least heard of her brother, even after she told him her name, he had no idea who she was. In particular, he did not realize that she was a woman of color.[11]

After years of prosperity, freedom, and equality in Paris, Madame Decuir now struggled with financial difficulty as well as rising restrictions placed on people of color in Louisiana. The proceedings over her husband's succession had dragged on for years. She no longer trusted the local lawyers who had been representing her. One of her husband's creditors—Dr. Leon Ferrier, with her lawyers' cooperation, and pursuant to court order—had gained control over the property of the estate. Ferrier distributed it according to the tableau.[12] Madame Decuir felt her interests had been ignored. Her purpose in hiring Washington was to see what, if anything, could be done to reverse the distribution. Washington may have been her last hope.

E. K. Washington

The historical record does not reveal what led Madame Decuir to Washington. Although Washington was an active lawyer, representing numerous clients in a wide variety of disputes during the 1870s, he was not a particularly prominent or distinguished member of the New Orleans legal community. In fact, he may have been a subject of gossip and ridicule due to embarrassing divorce proceedings he went through in the late 1860s and early 1870s.[13] The most likely explanation for Madame Decuir's decision to see

Washington was that her brother Antoine suggested, or even demanded, that she consult him because Washington had a colored associate, S. R. Snaer, who was known to Antoine. Perhaps Louisiana's former attorney general Simeon Belden, a professional associate of Washington's with whom Snaer was reading law, joined in the recommendation.

E. K. Washington was born in Philadelphia, Pennsylvania, in either 1823 or 1824 and died in New Orleans in 1882 at the age of fifty-eight. He lived in New Orleans for at least three decades, marrying Mary Cady there in 1864 and serving in the Louisiana militia during the Civil War.[14]

Washington had a varied law practice, including litigation involving business disputes, divorce, and property succession. Between 1871 and 1881, Washington was listed as counsel on twenty-eight reported cases in the Louisiana Supreme Court, including three arising out of his representation of Madame Decuir, two concerning her husband's succession and the third the Louisiana court's decision in her case against Captain John Benson. Six of the cases involved regulation of slaughterhouses under the statutes that were challenged in the *Slaughter-House Cases*, in which the US Supreme Court first construed the Privileges or Immunities Clause of the Fourteenth Amendment.[15] It seems that Washington represented butchers opposed to the monopoly granted by the Slaughterhouse Act to the Crescent City Livestock Association. Although he worked together with the mixed-race lawyer Snaer and represented Madame Decuir in her race discrimination case, it does not appear that his views on race were particularly progressive, once characterizing himself as "perhaps a worse rebel than you are," referring to opposing counsel in Madame Decuir's case.[16]

Washington must have been an interesting character. In the late 1850s, he traveled to Europe and published a detailed travelogue of his journey, including descriptions of many familiar tourist attractions.[17] In addition to his travelogue, he wrote poetry that was reviewed favorably in New Orleans newspapers.[18]

Washington's travelogue, *Echoes of Europe, or Word Pictures of Travel*, published in 1860, related eleven months of travels that occurred sometime shortly prior to publication. The book contains some interesting suggestions concerning Washington's views and personality. Washington began his journey by visiting Washington, DC, where he went to "pay his respects" to President Buchanan.[19] During the era of open office hours, many people would come to see the president, often to seek government employment.[20]

(Later, President James Garfield was assassinated by a disappointed job seeker.) Washington told Buchanan that he and his companion, who was never named, were "friends to his administration," and they had a brief discussion of Washington's travel plans. Buchanan is widely regarded as one of the worst presidents in US history, largely due to his behind-the-scenes efforts to engineer a pro–Southern decision in the *Dred Scott* case and his failure to make serious efforts to preserve the Union. In the book, Washington commented on the merits of members of Buchanan's cabinet and lamented the emergence of political parties in the United States, which he believed caused corruption and impeded loyalty to the president by placing a large portion of the people in opposition, hoping that their party would prevail in the next election.[21]

The travelogue contains some disturbing comments on slavery and racial matters. Washington had clearly adopted the Southern view of slavery, defending it as a benevolent institution that elevated the slave by exposing him to Christianity while at the same time relieving the slave of anxiety caused by worry about wages and providing for his family. He compared the class system in Europe unfavorably to slavery. According to Washington, European peasants and laborers were not in any way elevated by their work, their social position was a permanent state of inferiority, their employers did not care at all about their long-term welfare, and they were in a constant state of anxiety over the necessity of supporting their families. Slaves, on the other hand, were happy and carefree because their masters looked out for them and supplied them with all of their worldly needs. He also observed that slaves' living conditions were better than those of European peasants and laborers.[22]

A trip to Europe made far different impressions on antislavery senator Charles Sumner. Sumner, who was born and raised in Massachusetts, traveled south in the United States and was deeply disturbed the first time he saw slaves. He later traveled to Paris, where he observed Black students in classrooms at the Sorbonne, and it was then that he became convinced that the status of Black people in the United States resulted from lack of education rather than any natural inferiority. As a senator from Massachusetts, Sumner relentlessly attacked slavery and racist Southern politicians and institutions, leading to the famous incident in 1856, in which a member of the House of Representatives beat and severely injured Sumner with his cane in the Senate chamber.[23]

Washington criticized abolitionists as "magnifying slavery into untold

horrors" and for not understanding that slavery was "a progressive and natural civilization and amelioration of a race which, in two thousand years
of trial, have shown themselves insusceptible of improvement by any other
means." Consistent with his apparent worldview, Washington also expressed
negative views on Native Americans: "Our real greatness is in our Protestant
diffusion of the Bible, in our giving homes to all nations, in our civilizing
and improving the African race, in driving off and exterminating the unim-
provable Indian races, and reclaiming lands useless for ages." Washington
attributed the success of the United States to divine providence, finding in
public officials, members of Congress, and state legislators qualities that res-
onate with current views, especially of Congress: "The mean, ignorant and
vicious office-holders, the corrupt, pandering, sapheaded simpletons who go
to Congress and the State Legislatures, would drag down any Government
on earth; and ours is only kept up because supported and freighted by an Al-
mighty destiny." Although more than once in the book Washington praised
the United States as a great country, his views on slavery make it unsurpris-
ing that he served on the Confederate side during the Civil War.[24]

If Washington's personal life was widely known in New Orleans, he might
have been a comic or tragic figure. Very soon after his October 1864 wedding
to Cady, who needed written permission from her stepfather John Washington (no relation to E. K.) to marry, the parties became tangled up in divorce
proceedings that did not conclude until 1872. John Washington was the fifth
husband of Mary's mother Elizabeth, and while the two Washingtons were
not related, the Washington family into which E. K. Washington's mother-
in-law married figures prominently in his divorce.[25] E. K. Washington and
Cady ultimately went through three separate divorce proceedings, including one in which she charged him with impotence and another in which he
charged her with bigamy and adultery.[26]

Washington and Cady did not live together as husband and wife for very
long; by her mother's account, it was only six or seven months. When they
were together, they lived in a boardinghouse owned by her mother that was
located on Canal Street, just west of the northern section of the French Quarter. When Cady sued for "separate bed and board" in May 1866, she alleged
that Washington treated her with "marked disrespect, chilly indifference, and
intentional neglect," that he "never did support her according to his or her
place in society and in proportion to his pecuniary means," that he was "jeal-
ous without cause, . . . that he publicly defamed her character by foul judicial

libels and open slander . . . and finally that the excesses of her husband's lax treatment to petitioner, his wife, render them living together impossible." In late June 1866, Cady supplemented her petition, alleging that Washington "did not supply her with the necessaries of life and he refused to supply her with comfortable clothing." (Cady claimed that Washington took back some furniture he had bought for their living quarters in the boardinghouse, and that when she told him she needed clothing, he gave her $1.20 for fabric to make herself a dress.) In December 1866, Cady filed another petition requesting that the marriage be "declared to be an absolute nullity" on the ground that the plaintiff falsely claimed "to belong to the family of George Washington, the father of his country." It was not simply that he falsely claimed a familial connection. Cady alleged that his real name was Eugene Keepers and that he had fraudulently assumed the Washington name. Reminiscent of the twenty-first-century case of Clark Rockefeller, Cady claimed that E. K. Washington was an imposter. In April 1867, Cady filed one last petition for divorce, asking that the marriage be annulled "on the ground that the defendant is impotent."[27]

Washington denied all of these allegations, claiming that his wife was better treated than any of the other wives in the boardinghouse (including her mother), and he countered that Cady had been pregnant by him once but had miscarried, and that she had abandoned him and their marriage vows. He forced her to undergo a humiliating virginity examination, the results of which were discussed in testimony. Washington also addressed the allegation of fraud in the inducement of the marriage, stating, "In the year 1864—being desirous of marrying and perpetuating the elder line of the Lund Washington family, to which petitioner belongs," he and Mary Cady were married. Lund Washington was a cousin of George Washington who managed Mount Vernon for the president during some of his time away in public service.[28] Washington supported his claim to be a member of the family of George Washington with answers to interrogatories by several friends and relatives from Pennsylvania, including a half-sister, detailing Washington's familial connection to Lund Washington.[29] Washington also included evidence of a physical exam he underwent to prove he was not impotent and described his wife hugging and kissing other men in the boardinghouse.

Mary Cady was awarded a divorce by the New Orleans District Court, but the judgment was reversed in January 17, 1870, in an unpublished and unreported decision of the Supreme Court of Louisiana. Chief Justice John T.

Ludeling, who later wrote that court's opinion in *Decuir v. Benson*, wrote an opinion explaining the denial of the divorce. The Court held that impotence was no ground for "nullity" and concluded that a careful review of the facts revealed that the conduct alleged as grounds for separate bed and board occurred mainly after Cady wrongfully left Washington and refused to see him. In holding that Washington's alleged impotence was no ground for nullifying the marriage, the Court noted that physicians testified on both sides in the matter and that courts would be forced to decide based on conjecture, lacking clear evidence one way or the other.[30]

Cady then went to Chicago with a family friend, claimed residency at the Tremont Hotel in that city, and on January 26, 1870, filed for divorce in the circuit court of Cook County, Illinois, falsely claiming to have been living in Chicago "for more than one whole year prior to filing." Notice to Washington was by publication, and a divorce was granted on April 5, 1870. After the decree was rendered, Washington traveled to Chicago, hired an attorney, and unsuccessfully attempted to reopen the judgment on the ground that the Illinois court lacked jurisdiction. Meanwhile, on August 17, 1870, Mary Cady traveled to Mobile, Alabama, and, in reliance on the Illinois divorce decree, married Henry T. Washington, the son of her mother's husband John, yet another marriage between a Cady woman and a man named Washington.

E. K. Washington's reaction to his ex-wife's remarriage was, on August 25, 1870, to file for divorce in Louisiana, alleging bigamy, adultery, and incest on the part of his wife. Bigamy and adultery because, he claimed, the Illinois divorce was invalid, and incest because her new purported husband was also her stepbrother. He also alleged that she had aided and abetted her stepfather's attempt to shoot him sometime in 1866. During the proceedings, Washington characterized Chicago as a "divorce hole," perhaps the Reno, Nevada, of its time. Washington attempted to prove that Cady committed fraud on the Illinois court with false evidence of residence.[31] Things apparently got ugly, and father and son John and Henry Washington allegedly attempted to choke E. K. during one of the depositions, prompting E. K. to ask the Louisiana District Court to hold them in contempt. Although the Court's reaction to that request is unknown, the trial court ruled against Washington's request for a divorce.[32] Meanwhile, he had also filed a criminal charge of bigamy against Cady: the *Daily Picayune* reported that charges of bigamy brought against "Mrs. Henry Washington" were dismissed. Washington pressed the matter and unsuccessfully attempted to procure an indictment from a grand jury.[33]

When Washington appealed the rejection of his petition for divorce, the clerk of the trial court, William Woelker, refused to release the transcript of proceedings until Washington paid certain court costs. This was apparently not the first time a Louisiana district court clerk had done this, and Washington's only remedy was to seek an order of "mandamus" from the Louisiana Supreme Court ordering the clerk to deliver the transcript.[34] In his petition, Washington alleged that he had given Woelker twenty dollars, which he claimed was all that the clerk was legally entitled to for the service of preparing the transcript of appeal, based on the number of pages and words in the record. Washington stated that he had provided an appeal bond of $300, "the Hon. S. Belden being the security."[35] S. Belden was Simeon Belden, the Louisiana attorney general at the time, with whom Washington's associate Snaer studied law and who was also a party named in the *Slaughter-House Cases* as acting on behalf of the state of Louisiana. Washington argued that the clerk of court had demanded "enormous, extortionate and illegal fees." Woelker replied that the dispute arose because he had done Washington a favor by not requiring Washington to post security for costs at the outset of the litigation: "At the time and prior to the filing of the suit of the said Washington this respondent knows him to be a member of the Bar, and believing him to be a man of limited means and being willing to aid and assist him on that account, entered into a contract with him in relation to the payment of Clerk's costs." The contract, according to Woelker, provided that Washington would pay only the actual costs incurred, which amounted to $144.75, including the fee to the Court stenographer.[36]

Despite Woelker's protestations, the Louisiana Supreme Court ordered him to deliver the transcript. Washington's divorce appeal was finally heard in 1872, and it was denied. Although the Louisiana Supreme Court issued no opinion in the case, it is likely that it decided not to question the validity of the Illinois judgment, perhaps because Washington appeared there, albeit after the entry of judgment, to challenge the Illinois court's jurisdiction.

Washington did some criminal work, and in one 1871 case, his opponent was Belden, who at the time was serving as guarantor on Washington's appeal bond in his divorce case. Washington and Belden also worked together on some cases in the 1870s, and Washington represented Belden in a business dispute that was resolved against him by the Louisiana Supreme Court in 1875.[37] Belden had been elected the attorney general of Louisiana on the Republican ticket in 1868, serving until 1873. In 1873, the Louisiana legislature passed a statute requiring Belden to turn over all books and furniture purchased with an appropriation that it had made for that purpose in September 1868.[38] This statute was passed based on the representation of Belden's successor, Alexander Pope Field, that no books or furniture had been turned over to him by his predecessor in office. Belden was also held in contempt of court and sentenced to ten days in jail by Florida district judge Charles Swayne, a case that was one of grounds upon which Swayne was later impeached.[39] After his public service, Belden practiced law and appeared in many reported cases in Louisiana, both civil and criminal, right up to the year of his death in New Orleans in 1906, including at least one case in which he represented a colored man suing over his exclusion from a place of public entertainment.[40]

Washington died on January 28, 1882, and his funeral was held the next day "from the late residence of the deceased, St. Claude Street, between Clouet and Louisa." On March 17, 1882, Washington's law books and office furnishings were auctioned on behalf of his succession. Washington died unmarried and childless. His sole heir was Louisa Washington Robb, a half-sister living in Missouri, formerly of Illinois, who had testified in Washington's divorce litigation in support of his membership in the family of George Washington.[41]

S. R. Snaer

S. R. Snaer was Washington's cocounsel in *Decuir v. Benson* in the Louisiana state courts. Like Madame Decuir, Snaer was French-speaking and of mixed racial heritage. Although his year of birth is sometimes listed as 1847, New Orleans birth records list his date of birth as June 23, 1845.[42] His race was listed as "M" in the census, meaning "mulatto." Born Seymour Rene Snaer, he was apparently named after the pirate Rene Beluche, a member of his mother Emiren Beluche's family who may have transported an earlier generation of Snaers from Cuba to New Orleans. S. R. Snaer did not like this association and, as an adult, used the name Seymour.[43]

Although he signed the complaint and participated in the litigation in the Louisiana courts, Snaer is not listed as counsel in *Hall v. Decuir* at the US Supreme Court, perhaps because he might not yet have met the qualifications for membership in the Supreme Court bar. There are four reported

Louisiana cases in which Snaer worked together with Washington, including the appeal in *Decuir v. Benson* and one case involving the Decuir succession. Washington and Snaer also worked together on two cases involving successions not related to the Decuir litigation. On one 1878 case, Simeon Belden, by then former Louisiana attorney general, joined them as cocounsel.[44]

The Snaer family's interesting history has been chronicled by Mary Frances Berry in her book *We Are Who We Say We Are*.[45] Snaer and Snaer's older brother Louis very likely knew Madame Decuir's brother Antoine Dubuclet, the state treasurer. Louis A. Snaer served on the Union side in the colored militia that was mustered shortly after New Orleans was taken by the North in 1862, after having served in the 1st Louisiana Native Guard beginning in 1861.[46] (The Native Guard was a colored militia created by the government of Louisiana, presumably to defend against Northern aggression. Many non-White Louisianans were torn between defending what they considered their native land and the hope, however small some of them thought it to be, that a Union victory would result in freedom for slaves and greater personal dignity and respect for their rights.[47]) In the US Army, Louis attained the rank of major after being seriously wounded in the battle of Fort Blakeley in April 1865. He was a captain at the time of the battle, reputed to have been the only "Colored Creole" officer on that battlefield, and afterward, President Andrew Johnson promoted him to the rank of major in recognition of his conduct in helping capture the fort. Louis was politically active after the war, serving on the constitutional convention that produced the Louisiana Constitution of 1868 and in the state legislature from 1872 to 1879, representing Iberia Parish, which is west of New Orleans and south of Pointe Coupée Parish.[48] Sometime later, Louis A. Snaer moved to Oregon to escape the limitations of his status as a man of color imposed upon him in Louisiana. Although he lived as a White man in Oregon and his children were able to attend public school there, homesickness and the cold weather led him to move temporarily back to Louisiana. Ultimately, he relocated to California and died in the Oakland area in 1917, having lived there for years as a White man.[49]

S. R. Snaer was also politically active. The earliest hint of this in the historical record consists of his December 27, 1866, testimony in New Orleans before a committee of Congress on what became known as the New Orleans massacre of July 30, 1866. Snaer informed the committee that he was of French and German descent, belonged to the Republican party, was in favor of "negro suffrage," and in favor of keeping those who were engaged in the rebellion from voting.[50] The New Orleans massacre swung nation-wide public opinion toward the Republican Party and was a precipitating factor behind the passage of the federal Civil Rights Act of 1866. This riot erupted when Republicans—White, colored, and Black—reconvened a constitutional convention in the Mechanics Institute in New Orleans, after the Louisiana legislature enacted post–Civil War Black codes. Snaer testified that the police violently attacked the meeting, including shooting Black people who were parading in front of the hall in which the convention was being held. Ultimately, according to Snaer, "Every one who went out from the Institute was shot and killed." Snaer said he saw "about forty or fifty killed or wounded" and that the attackers included policemen and firemen. It is believed that some Black people were murdered in cold blood behind the Mechanics Institute. *Harpers Weekly* called it a "massacre."[51]

Snaer began practicing law and working on cases with E. K. Washington sometime in the early 1870s. He was reportedly admitted to the Louisiana bar in 1873, although another report has him admitted to the bar by June 24, 1871.[52] Despite documented history of having practiced law in the 1870s in New Orleans, Snaer is not mentioned in any scholarly books or articles on the nation's and Louisiana's earliest Black lawyers. If the 1873 date is correct, based on the dates that other early Louisiana lawyers of color are reported to have become members of the bar, Snaer would have been the third or fourth, after both C. Clay Morgan, who was a lawyer by 1860, and Louis A. Bell, a Howard Law graduate admitted in 1871, and during the same year as Thomas Morris Chester. If the 1871 date is correct, he would have been second or third.[53]

At the time, the most common way of becoming a lawyer was to study (or "read the law") with a practicing lawyer, although Bell had attended law school at Howard, and several of Louisiana's early colored lawyers attended Straight University Law School, which Bell helped found. In 1875, an article published in the *Terrebonne Republican*, and reprinted in the *Louisianan*, a New Orleans newspaper serving the colored community, welcomed Snaer ("a capable, honest and independent attorney") to town in Terrebonne Parish, reporting that Snaer had read law with former Louisiana Attorney General Simeon Belden and had been practicing in New Orleans since his 1873 admission to the bar. The article characterized Snaer as "active, able, industrious and sober." Further singing his praises, the article went on: "When we state that Mr. Snaer has passed his examination in open court with the highest compliments of the bar, our readers will at once understand that Mr. Snaer is prepared to take charge of any suit."[54]

The 1877 New Orleans city directory lists Snaer as a lawyer residing at 232 St. Claude Street, likely in a neighborhood a bit east of the French Quarter, close to the future residence of Madame Decuir and her daughter.[55] In addition to the private practice of law, Snaer engaged in substantial public service. He was twice elected district attorney for Terrebonne and Lafourche Parishes, beginning in 1877. That is pretty late for a colored man to be elected in Louisiana, but he may have been an exceptional figure, and his light skin may also have helped. In an article discussing his candidacy, Snaer was characterized by the *Weekly Louisianan* as an "honor to our race" and expressed the hope that others will follow the precedent set by Snaer "by putting intelligent colored men on their local tickets." Before his election as district attorney, Snaer ran unsuccessfully for the state house from New Orleans's fifth ward on the "radical" ticket.[56]

On Friday, June 13, 1873, another of Snaer's brothers, Alexamore, a storekeeper, was murdered at his shop along with his business partner, a White man named Daniel Francois Lanet. Based on a description, an African American named Polycarp was suspected of the crime. At a coroner's inquest held the following Tuesday, Polycarp denied involvement, "but upon being closely questioned by a brother of one of the murdered men, Mr. Seymour Snaer, . . . he confessed to having been at the store when the deed was done, but had no hand in it."[57] Polycarp named three others as the robbers and murderers, and those three men were arrested that day. While at first they denied the charges, by 5 p.m. that day they confessed that they had "felled [Lanet and Snaer] to the floor by hickory clubs," stole $600 in currency and $200 in gold and silver from the safe, slit their victims' throats, and set the bodies and the store on fire.

A mixed-race crowd of between fifteen hundred and two thousand people clamored for an immediate hanging, but Snaer would not allow it. After Snaer left, however, the mob succeeded in seizing the three identified by Polycarp as the killers, and they were hanged. Although they had confessed their crimes, during the process of being hanged, one of the three claimed that it was Polycarp who actually cut Laret's throat. Polycarp was apparently not lynched, as Snaer had protected him in exchange for naming the other three murderers. The lynching story was reported nationally, including in the *Chicago Daily Tribune* on June 18, 1873, and the *Jackson City (Michigan) Patriot* on June 19, 1873, along with a story about the lynching of a horse thief in Marion County, Missouri.[58]

It does not appear that Snaer was what today would be termed a "cause" lawyer in the sense of seeking out civil rights cases like Madame Decuir's, but given his mixed-race identity and his political involvement, he likely viewed the case as more than simple work for a paying client. He must have been sympathetic with Madame Decuir's cause. It is unclear how extensive Snaer's role was in the litigation in *Hall v. Decuir*. His signature appeared above Washington's on Madame Decuir's complaint. He was present for at least some of the proceedings, translating French testimony into English and testifying about his role in the events leading up to Madame Decuir's trip on the *Governor Allen*, but he did not question any witness.[59]

Snaer and Washington worked on a few more reported cases, but once Snaer became district attorney for Terrebonne and Lafourche Parishes, the professional association was mostly over. He married twenty-year-old Marie Lalande, the daughter of Euphraisie and Louis Lalande, on January 16, 1877, at St. Augustine Church in New Orleans, established as a place of worship by Antoine Blanc, the first Catholic Archbishop of New Orleans for the city's free people of color.[60] Perhaps his move out of New Orleans was precipitated by the marriage. They had one child, Seymour Louis Snaer.

Snaer's life turned tragic shortly after his marriage. Marie died in 1879 when their boy was two years old, and Snaer raised his son either in the family home on St. Claude Street or in Bayou Blue, Terrebonne Parish. He was listed in census records and directories at both addresses. Although in 1880 he apparently had plans to remarry, he began suffering from epilepsy and some sort of mania that led to his removal from office and commitment to a state mental hospital where he died in 1885 at approximately forty years old, with an estate valued at $450.[61]

After listening to Madame Decuir's story, including that she felt that she had been cheated in the succession proceedings, Washington agreed to represent her and told her that he and Snaer would have to travel to Pointe Coupée Parish to review the records there to determine if anything could be done. Travel from New Orleans to Pointe Coupée Parish was by riverboat to Hermitage Landing, then either by boat through the Chenal or by wagon overland. Today, the one-hundred-mile trip on interstate highways takes a little more than two hours. But at that time, New Orleans to Hermitage Landing was an overnight riverboat journey of about sixteen or seventeen hours. Getting from Hermitage Landing to New Roads, the location of the Parish courthouse, likely added several more hours. Washington told Madame Decuir that he would let her know when he was ready to make the trip. Even after hearing her story and agreeing to represent her, and despite all of the likely connections between Snaer and Madame Decuir, Washington would later insist that at this point, he did not realize that his new client was a woman of color.[62]

3

Madame Decuir's Journey and Reconstruction

Sometime during the week of July 14, 1872, E. K. Washington sent Madame Decuir a message informing her that he and S. R. Snaer would travel to Pointe Coupée that weekend to investigate the handling of the succession of her late husband Antoine. The plan was to travel upriver by steamboat on Saturday evening, July 20, to arrive Sunday, July 21, at Hermitage Landing, and then travel to New Roads. Madame Decuir informed Snaer that she would accompany them to help with logistics and answer any questions that may arise. Because there was constant steamboat traffic from New Orleans to points north, there was no need to book the travel in advance.

Saturday the twentieth was a typical July day in New Orleans—hot, with a mean temperature of seventy-nine degrees, and humid, with a tenth of an inch of rainfall that day in a month that would see nearly six and a half inches of rain, about the norm. The weather may have been threatening; on the following day, the temperature would be slightly warmer and a quarter inch of rain would fall.[1] Washington arrived at the levee at about 5 p.m., saw the *Governor Allen*, and, knowing it by reputation to be "a very good boat," went aboard to book passage. This was a promising trip—he had a new client and a case in a distant parish, outside of his usual humdrum of New Orleans commercial and family disputes, and there would be ample time on the boat for Washington and Madame Decuir to discuss the case and plan research in Pointe Coupée.[2]

After booking passage, Washington came off the boat hoping to find Madame Decuir when he ran into Snaer, who would also be traveling to Pointe Coupée. When Washington told Snaer that he had booked passage for himself and Madame Decuir on the *Governor Allen*, Snaer became agitated. After some hesitation, Snaer told Washington that Madame Decuir would be "mortified" if she went on the *Governor Allen* and that he would be going on a different boat. Washington did not immediately understand why, on either count, until, at last, as he put it, he "apprehended" that Madame Decuir was "a woman of color" who would object to the boat's segregation policy, which was more stringent than some of the other boats on the Mississippi. While on some boats, special arrangements were made for high-status people of color like Madame Decuir, on the *Governor Allen*, all colored passengers desiring sleeping accommodations, regardless of economic and social class, would be segregated to the colored-only bureau and barred from the ladies' cabin. Given that he claimed to have not known that she was a woman of color, Washington was certainly unaware of the previous occasions on which Madame Decuir had rejected accommodations in the bureau reserved for colored passengers, or violated rules of segregation on riverboats.[3]

Washington suddenly saw that he would have a big problem on his hands if Madame Decuir joined him on the *Governor Allen*.

Earlier on the twentieth, Madame Decuir packed a trunk and made her way by horse-drawn wagon to the levee, resolute not to wind up in the bureau, the area set aside for colored travelers. The first-class ladies' cabin, not the bureau, was suited to a woman of her social standing, and she may not have felt welcome in the bureau anyway since she had once been a slave owner herself.[4] Perhaps not knowing of the inflexible racial rules on the *Governor Allen*, Madame Decuir had a porter take her trunk on board, then boarded herself, taking a seat in the lounge of the ladies' cabin. Perhaps she thought that she would be treated properly, in line with her high social status. On the steamer *Lafourche*, in 1866 or 1867, she had been provided with a room in the ladies' cabin, although she was not allowed to enter the common area or eat at the table with the White passengers. Maybe she hoped she could pass as White and take her meals along with the other ladies and gentlemen of her class. Or perhaps she knew of the policy of segregation on the *Governor Allen* and was preparing to fight the inevitable demand that if she wanted a stateroom, it would have to be in the bureau, not the ladies' cabin.[5]

A significant proportion of Madame Decuir's encounters with discrimination likely occurred when she needed to travel. Transportation systems have long been points of racial friction. While Whites might have been able to exclude non-Whites from restaurants, hotels, theaters, and parks, and Blacks could avoid them, the cost and impracticability of constructing separate systems of transportation and the absolute necessity of travel for people of all races meant that White and non-White people were constantly traveling together. As Blair L. M. Kelley reports, "Segregation was not a southern invention and" was common throughout the United States on "railroads, streetcars and ferryboats" long before the Civil War.[6]

Before the Civil War, transportation segregation did not present much of an issue in the South because most non-Whites on trains or steamboats were slaves traveling with their owners. When wealthy free men of color like Madame Decuir's brother Antoine Dubuclet and P. G. Deslonde, future secretary of state of Louisiana, traveled by boat, they were sometimes permitted in the cabin with White travelers, although for the most part, segregation was the norm and accommodations for free people of color were inferior to those provided to Whites. After the Civil War, with much higher numbers of Black people traveling, the situation became more complicated. In line with pervasive racism, Whites did not want to share sleeping quarters or eat at the same table with Black people—at least not in a public place like a steamboat or a train.[7]

In the aftermath of the Civil War, after emancipation and constitutional amendments that purported to grant equal rights to all Americans, Black people in New Orleans and elsewhere resisted segregation in transportation. For example, in the late 1860s, New Orleans was covered by an extensive network of mule-drawn streetcars. The cars were segregated, with people of color confined to cars painted with large black stars, although Whites were allowed to ride in both starred and non-starred cars. In May 1867, Black people began agitating against segregation, and after a mass demonstration in which they exhorted each other to ride in any car they wanted, the streetcar companies, with the agreement of the chief of police, abolished the star-car system. While this did not completely end streetcar segregation, it did remove the official stamp of approval from this daily affront to the dignity of non-White streetcar riders.[8]

Long-distance transportation in Louisiana in the 1860s and 1870s was provided by steamboats and railroads. For Madame Decuir, whose life was centered in locations along the Mississippi River, steamboats were most convenient, and she traveled on them often. There were numerous boats running up and down the river, serving New Orleans and Pointe Coupée Parish, including Hermitage Landing, which was along the river directly east of the False River and the area of the Chenal to which Madame Decuir's family had relocated in the mid-1850s.

After the war, most steamboats provided separate sleeping areas for White and Black people. First-class sleeping accommodations for Whites were provided in what was often referred to as the "cabin," or in the case of White women, the "ladies' cabin." Most commonly, the sleeping area for non-Whites was a separate cabin referred to as the "bureau," an ironic reference to the post–Civil War freedmen's bureaus. On some boats that had few non-White travelers desiring sleeping accommodations, the arrangements were somewhat ad hoc, with non-White passengers accommodated in areas normally used by crew members or in areas not usually used for sleeping.

In addition to segregated sleeping arrangements, segregation in dining was strictly observed. On some boats, there were separate tables for Whites and non-Whites. On boats with only one dining table, Whites ate first and non-Whites were served at the same table after the Whites were finished, or non-Whites were fed in their rooms or on the outside areas of the boat called "the guards."

One important difference between the accommodations for White women and women of color was that the separation of the sexes was not observed in the area reserved for non-White travelers. This was intolerable to many women of color who would suffer the sting of the devaluation of their sexual autonomy, which was an aspect of slavery they would just as soon forget. On the railroads, women of color suffered a similar fate when they were forced to travel second class, which usually meant a seat in the smoking car, which was an especially uncomfortable place for a "lady" and the children who might be along for the journey. Men would smoke, chew and spit, curse and gamble, and make crude comments about female travelers. Overall, the treatment of non-White female travelers was an even greater affront to their dignity as it was to the men of color who were also subjected to segregation, although men also suffered from the sense that they were unable to protect the female members of their community.[9]

After the war, the practice on some boats of making special arrangements for high-status colored passengers continued. Captain V. B. Baranco of the steamboat the *Bart Able* recounted that on his boat, two rooms in the cabin were set aside for non-White travelers. The inner doors of these rooms were locked so the occupants could not enter the common area where White people would receive their meals. Food would be brought directly to the rooms occupied by non-White travelers and they were allowed to enter and leave their rooms only through a second door that led directly outside to the guards.[10]

Madame Decuir had traveled with Captain Baranco more than once, and Baranco recalled that sometime during the period 1866 to 1867, on a boat called the *Lafourche*, she was provided with one of the rooms reserved for high-status people of color on the condition that she not enter the common area where the White passengers took their meals, but go in and out through the outer door (on the guards) rather than the inner one leading to the common room. Her meals would be served in her room, or on the guards to the outside of the boat. During this trip, Madame Decuir complied with Captain Baranco's instructions and had her meals in her room. Other colored people, according to Baranco, ate outside on the guards. While preferable to the Bureau, it must still have been humiliating, a mark of supposed inferiority.[11]

On another trip with Captain Baranco, Madame Decuir resisted her second-class treatment. After Baranco provided her with one of the rooms reserved for higher-status people of color, Madame Decuir went into the common area of the cabin and "sat there rocking herself to and fro." After letting a few minutes pass while there were no White ladies yet on board, Captain Baranco sent Madame Decuir a note telling her to either go into her room or out on the guard, that she was not allowed inside the ladies' cabin. In response, Madame Decuir sent for Captain Baranco and tearfully pleaded with him to treat her as a White person as she had been treated in France, reminding him of his long acquaintance with her and her late husband. Captain Baranco replied that his rules and regulations required that passengers observe the custom of segregation. Madame Decuir complied, and that was the end of the matter, but it was not the last time Madame Decuir resisted being treated in this manner on a boat.[12]

J. H. Mossof, clerk of the steamboat *Robert E. Lee*, recounted how Madame Decuir resisted segregation, possibly also in the summer of 1872 when Madame Decuir's case against Captain Benson arose. At the time, Mossof was the clerk of the *Ouachita Belle* when Madame Decuir took that boat from Pointe Coupée down to New Orleans. On the *Ouachita Belle*, there were no special accommodations made for higher-status passengers of color—it was a room in the bureau or nothing. Mossof offered Madame Decuir a room in the bureau, but she refused it and chose to sit for the entire trip in the "recess," which is a semipublic area behind, but close to, the ladies' cabin.[13]

Madame Decuir's Journey on the *Governor Allen*

After boarding, Madame Decuir sat in the common area of the *Governor Allen*'s ladies' cabin and waited for her new lawyer to arrive. In the meantime, Washington asked the ship's clerk, D. E. Grove, if "a person of color and a very respectable person," Madame Decuir, might be accommodated in the ladies' cabin. Grove said no.[14] Washington then hurried off the boat to ask Snaer to tell Madame Decuir she should not travel on the *Governor Allen.* Snaer was nowhere to be found, and as the time for departure neared, Washington reboarded, only to encounter "a party whose appearance seemed somewhat familiar," as he described it, in the ladies' cabin. When he realized it was Madame Decuir, he was startled and distressed to find her there. Washington then tried to get her off the boat, but it was too late. It was setting out on its journey north.

Washington made two more efforts to secure accommodations for Madame Decuir in the ladies' cabin: first by asking Grove again. He explained to Grove that Madame Decuir was in ill health and that he hadn't realized that she had already come on board—might not he reconsider the policy? Grove would not depart from boat rules. Washington then collared another random official whose response was no different.[15]

In the meantime, recognizing that she was not welcome in the ladies' cabin, Madame Decuir took a seat in a chair in the recess. The recess was described as a semipublic area through which people would pass and ladies staying in the cabin might lounge along with governesses and children. This is where Madame Decuir sat on the *Ouachita Belle* after being excluded from the ladies' cabin on that boat. As on the *Ouachita Belle*, the steward of the *Governor Allen,* John Cedilot, sent a cot and meals to the recess for her, even though she said she did not want either of them.[16]

Madame Decuir chose the recess not only for its proximity to the ladies' cabin. After she refused a room in the bureau, she was offered a choice of accommodations either in the "chambermaid's apartment" or the recess, and she chose the recess. In fact, it may have been customary to offer colored passengers a bed in the recess on boats without a bureau. Washington found her there and informed her of the failure of his efforts. As he did so, Madame Decuir was visibly upset, apparently crying. This indignity was unbearable. The journey would underscore her sense of loss and frustration at her reduced circumstances. Washington resolved to appeal to the boat's captain, John Benson, to plead his client's case.[17]

At suppertime, as Madame Decuir ate fried oysters, baked potatoes, warm rolls, and waffles in the recess, Washington went in search of Captain Benson, whom he located on an upper deck.[18] Benson had purchased the *Governor Allen* in September, 1871, less than a year before Madame Decuir's journey. Prior to that, Benson captained the *Kilgour*.[19] Washington was concerned not only for his client's welfare, but also that he might be blamed for instigating a confrontation by suggesting that they travel on the *Governor Allen*. He told Benson that he had tried to keep her off the boat and, by no fault of his, she had wound up on it anyway. He pleaded that in consideration of her high social status and her ill health, might Benson please accommodate her in the ladies' cabin. The two argued for a short time and Benson firmly refused, explaining that allowing her into the ladies' cabin would damage his business and that she would be well cared for in the bureau reserved for colored passengers.[20]

In his testimony in Madame Decuir's case, Benson explained that before the Civil War, Black people were not provided with rooms on boats like the *Governor Allen* at all, because, other than slaves traveling with their owners, so few traveled. Rather, they would sleep here and there, wherever open space and operations permitted. He did not describe any special accommodations for high-status free people of color. It was only after the Civil War that the issue was presented with enough frequency to require the development of a clear social practice.[21]

Captain Benson (and other officials on the *Governor Allen* and the captains of other boats who testified in the case) claimed that the accommodations for non-Whites were equal to the accommodations provided for Whites, including both the rooms they slept in and the food they were served. John Cedilot, the *Governor Allen's* steward, race unspecified, stated that the Black people ate at the same time as Whites in the common room in the bureau, contrary to the practice on some boats on which Blacks had to wait until Whites were finished eating. Benson stated that he had never had a complaint about the food. He stated, with apparent pride, using language that today would be found quite offensive, that

I know, and reckon, it is as good as these hotels generally give a guest. I never heard any fault-finding. . . . All that I have ever cared for have always been pleased, and always anxious to travel on the boat again, when they are going on the same way we are going. I don't suppose there is a boat on the river that fed the darkies as well as the Allen. I know there is not.[22]

Echoing these sentiments, Cedilot stated that Black people received

the same food, the same dessert, the same pies, the same of everything. Fruits and everything the same, even coffee, if they wish it. Anybody can get a cup of coffee at dinner time if they ask for it. . . . She [the *Governor Allen*] feeds the colored people better than any other boat on the Mississippi River, which I will say to everybody else, as well as say here. They get all kinds of dessert the same as the White people. That is what the "Lee" doesn't do and the Natchez doesn't give it.

When pressed on cross-examination, both Benson and Cedilot insisted that the facilities for Black and White ladies were equal.[23] It is not clear whether Benson and Cedilot were being honest about the equality of the accommodations for White and colored travelers on the *Governor Allen.* There is little in the historical record about that particular boat. More is known about the general situation, and the record is mixed. James Moore, a colored New Orleans policeman who had worked on various steamboats as a cabin boy and steward, stated that while on some boats the bureau was fine, generally it was "very bad." For example, the bureau on the steamship the *Sue* was described by a plaintiff in a suit involving accommodations on that boat as "not fitten for a dog."[24] Specifically, ventilation, which was very important in the Louisiana summer, was worse in the bureau than in the ladies' cabin, basically because the bureau was usually on a deck below the cabin. On the *Governor Allen,* the rooms in the bureau did not have windows, which would virtually guarantee poor ventilation. The rooms in the bureau were generally smaller, and the appointments were often not as nice. Further, there was less attention paid to separating the sexes in the bureau than in the ladies' cabin, which was very important to the dignity and well-being of travelers and an illustration of the lack of concern White boat captains had for their non-White female passengers.[25]

Class consciousness clearly played a role in Madame Decuir's rejection of accommodations in the Bureau. P. G. Deslonde, Madame Decuir's cousin, a wealthy man of color from Madame Decuir's native Iberville Parish and newly elected secretary of state of Louisiana at the time of the trial of Madame Decuir's case, characterized the bureau as "a back room somewhere in the back part of the boat where they generally pen up colored passengers. . . . A dark place like a kind of prison. . . . I deemed it not a place for a man of my standing. . . . It was dirty for a man of my standing. . . . I never went into them only when I was forced to do so. . . . I know it was no place for me."[26] Deslonde preferred to sit in a chair outside on the guard rather than go into the bureau.[27]

Deslonde was even more emphatic about the inappropriateness of the bureau for a lady of Madame Decuir's status. When asked at trial whether he would let his wife go into the bureau, he stated that he would be mortified if she went in there, because "she was raised in another sphere from that to be classed as such." Deslonde found a great deal of difference between the "comfort and eligibility and convenience" of the bureau as compared to the ladies' cabin.[28]

Disputing Deslonde's reaction, Captain Thomas Leathers, a lifelong steamboat operator and "master of the Steamer Natchez, a weekly packet between New Orleans and Vicksburg," at the time of Madame Decuir's journey, reported that some high-status men of color accepted, and even preferred, accommodations in the bureau. In particular, Leathers stated that his colored passengers, including Louisiana lieutenant governor Oscar Dunn, who died in November 1871, and Mississippi's United States Senator Hiram Revels, who served in 1870 and 1871, preferred the bureau. Revels was the first African American to serve in the United States Senate. He was elected by Mississippi's Reconstruction legislature and seated after a Senate debate in which Democrats, relying on the *Dred Scott* decision, argued that as a former slave, he did not meet the Constitution's nine year citizenship requirement for service in the Senate because he became a citizen of the United States only when the Fourteenth Amendment was ratified in 1868, two years before his election to the Senate. Leathers stated that he also "frequently had other Colored members of the Legislature of both Louisiana and Mississippi and always put them in the colored cabin and never heard any complaint from them on that score."[29]

Nevertheless, Deslonde asserted that the situation for colored travelers like him had become worse since the end of the war, and he attributed it to racial prejudice:

I saw a prejudice from here to Louisville but just as quick as I took the cars to go to Washington I discovered I was treated with the proper respect, having the full accommodation of the first fare, but down here South, I never met it yet in my life and I was bred and born here. . . . Providing your skin is White you can get everything, but while my pocket was full of gold I could not get no fare.[30]

Deslonde's comments are consistent with the dignitary aims of the reformers who pressed for equality and integration in the public sphere. Rebecca Scott characterizes the rights sought by Deslonde, Madame Decuir, and others as "public rights" (i.e., rights that would "encompass the[ir] dignitary and anti-discriminatory concerns").[31] It may be that the grievances of high-status people of color were augmented by resentment over being considered colored by White society when they did not see, in themselves, the characteristics of the dark-skinned Black people who had been enslaved. Both Deslonde and another of Madame Decuir's witnesses at trial, Aristile Duconge, who identified himself as a former merchant born and residing in New Orleans, were clearly seething with anger over their treatment as second-class citizens. Duconge was a prominent member of the French-speaking community of color. In 1868, he, together with Louis A. Snaer, the brother of Madame Decuir's attorney S. R. Snaer, was accommodated with the White travelers on the steamboat *Mississippi* from New Orleans to St. Louis. Although physically the two may have been able to pass for White, it was probably known that they were colored; due to his military and government service, Louis A. Snaer was a well-known figure in New Orleans. Duconge acknowledged that he was reputed to be a man of color but did not take the bait when asked to elaborate on what physical features separate the White from the non-White race.[32]

It is clear that the policy of riverboat segregation was designed to satisfy White travelers' demand that they not be forced to travel in close proximity to non-White passengers. As Barbara Welke has so thoroughly and persuasively documented, this was due to two related factors: the perception that integration, especially in the ladies' car, was a threat to White supremacy; and the consensus among Southern Whites that their "ladies" had to be protected from Black men. Whites constituted about 80 percent of the steamboat travelers in postwar Louisiana, and the boat owners all stated that they would lose a substantial portion of their business if they did not segregate passengers by race. What is less clear is the reason for the claim of equal treatment. Perhaps those defending segregation thought that equal treatment would satisfy Louisiana's laws prohibiting discrimination, but in Madame Decuir's case, that legal point was not argued. Perhaps the boat owners were in competition for the business of non-White travelers and wanted to reassure them that they would be well taken care of on their boats. For whatever reason, Captain Benson's rejection of Washington's request that Madame Decuir be accommodated in the ladies' cabin was based, at least in part, on his assertion that her treatment in the bureau would be equal to the treatment of White women in the ladies' cabin.[33]

Madame Decuir remained overnight in the recess, sitting up the entire night in a chair and taking her meals in this nonprivate area. She did not avail herself of the cot to sleep, finding it impossible to undress in an area open to other passengers. The ladies' cabin being just next door, she would have watched as the White women on the boat went to and fro, taking their children into the recess to play or relax after dinner, adding to her discomfort as the night wore on.[34]

Washington, while upset over his client's distress, probably had a pleasant, if somewhat hot, night on the *Governor Allen*. There was plenty of food and coffee available and interesting passengers to talk to. Washington and Madame Decuir may have spent some time discussing her husband's succession matters, or her brother Antoine, or the indignity of her situation. Very likely both knew that segregation on the *Governor Allen* was illegal under Louisiana law. They were almost certainly aware of Sheriff Charles Sauvinet's case challenging his exclusion from the Bank Coffeehouse. While that case involved exclusion and not segregation, the statute under which Sauvinet sued, which prohibited race-based exclusion from places open to the public and from places licensed by state and local government, was the very same statute that prohibited discrimination on common carriers such as the *Governor Allen*. Madame Decuir and Washington may have viewed that episode as a precedent supporting their conclusion that Captain Benson was violating Louisiana law. Given how quickly Madame Decuir filed suit against Captain Benson, the decision to sue was likely made on his boat as Madame Decuir rode in exile in the recess behind the ladies' cabin.

When the *Governor Allen* arrived at Hermitage Landing in the morning, Madame Decuir paid for her freight and the lower fare charged to colored passengers. She disembarked and joined her lawyers, including Snaer who had traveled at the same time on a different boat, for the journey to the New Roads area. There, the lawyers probably spent a day or two looking through court files and Antoine Decuir's financial records. There may have been unpleasant interactions with Madame Decuir's prior lawyers, given that Washington would have needed access to their files to evaluate Madame Decuir's claims.[35]

We do not know if Madame Decuir returned to New Orleans with

Washington and Snaer or if she stayed on in Pointe Coupée Parish. There is no record of what boat they took back down to New Orleans or whether she even went back down after Washington and Snaer finished their investigation. When the two lawyers arrived back in New Orleans, they began working on a lawsuit over Madame Decuir's treatment on the boat, as well their efforts to reopen the succession proceedings.

On July 29, 1872, eight days after her trip on the *Governor Allen*, Madame Decuir, represented by Washington and Snaer, filed suit against Captain Benson in the Eighth District Court for Orleans Parish.[36] Before examining Madame Decuir's lawsuit in detail, it is important to pause to consider how the 1869 antidiscrimination statute under which she sued came to be. The short version is that in the late 1860s and early 1870s, the government of Louisiana was controlled by Republicans, including freed and colored men, committed, in varying degrees, to the cause of racial equality. The complete story is more complicated and reveals a great deal about the process of Reconstruction in postwar Louisiana.

The Reconstruction Background

Louisiana seceded from the Union in 1861 and adopted a new constitution to reflect its status as one of the Confederate States of America. In April 1862, Union forces took New Orleans and used it as a combat base for the remainder of the war. For most of the war, the Union controlled New Orleans and nearby territory along major waterways, including the Mississippi River. In 1864, the United States government designated those parts of Louisiana under Union control as a separate state, and that same year, the federally approved government adopted a new constitution abolishing slavery, granting voting rights to some Black men, and providing for public education for children of all races between the ages of six and eighteen.[37] On April 11, 1865, in the last speech he gave before he was assassinated, President Abraham Lincoln urged Congress to readmit Louisiana's government to the Union, highlighting the fact that its constitution granted limited Black suffrage.

In the South more broadly, defeat in the Civil War and the freeing of nearly four million slaves made it necessary for Southern society to adjust to new realities on multiple fronts. Millions of former slaves of African descent were now free and on their way to becoming citizens of the United States.

Race had always been an organizing principle in the social, legal, and economic life of the United States, especially in the South. Would it remain so? What legal rights would the freedmen have? What about their social status? What would happen to labor markets in the South with the end of slavery? Southern society settled on exclusion when possible, segregation when exclusion was not possible, and legal, social, and economic inferiority for people of color, whether they had been free or enslaved before the war.

After Lincoln's assassination, President Andrew Johnson's plan for Reconstruction, which has been termed "Presidential Reconstruction," allowed the South's White establishment to regain power, with only leading rebels disqualified from participating.[38] On May 29, 1865, Johnson issued a blanket pardon to all participants in the rebellion, White and colored, except for a relatively small group of high-ranking Confederate officials and others who had actively participated in or aided the rebellion. And many of those who were not included in the blanket pardon successfully petitioned for individual pardons. On the political scene, racially exclusionary governments composed largely of antisecession White Southerners gained power, while in Louisiana secessionist Democrats took over "on a platform declaring that Louisiana government should be 'perpetuated for the exclusive benefit of the White race.'"[39] Thus, in the early postwar period, Southern resistance to equal rights for people of color was enabled to a great extent by the lack of forceful action to protect civil rights by the executive branch in Washington.

During this period of presidential Reconstruction, Southern state governments began passing Black codes, which were designed to keep the newly freed slaves in a perpetual state of indentured servitude. The government of Louisiana quickly adopted a Black code, which severely restricted free Black labor and political participation.[40] Large numbers of Black people were jailed for vagrancy, and in some communities, former slaves needed permission from their former owners to work for anyone else.[41] Even where laws were racially neutral, they were enforced in a discriminatory manner in order to preserve as much of the prewar status quo as possible.[42]

The Louisiana Black code of 1865 created a system of legally enforced apprenticeship for minors whose parents were unable to provide for them, and also legalized five-year binding employment arrangements that would be virtually indistinguishable from slavery. In general, the Black codes closed many occupations to people of color and prohibited them from owing firearms. Individual parishes in Louisiana enacted their own Black codes. For example, in St. Landry Parish, the site of an 1868 massacre of Blacks described later, the local Black code required "Negroes" to obtain a permit to enter the parish, prohibited them from owning or leasing property, and required them to work for a White person. The code also restricted the mobility of Black people's labor, providing that the "employer or former owner may permit said negro to hire his own time by special permission in writing, which permission shall not extend over seven days at any one time."

Other legal reforms were also aimed at suppressing the ambitions of the newly freed. Heavy taxes were placed on labor, as compared with lower taxation of real property. Laws on grazing animals were reformed to prevent Black people without property from competing with White property owners. Rather than adapt to the reality of free labor, Southern leaders worked to recreate, as nearly as possible, the system of slave labor.

Even in the North, Johnson's program enjoyed a great deal of support. Some Northerners thought it showed the greatest promise for reviving the Southern economy, especially cotton production, which would in turn support Northern textile, export, and banking interests.[43] Black suffrage did not enjoy majority support in the North, and, for a time, it seemed that Johnson's plan and all of its consequences would prevail. However, there was always a core of Radical Republicans that advocated equal rights for all and thus opposed enabling Southern governments to rejoin the Union without purging all remnants of the slave system. News of violence directed at Black people across the South and the oppressive terms of the Black codes steadily broadened support for the radical position. The result was a more Radical Reconstruction led not by the president but by Congress.

Beginning in 1866, Congress enacted a series of civil rights laws culminating in the Civil Rights Act of 1875, under which numerous criminal prosecutions and civil actions against racial segregation and exclusion were brought. These reforms resulted in increased political participation for Blacks and other citizens of color.[44] As noted, the convulsive legal changes that occurred in the immediate aftermath of the Civil War, mainly during, have been termed a "second founding" by historian Eric Foner.[45] Three constitutional amendments and four civil rights statutes were enacted into law in the period from 1865 through 1875, forever changing the status of the people of color in the United States. These legal reforms were seen as finally translating the Declaration of Independence's principles of liberty and equality into positive law. The Thirteenth Amendment abolished slavery and, in a move seen by some as even more revolutionary, granted Congress the power to enforce the amendment by "appropriate legislation." Significantly, the Thirteenth Amendment did not address voting rights. Congress then enacted, over President Andrew Johnson's veto, the Civil Rights Act of 1866, which purported to extend US citizenship to "all persons born in the United States" (except Native Americans living under tribal sovereignty and offspring of foreign diplomats). The act also extended to all citizens, "of every race and color," the same basic rights associated at the time with citizenship as "enjoyed by white citizens," including the right "to make and enforce contracts, to sue, give evidence, [and] to inherit, purchase, lease, sell, hold, and convey real and personal property." For the first time in a federal law, the act invoked the concept of racial equality, guaranteeing to all citizens "the full and equal benefit of all laws and proceedings for the security of person and property." In another startling provision, the act declared that it would be lawful for federal authorities and the president to enlist "the land or naval forces of the United States, or . . . the militia" to enforce the act. The act also contained detailed instructions for the enforcement of its civil and criminal provisions in court and by federal district attorneys and marshals.[46]

Doubts about whether there was an adequate constitutional basis for the 1866 act, and concern that a future Congress might repeal it, led civil rights advocates in Congress to draft and propose the Fourteenth Amendment. Ratification was complete in 1868. This amendment, which also includes a clause giving Congress the power to enforce it by "appropriate legislation," amalgamated several disparate concerns. Its most familiar provisions established birthright citizenship and guaranteed all persons the right to due process and equal protection. Although it did not address the right to vote directly, the amendment also promised to reduce the representation in Congress of any state that denied the right to vote to "any of the male inhabitants of Such state, being twenty-one years of age, and citizens of the United States." This provision was important because, as members of Congress recognized at the time, once former slaves were granted citizenship, they counted as whole persons in the census, rather than three-fifths under prior law, thus increasing Southern states' representation in Congress.[47] A further provision disqualified former rebels from holding federal or state office unless this "disability" was removed by a two-thirds vote of each house of Congress. Further provisions of the amendment proclaimed the validity of the federal debt and declared void all debts incurred "in aid of insurrection or rebellion" or based on claims for compensation for freed slaves.[48]

The final Reconstruction-era constitutional amendment was the Fifteenth Amendment, which became law in early 1870. This amendment prohibited states from denying to any citizen the right to vote based on "race, color, or previous condition of servitude."[49] After these constitutional amendments became law, and as conditions for people of color in the South continued to deteriorate, Congress began to pass legislation enforcing them. The Enforcement Act of 1870 re-enacted the 1866 act (now on a more secure constitutional footing) and included civil and criminal penalties against officials, state and federal, who violated or failed to enforce various provisions of the Reconstruction-era constitutional amendments and statutes, including voting rights and bars on public service for formal rebels. This act, and the two civil rights statutes that followed it, were signed into law by President Ulysees S. Grant, who was much more sympathetic to the cause of equal rights for people of color than his predecessor had been.

The Civil Rights Act of 1871 created a federal civil remedy against state officials who, acting under color of state law, violated the federal rights of "any person within the jurisdiction of the United States." It also created civil and criminal liability against "two or more persons [who] conspire . . . or go in disguise upon the public highway or upon the premises of another for the purpose, either directly or indirectly, depriving any person or any class of persons of the equal protection of the laws, or of equal privileges or immunities under the laws." These provisions were inspired by extensive evidence that had been presented to Congress that state and local officials either stood by or were in league with the Ku Klux Klan and similar organizations that were terrorizing people of color throughout the South. The "under color of law" provision, now known as "section 1983," remains a fertile source of federal civil rights actions, including, inter alia, claims alleging excessive force by police.[50]

Louisiana's Reconstruction-Era Reforms

In line with Congress's plan of Reconstruction, in 1868, Louisiana's government under the constitution of 1864 was declared invalid under federal Reconstruction legislation, and a constitutional convention was held in New Orleans to form a new government that would be acceptable to federal authorities. This time, radical Republicans, Blacks and mixed-race men of color, dominated the proceedings, producing a constitution that granted citizenship to all people of color and voting rights to Black men. They repealed the Black codes and continued the exclusion of former rebels from voting and office holding.

Most directly relevant to Madame Decuir, the constitution of 1868 prohibited racial discrimination in public accommodations, providing for

equal rights and privileges upon any conveyance of a public character; and all places of business, or of public resort, or for which a license is required by either State, parish or municipal authority, shall be deemed places of a public character, and shall be opened to the accommodation and patronage of all persons, without distinction or discrimination on account of race or color.[51]

In the first election held under this constitution, also in 1868, White Republican Henry Clay Warmoth was elected governor and Oscar Dunn, a man of color and former slave, was elected lieutenant governor, the first African American to hold that post in any state.[52] The legislature was controlled by the Republican Party, and between 1869 and 1871, it passed three statutes that became relevant to Madame Decuir's case. The most important was the 1869 prohibition on race discrimination in modes of transportation in Louisiana, known as Act No. 38 of 1869.[53] Section 1 provided

that all persons engaged within this State in the business of common carriers of passengers shall have the right to refuse to admit any person to any railroad cars, street cars, steamboats or other water crafts, stage coaches, omnibuses or other vehicle, or to expel any person therefrom after admission, when such person shall, on demand, refuse or neglect to pay the customary fare, or when such person shall be of infamous character, or shall be guilty, after admission to the conveyance of the carrier, of gross, vulgar or disorderly conduct, or who shall commit any act tending to injure the business of the carrier, prescribed for the management of his business after such rules and regulations shall have been made known; provided, said rules and regulations make no discrimination on account of race or color.[54]

Section 4 of the act specified the remedies for a violation of the act: "For a violation of any of the provisions of the first and second sections of this act, the party injured shall have the right of action to recover any damages, exemplary as well as actual, which he may sustain, before any court of competent jurisdiction." Section 2 was a comprehensive public accommodations law, providing that "no person shall be refused admission to any public inn, hotel or place of public resort within the state." Section 3 provided that any licensed establishment that is not "open to the accommodation and patronage of all persons without distinction based on race or color" shall "be punished by forfeiture of his license, and his place of business or of public resort shall be closed." Similar statutes were passed in many of the Southern states that, at the time, were governed by progressive coalitions of Republicans and people of color, including South Carolina, Texas, Arkansas, Florida, and Mississippi.[55]

Not surprisingly, New Orleans White society did not embrace these provisions of law or the cause of racial equality underlying them. In the *Daily Picayune*, the law was decried as "the work of misguided blackmen and very worthless and wicked white ones," while the *New Orleans Bee* predicted "it will be defied and condemned by every white man who has any sense of dignity and superiority of his race over that of the negro."[56]

Subsequently, the Louisiana general assembly enacted two procedural statutes to support enforcement of Act 38. In 1870, the legislature passed a statute granting priority to cases brought under civil rights statutes, including Act 38 of 1869.[57] Madame Decuir's lawyer E. K. Washington successfully invoked this provision in the Louisiana trial court and Supreme Court. Recognizing that it might be impossible to get a unanimous verdict in a discrimination case from a jury that included White members, in 1871, the Louisiana legislature provided in a statute that if a jury in a discrimination case does not come to a unanimous verdict for either party, "it shall be the duty of the judge to decide the case at once, without any further proceedings, arguments, continuance, or delay; each party having the right to appeal to the Supreme Court in all cases where an appeal is allowed by law." This statute was applied in Sheriff Sauvinet's challenge to his exclusion from the Bank Coffeehouse, although the judge in that case allowed the parties to file briefs before he rendered his decision, violating the statute's requirement to decide the case "at once, without any further proceedings."[58]

Captain Benson's refusal to accommodate Madame Decuir in the ladies' cabin on the *Governor Allen* was an affront to her dignity and appeared to her and her lawyers to violate her rights under Louisiana law. Once she filed suit, the proceedings went relatively quickly, and it was clear from the outset that *Decuir v. Benson* was a test case on the application and viability of Louisiana's Reconstruction-era effort to prohibit racial discrimination.

4

Madame Decuir's Suit against Captain Benson

News that Madame Decuir had filed suit against Captain John Benson on July 29, 1872, was carried the next evening in the *Picayune*, the most widely read newspaper in New Orleans, on the same page as an advertisement for the *Governor Allen*'s weekly trip from New Orleans to Vicksburg.[1] The case was important to both plaintiff and defendant, but for different reasons. Madame Decuir was seeking to vindicate her personal dignity and her rights as a citizen of the United States, which she felt had been denied since her return from Paris. Owing to her precarious financial situation, the potential for a substantial damages award was likely also an incentive to sue. Captain Benson, and his fellow steamboaters, were seeking to preserve their authority to segregate the races on their boats, both because of support for segregation that was widespread among the White community and out of possible concern that enforcement of Louisiana's ban on segregation would deter Whites from traveling by riverboat and thus cut into their income.

The case was also potentially important to millions of people throughout the South. The outcome of the Civil War had set two world views, racial equality and White supremacy, on a collision course. After the 1865 assassination of President Abraham Lincoln and the ascension of Vice President Andrew Johnson to the presidency, the federal commitment to protecting Blacks wavered, with Congress forced to take the leading role after President Johnson embarked on his lenient program of presidential reconstruction. Racial segregation and outright exclusion were developing as postwar norms and they were being applied equally to freed slaves and never-enslaved people of color. Madame Decuir's lawsuit sought to enforce the counter norms of integration and full equality, as embodied in the Louisiana Constitution of 1868 and the statutes passed under it. Victory could add momentum to the movement for equality that sought to end exclusion and segregation. Insofar as they knew about the suit, Southern Whites would have been concerned that integration was contrary to their worldview. The steamboating community was certainly concerned about the effects the case might have on their business and their ability to behave consistently with the norm of White supremacy.

Madame Decuir's Claims

Because she did not testify when her case was tried, Madame Decuir told her story primarily through her complaint. The handwritten complaint, signed by S. R. Snaer and E. K. Washington, set forth that the *Governor Allen* was a common carrier operating between New Orleans and Vicksburg and that it was subject to the nondiscrimination requirements of Louisiana law. It told the story of Madame Decuir's journey, emphasizing that Madame Decuir was "expressly denied, though in ill-health at the time, the privilege of even a state room in the cabin, or a seat at the table to take her meals on said boat." Rather, "she was forced to remain in a small compartment in the rear of said boat, which was a public place, without the common conveniences granted to the other passengers, on the sole ground . . . that she was a colored person." She further alleged that "her meals . . . were brought out to her to said place after all the cabin passengers, officers, and servants had sat at the table and eaten, and she was thus compelled to eat on a chair." Adding to her discomfort,

Adding to her discomfort, "she was forced to set up all night, although a bed was offered to her on the floor of said boat, which she refused for the reasons that the place was public, and a place of passage for the officers, of the boat and every one, and she could not, on account of delicacy, disrobe herself or be exposed to the sight of every one." She also claimed that she was "exposed to the vulgar conversation of the crew and every one on said boat."[2]

In short, the boat's policy of segregation, she claimed, was distressing and illegal. She pled that she was "a native of the State of Louisiana; that her husband was a large land-holder in the parish of Pointe Coupée . . . that she is well educated; that she resided more than twelve years in the city of Paris, France . . . that she has always demeaned herself with propriety, decorum, and respect . . . [and] that she was not guilty of any gross, vulgar or disorderly conduct." Her trip on the *Governor Allen* had been on "legal business of importance in the matter of the succession of her late husband." Stated most simply, she wanted to be treated like a lady, with respect and concern for her well-being.[3]

These pleadings were essential to her claim. The 1868 Louisiana statute prohibiting discrimination on riverboats expressly recognized the carrier's common-law right to establish and enforce rules and regulations, specifically the right to "refuse to admit" or "expel" any "person . . . of infamous character, or [who] shall be guilty, after admission to the conveyance of the carrier, of gross, vulgar, or disorderly conduct, or who shall commit any act tending to injure the business of the carrier, prescribed for the management of his business, after such rules and regulations shall have been made known." By alleging that she was well educated and had always behaved with propriety and decorum, she helped establish that the only reason she had been excluded from the ladies' cabin was her race, in direct violation of the statute's requirement that carriers "make no discrimination on account of race or color."

She also alleged that her legal rights were violated and that she suffered damages due to the violation. Legally, her complaint stated that

she was denied the equal rights and privileges granted to all persons under the provisions of article 13th of the constitution of Louisiana, in regard to the equal rights and privileges of all persons, irrespective of race and color, and under the laws of the United States, and under the provisions of act No. 38, of the general assembly of 1869, on the sole ground of her being a person of color.

In support of damages, she alleged that

she was greatly insulted and wounded in her feelings, . . . that the treatment above alluded to is not only a gross infraction of the constitution and laws of this State and those of the United States, but is also a gross indignity to her personally; and for this denial of equal rights and privileges on the part of said officers of the steamboat Governor Allen, was such a shock to her feelings, and occasioned so much mental pain, shame, and mortification, that her mind was affected.[4]

And she claimed—falsely, it would appear, given that this was at least her third attempt to be treated as White on a Mississippi River steamboat—"that in all her travels on different steamers and public conveyances, both in this country and Europe, she has not met a like indignity as on the steamer Governor Allen." The complaint requested $25,000 in actual damages and $50,000 in punitive damages, which Act 38 specifically allowed, for a total of $75,000.[5]

Before filing suit, either Madame Decuir or her lawyers consulted with Madame Decuir's brother Antoine Dubuclet, Louisiana state treasurer, who promised to guarantee costs in case they did not prevail. This promise was set forth in a document attached to Madame Decuir's complaint, which Dubuclet signed, stating simply, "I am surety for cash trust in the above entitled suit."[6] Dubuclet may have encouraged his sister to take action to establish the principle that Captain Benson could not ignore the law of Louisiana and continue racial segregation. In fact, Decuir family descendants have expressed the opinion that a Decuir would have been unlikely to bring suit without encouragement or even incitement from someone outside the Decuir family such as Dubuclet.[7]

Madame Decuir's case was assigned to Henry C. Dibble, judge of the Eighth District Court in New Orleans. This was promising. Judge Dibble was "an early adherent of Louisiana's Radical Republican party." He was an active supporter of Henry Clay Warmoth's campaign for governor of Louisiana and was rewarded by Warmoth with an appointment as judge of the newly created Eighth District Court. He had presided over Sheriff Charles Sauvinet's successful suit under the same statute invoked by Madame Decuir. After his judicial service in Louisiana, the end of which was quite dramatic and is recounted below, Judge Dibble relocated to California where, as a legislator, he authored a civil rights law (informally known as "Dibble's Law") passed in 1897, which outlawed race discrimination in places of public accommodation and amusement.[8]

Captain Benson brought the complaint to his lawyer Bentinck Egan, a respected admiralty practitioner, experienced litigator, and one of the leading lawyers in New Orleans at the time, who represented a wide range of clients in business and personal disputes.

Bentinck Egan

Egan was born in 1834 or 1835—the 1860 federal census lists him as twenty-five years old, a lawyer, and living at the same address as his parents, three younger siblings, and an Irish servant named "Brigitt." It is unclear whether Egan was born in New Orleans or elsewhere. He may have been born in Canada where his father was a surgeon, or in Vermont, where his father was reportedly from. His mother was the daughter of an Irish lord, and his father must have been successful, as his personal estate in that 1860 census was valued at $20,000, a tidy sum at the time.[9]

In addition to admiralty matters, Egan also represented clients in typical commercial and personal matters such as breach-of-contract cases and succession proceedings. Egan initially practiced law together with his younger brother Henry who died in the Civil War, as did another brother Yelverton, named for his mother's noble family. Henry was killed at age twenty-four at Amelia Springs, Virginia, on April 6, 1865, very close to the end of the war while commanding sharpshooters protecting the retreat of Robert E. Lee's army. Yelverton also died at age twenty-four, at the battle of Sharpsburg, Maryland, in September, 1862. Both of Egan's parents outlived all six of their sons, and Bentinck's only surviving sibling at the time of his death in 1881 was his younger sister Louisa. Bentinck Egan never married or had children.[10]

Although his sympathies were likely with the Confederate side during the Civil War, and there is no indication that his attitude toward Black people was any different from the average Southern White at the time, it does not appear that Egan was especially devoted to defeating civil rights claims. Rather, he was one of New Orleans's leading admiralty and commercial lawyers and may have been Benson's everyday lawyer. Certainly his reputation as a top admiralty lawyer and as "devoted to the interest of [his] clients" would have made him a logical choice to represent Benson, especially since the entire community of steamboat owners and operators was keenly interested in the case. He was known as a zealous advocate—a tribute after his death reported that he was "pernicious in his arguments; he never gave up a case in which he was engaged until every argument and authority had been successfully combated, and so earnest and persistent was he in pressing his points as at times to risk the displeasure of the Court."[11] This character trait may explain why Egan may have attempted to file a brief in Benson's defense in the US Supreme Court even though another lawyer, Robert H. (R. H.) Marr, had taken over when the case reached that court.

Egan's life was decidedly unremarkable other than when, as a teenager in 1849, he went to California to join the gold rush. Shortly thereafter, Egan returned to New Orleans "after many sufferings and hardships." The return trip was by foot. It was said that Egan was captain of a party that set out from California for New Orleans, and that only four of the group survived the journey. He may have had little social life outside a small circle of family and close friends. As the tribute reported, "His pleasures consisted in the study of his cases; among his leisure hours he was to be found at his home surrounded by his books." He was financially successful, leaving a substantial estate to his parents and sister: "As a son his devotion to his parents was simply beautiful; as a brother he was kind, affectionate and loving, to his only sister, who in return seemed wedded equally to him."[12]

In addition to admiralty cases, Egan handled all manner of commercial and personal disputes. A particularly interesting example is a breach-of-contract case Egan won on appeal to the Louisiana Supreme Court in 1874. In 1868, plaintiff Eliza V. Mahood sold furniture to defendant Ida T. Tealza with a purchase price of $5,500, or approximately $90,000 in current dollars. It was apparently a large amount of furniture, used by both women in the pursuit of their businesses: running houses of prostitution. After Tealza stopped making required monthly payments, Mahood "sequestered" the furniture (although not all of it since the defendant had allegedly disposed of some of it) and sued Tealza for the remaining balance of $1,500.[13]

In the trial court, Tealza prevailed on the ground that the furniture was being used to further the illegal and immoral business of prostitution. As Supreme Court justice James G. Taliaferro explained, "The defendant, avowing her own infamy, invokes the maxim ex turpi pacto nil oritur action [on an immoral contract no action lies]." Justice Taliaferro and the Court majority rejected application of the maxim to the case, citing two then-recent Louisiana Supreme Court decisions enforcing contracts in virtually identical circumstances, including one in which he wrote the Court's opinion. Perhaps not wanting to create insecurity in an important sector of the New Orleans economy, Justice Taliaferro's opinion found that they "must, therefore, reject the plea of contra bonos mores, examine this case on the merits, and determine it according to the law and evidence." And on the law and evidence, Egan prevailed, his client was awarded a judgment in the full amount of $1,500 and he was given permission to sell the seized furniture to satisfy the judgment.[14] The decision was not unanimous. Justice Phillip H. Morgan, joined by Justice Rufus K. Howell, observed in dissent that in cases concerning contracts to advance immoral activities, "the law, I think, leaves such people where it finds them, and takes no interest in their disputes."[15]

Egan was so well respected that on a Monday shortly after he died, both the state and federal district courts "adjourned out of respect to the memory of Mr. Bentinck Egan." As the tribute in which this was reported continued: "All who knew this gentleman respected him due to his sterling worth, and recognized him as a lawyer of great ability and integrity. . . . To those who knew him best, his virtues will long be remembered, and as a tribute to his memory, let it be said with truth—he was a noble, kind and good man."[16]

Madame Decuir's suit shaped up quickly as a test case over segregation. The defense readily admitted that Madame Decuir had been barred from the ladies' cabin due to her race but argued that Captain Benson had the right as a common carrier, protected by federal law, to make reasonable rules governing conduct on his boat, including the right to assign passengers to different cabins based on their race. Although Egan did not argue that equal, but separate, accommodations satisfied Louisiana law, he apparently intended, in some undefined way, to pit the custom of segregation against the statutory prohibition of racial discrimination. In August, 1872, Egan filed a motion denominated "exceptions" to dismiss Madame Decuir's case, raising mainly federal grounds along with two technical state law defenses that did not address race discrimination.[17]

After arguments on December 2 and December 11, 1872, before Judge Dibble, the motion to dismiss was denied, but in the meantime, the case had been transferred for further proceedings to the Fifth District Court where Egan was allowed to replead his defenses in his answer to the complaint.[18] The record does not reveal a reason for the transfer, but Louisiana's government, including the courts, was in turmoil after the election of 1872. Both Republicans and Democrats had claimed victory. Judge Dibble apparently lost his judgeship in the election, but the transition did not go smoothly. Judge Dibble, accompanied by Sheriff Sauvinet, who had also lost his bid for re-election, refused to acknowledge the vote of the election and attempted to retain his seat. When the newly elected judge W. A. Elmore rejected Judge Dibble's demand to vacate the courtroom, Judge Dibble ordered Sheriff Sauvinet to arrest Judge Elmore. When that did not happen, Judge Dibble and

Sheriff Sauvinet left to seek relief in the Louisiana Supreme Court, and Judge Elmore commenced to conduct the Court's business. The state legislature then held an extra session, and on December 11, 1872, it abolished the Eighth District Court and replaced it with a new "Superior District Court."[19]

The transfer placed Madame Decuir's case before the newly elected judge E. North Collum of the Fifth District Court, who took his seat on the morning of November 21, 1872, without incident.[20] The sparse historical record indicates that Judge Collum was a Democrat, perhaps with somewhat liberal attitudes on race. Before being elected judge, he practiced law with his father Francis Collum, who had a long career as a carpenter before becoming a lawyer in 1845. While still a carpenter, Francis Collum participated in an effort to prevent a Black man, Daniel Hancock, from regaining his freedom. Hancock was born free in Connecticut and served from 1815 through 1817 in the US Navy. After his service, Hancock relocated to Louisiana where, in 1823, he was sold into slavery by his employer and delivered into possession of another carpenter, John Davis. Hancock sued for his freedom, and at the onset of proceedings, the trial judge allowed Davis to retain possession of Hancock on the condition that Davis post a bond sufficient to guarantee that he would produce Hancock in court for the trial and comply with any judgment issued in the case, including possible retroactive wages for Davis. Francis Collum helped Davis post the bond and, when Davis died during the litigation, Collum participated in the inventory and valuation of Davis's estate. Hancock won his case for freedom based on extensive evidence gathered in Connecticut and New York, but ultimately, he collected very little in damages for the time he spent in legally unauthorized bondage.[21]

Judge Collum was a respected member of the New Orleans legal and political community. In September 1868, he addressed a meeting of the Crescent City Democratic Club, and in promotional material for the event, he was characterized as "a man of rare attainments and eloquence."[22] He was part of the Democratic Party's effort to attract non-White voters in the 1876 election. Once, after his involvement with Madame Decuir's case was over, together with a member of Captain Benson's Supreme Court litigation team, he addressed a political meeting in 1876, urging Whites to treat Blacks "kindly and endeavor to make them understand that their interests were common; to open their doors to the colored people and invite them to take part in their proceedings, and thereby convince the colored voter of the sincerity of the words embodied in the Baton Rouge platform," as that year's state Democratic Party platform was called.[23] This platform included language promising fair treatment for Louisiana's colored people. Judge Collum served as a judge for a long time, at least until 1897, when he was identified as the judge in a case appealed to the Louisiana Supreme Court from the superior court in the Parish of Natchitoches.[24]

Late in December, 1872, Egan filed Benson's answer to Madame Decuir's complaint in Judge Collum's court, reiterating and refining the defenses he had raised in the motion to dismiss. He argued that the *Governor Allen* was federally licensed and therefore the application of Louisiana's antidiscrimination laws violated "article 1, section 8, of the Constitution of the United States, giving Congress exclusive power to regulate commerce among the several states." He also renewed his argument that Madame Decuir's claims should be denied because she had paid only for bureau passage, not the fare charged to White passengers in the ladies' cabin.[25]

Egan also made an argument founded on the traditional common-law rights of common carriers that came tantalizingly close to an argument for "separate but equal." Egan argued that while common carriers like Captain Benson were required to serve all customers who tendered the required fare, they retained the right to establish reasonable rules and regulations governing their facilities and that racial segregation was a "reasonable, usual and customary" practice. Admitting Madame Decuir's central claim that she was denied a place in the ladies' cabin due to her racial identity, the answer asserted that colored passengers were "provided with state-rooms and all the conveniences of the cabin appropriated for the exclusive use of White persons." Egan's argument faced a substantial hurdle: Louisiana's 1869 statute explicitly allowed common carriers to make and enforce reasonable rules, but the legislation banned racial classifications: "*Provided*, said rules and regulations make no discrimination on account of race or color." Egan did not argue, as he might have, that "separate but equal" was not "discrimination." Thus, Captain Benson was asking the Court to ignore the statute in favor of a long-standing custom of segregation.[26]

Egan also made an argument founded upon the Due Process Clause of the Fourteenth Amendment, that private property such as the *Governor Allen* could not be regulated by government:

Said boat is private property and does not belong to the public and any law attempting to prevent him from regulating and managing said steamboat to the best advantage and for the interest of her owner would be in violation of Article 14 Section first of the amendment of the constitution of the United States prohibiting any State from depriving any person of his property without due process of law.[27]

Louisiana courts, affirmed by the US Supreme Court, had recently approved extensive regulation of slaughterhouses, so this argument must not have seemed too promising. It may have been more so a few years later when, during what has become known as the Lochner era, the Supreme Court interpreted the Due Process Clause to protect property and contract rights from what today is considered routine regulation.[28]

Some of Egan's allegations seem designed to reduce Captain Benson's exposure to damages. For example, Egan alleged that Madame Decuir knew before boarding that she would not be accommodated in the ladies' cabin of the *Governor Allen*. If Madame Decuir knew of the policy of segregation on the *Governor Allen*, she could have avoided it, and the humiliation she said it had caused, by simply taking a different boat. Had she accepted the offer of a room in the bureau, she would have had sleeping accommodations and meal service equal to that provided to Whites in the ladies' cabin. In short, Egan argued, if Madame Decuir suffered any injury, it was her own fault for choosing to travel on the *Governor Allen* or rejecting the room that was offered.

Judge Collum did not rule before trial on the sufficiency of Captain Benson's defenses, but rather set the case for an expedited hearing as required by Louisiana's antidiscrimination law. Neither party asked for a jury trial, so the case was conducted as a bench trial before Judge Collum. In other contemporaneous cases attacking segregation, the defendants sought jury trials, hoping for White jurors who would rule in favor of segregation. Public opinion among Whites was certainly on the side of segregation. Continuing its condemnation of the 1869 Louisiana equal rights law, the Picayune stated in 1874 that "the law itself is regarded by all thoughtful and well informed citizens as a violent infraction of constitutional rights" and it was thus no surprise that an "intelligent and respectable" jury would not rule in the plaintiff's favor in such a case. Benson's surprising failure to request a jury trial may indicate that from the outset, the defense viewed this as a test case, a vehicle to address the legal issues, primarily the constitutionality of applying Louisiana's antidiscrimination laws to boats operating on the Mississippi River.[29]

The Testimony in Madame Decuir's Case

For some unexplained reason, rather than holding trial in open court, most of the testimony in Madame Decuir's case was taken in private, in Egan's office. Transcripts of the testimony were later filed for the judge to read and placed in the public record of the case. Twelve witnesses testified, seven called by Captain Benson, including Captain Benson himself, and five by Madame Decuir, including both of her lawyers, Washington and Snaer. As noted, Madame Decuir did not testify. The record does not indicate why she did not. Louisiana law at the time did not prohibit people of color from testifying against Whites, and women frequently testified in court. Egan and Washington were present at all of the sessions held in Egan's office and in court, with Snaer missing for some of the testimony.

The testimony strikingly depicts the racial attitudes and views on segregation of the day among the White and colored communities of Louisiana, including those engaged in steamboating on the Mississippi River. The testimony for both sides centered on three main issues; namely, what happened to Madame Decuir on the *Governor Allen*, the custom of segregation on riverboats, and the quality of service provided to colored passengers in the bureau. There was also some curious testimony on racial identity.

Because no one disputed that Madame Decuir was denied accommodation in the ladies' cabin on account of her race, the events on the *Governor Allen* seemed to be an aside to the bigger social and economic issues of the case—the justice and economics of segregation. Benson's witnesses affirmed the widespread practice and the need for any viable steamboat business to conform to it or risk losing their White customers, while Madame Decuir's witnesses testified to the humiliation they suffered over the treatment they received on riverboats, and their perception that while accommodations were certainly separate, they were far from equal.

The social practices of racial segregation and exclusion were well-established long before Madame Decuir boarded the *Governor Allen* in 1872. What was new was the necessity of developing a legal justification for these customs in light of the abolition of slavery and the adoption of state and federal prohibitions against discrimination. It seems pretty clear that postwar defenders of segregation felt compelled to assert that their segregated facilities were equal, leading to the development of what ultimately became the doctrine of "separate, but equal." But in Madame Decuir's case itself, the defense did not explicitly argue that equal treatment satisfied the requirements of Louisiana's laws prohibiting discrimination. The kernel of that idea may have been in the minds of the defense, but it had not yet germinated into an express legal doctrine.

Madame Decuir's two lawyers, Washington and Snaer, were the only witnesses to testify on her behalf about what happened that day, although Snaer's testimony was limited to explaining that he took a different boat after encountering Madame Decuir and Washington, separately, on the levee. Washington testified first and began with a narrative of the events, which was the customary way testimony began in many courts at the time.[30] It is unusual for a lawyer to testify on behalf of his client, but then it is also unusual for the lawyer to witness the events leading to the suit. Washington sometimes undercut Madame Decuir's case by saying that she was treated courteously by the *Governor Allen*'s personnel, which contradicted her own assertion, in the complaint, that she was treated rudely. The contradictions may reflect Washington's perspective as a White man, but he also seems to have been concerned that it would harm his reputation if he were too closely identified with his client's cause. He testified, and Captain Benson confirmed, that he had tried to keep Madame Decuir off of the *Governor Allen* and that he personally had not set out to foment a racial confrontation during this tense period in New Orleans.[31]

Washington supported Madame Decuir's claim for damages by stating that when he encountered her in the recess and informed her that she would not be accommodated in the cabin, "she was very much mortified and seemed to be crying too, sitting on the chair in the back part of the boat alone very much mortified." Washington's testimony supported his client's contention that the recess was not a comfortable place to stay overnight, though, again, not her contention that she had been treated rudely.[32]

Madame Decuir's other witnesses, Aristile Duconge, P. G. Deslonde, and James E. Moore, all men of color, testified about conditions for colored travelers generally, attacking the practice of segregation. Their testimony was designed mainly to dispute Captain Benson's claim that the facilities for colored passengers were equal to those for Whites, and to establish that even high-status people of color who sometimes received special accommodations were unhappy with their treatment on segregated boats. Their testimony also illustrated that regardless of the quality of their accommodations, their legal rights, clearly established under postwar state law, were being violated, and Benson and his comrades should not be permitted to resist the changes in the law made during Reconstruction. Washington used Moore, a police officer and former boat worker, to establish that colored bureaus were inferior to the ladies' cabin.[33] Nearly all of Deslonde's testimony was about the quality of service in the bureau of steamboats generally. He clearly seethed with resentment over the discriminatory treatment he received, and there was also an undertone of general hostility between him and Benson's attorney Egan. His exchanges with Egan have the flavor of a political debate on segregation.[34] Duconge testified mostly about an episode in which he and Snaer's brother Louis were treated as if they were White on a different boat, the *Mississippi*. Perhaps the idea here was to dispute the universality of the custom of segregation or the notion that it was economically necessary.[35]

As defense witnesses, Egan assembled a group of experienced riverboat captains and other boat workers to explain and defend the custom of seg-regation. Egan called six witnesses. Three, including Benson, were captains of Mississippi River steamboats. Thomas Leathers, captain of the steamer *Natchez* and a close associate of Captain Benson, was on the *Governor Allen* for the first part of Madame Decuir's journey; the *Governor Allen* was, for some reason, temporarily taking the *Natchez*'s usual run between New Orleans and Vicksburg during Madame Decuir's journey.[36] John W. Cannon was captain and owner of the steamer *Robert E. Lee* and owner of the steamboat *Katie*.[37] Two were clerks on steamboats, including the clerk of the *Governor Allen*, D. E. Grove, and J. H. Mossop, clerk of the *Robert E. Lee*.[38] The remaining defense witness, Cedilot, was the steward on the *Governor Allen*.[39]

Captains Leathers and Cannon were celebrities. Cannon's *Robert E. Lee*, built just after the Civil War, was the most luxurious steamboat on the Mississippi. It was also among the largest, with sixty-one staterooms in the main cabin and rooms for fifty more passengers in a cabin next to the nursery. It could seat two hundred and forty at dinner in a single dining room. On July 4, 1870, Cannon and Leathers held a widely publicized race between the *Robert E. Lee* and the *Natchez* from New Orleans to St. Louis, which Cannon won with a time of three days, eighteen hours, and forty-one minutes, besting Leathers by about three and one-half hours.[40]

Leathers was known to be a strong supporter of the Confederacy, and he flew the Confederate battle flag on the *Natchez* long after the end of the Civil War.[41] He, and after him his son Bowling, owned numerous boats named the *Natchez*, but the *Natchez* that he raced against the *Robert E. Lee* was the most famous. The fame of the Leathers family was renewed when, in 1894, Bowling died and his wife Blanche took over as captain of the *Natchez*. She was the first woman to captain a steamboat on the Mississippi, which created a great deal of excitement in New Orleans. Her prized possession was a bottle of champagne given to her by former Confederate president Jefferson Davis in 1889 on his last trip to his home in Mississippi "to be used at the christening of [her] first baby." Blanche reported in 1927 that the bottle remained unopened.[42]

Testimony for the defense centered on two main themes: the strength of the custom of segregation on riverboats and the justifications for it. Subsidiary themes in the defense testimony were Madame Decuir's knowledge of the *Governor Allen*'s policies and the fact that she paid the lower fare charged to colored passengers, in essence agreeing to her treatment as colored on the *Governor Allen*.

Benson, Grove, and Cedilot described their interactions with Madame Decuir and Washington in detail and made no effort to dispute her allegation that she was refused a room in the ladies' cabin due to her race. Grove testified that it was he who instructed Cedilot to provide a cot and meals to Madame Decuir in the recess after she refused the offer of a room in the bureau. Benson portrayed segregation as benign and necessary to preserve both the comfort of all passengers and his ability to attract White customers.[43]

Benson, Grove, and Cedilot all testified that segregation was a long-standing, well-established custom on riverboats. They also testified to the reason for the custom. In Grove's words, "It is a reasonable regulation and made for the accommodation of the majority of the public. They would not travel on any boat where the white and colored passengers were mixed, because there is a public prejudice against associating with colored persons. If any boat was to attempt to mix the white and colored persons in the same cabin, I believe they would lose the white travel altogether." Cedilot echoed these sentiments, stating that if the White and colored passengers were mixed, "I think it would create a big fuss, for I think that the white people would take it in hands and create a big fuss on the steamboat, and somebody would be killed. . . . The white people wouldn't stand it." The possibility of violence was a justification used for decades to justify segregation in all sort of facilities, including the Separate Car Acts that many Southern states adopted to require segregation on railroads.[44]

One theme that was not raised as directly was the perceived need to protect White womanhood from Black men. Captain Benson hinted at the underlying Southern desire to protect White ladies, stating that during his encounter with Washington on board the *Governor Allen*, he "asked the gentleman if his wife was aboard of the boat, or his sister, how he would like to have Madame Decuir put in the room with them, and he said he wouldn't like it." This justification for segregation had powerful emotional appeal for many Whites long into the twentieth century, and the failure to separate the sexes in the bureaus illustrates that concern for the "fairer sex" did not extend to women of color.[45]

Captain Leathers had known Madame Decuir for twenty-five years, although he claimed he would not know her by sight, perhaps because she had spent much of that time in France. He was keenly interested in the outcome of the case since he had also been sued under Louisiana's 1869 antidiscrimination statute.[46] Leathers testified to the existence of the custom of segregation and its importance:

This regulation and custom . . . of keeping the White and Colored Cabin passengers separate has prevailed ever since I have been steamboating. I never have heard of any other. This regulation is made for the accommodation of the whole travelling community because there are a large majority of the White people who do not wish to travel mixed up with the Colored people, and the Colored people do not wish to be mixed up with the White people. It would be impossible to run a steamboat without this regulation. It is just as essential as to keep the gentlemen and Ladies Cabin separate.[47]

Leathers amplified on the economic reasons for the practice:

I think the Colored travel in my trade is between a fourth and fifth of the whole, that is the white persons traveling are about four fifths of the whole or near that. About one half of that travel is for pleasure. If I did not have rules and regulations for my boat and the accommodation of my passengers, I do not think that I would have any, either white or colored.

Captain Leathers also claimed that the colored cabin was as attractive as the White cabin and noted that "the white passengers are charged about twenty five percent more than the Colored passengers, though they get the same accommodation."[48]

Captain V. B. Baranco of the steamboat the *Bart Able* testified mainly about the custom of segregation on riverboats and also about Madame De-cuir's experiences on his boat. It was Baranco, when describing the custom of segregation on riverboats, who called the area set aside for colored travelers the "Freedmen's Bureau," a sarcastic reference to the federal government offices of the time that had been set up to help the former slaves transition to freedom. Baranco's custom regarding high-status colored passengers was more liberal than Leathers's and Benson's:

We have two special rooms in the cabin which we keep for colored people, some special people; but we don't allow them in the cabin, you understand. We lock the door inside generally, and let them go out on the guard when they want to leave the room. We carry their food into the room for these people, to take whenever they want to eat, and the colored people eat after all the white people are through in the cabin.[49]

Captain John W. Cannon was as clear as the others on the customs concerning segregation, stating that "since the negroes have been freed, we have had cabins for them. . . . In fact, they all seem to know where they belong when they come aboard." Like other witnesses, Cannon ascribed the custom of segregation to the unwillingness of Whites to travel together with colored passengers. He forthrightly attributed the custom to racial prejudice, stating:

I considered there was a difference between negroes and white people. I never put them together. No white people would travel on a boat at all if they knew that negroes were put in the same cabin with them, or even that they had stayed in the same state-rooms, where the white people would have to sleep after them.

He was asked whether there is "any prejudice in the public mind against associating with colored persons," to which he answered, "The greatest on earth, I suppose sir." He also stated that segregation was an economic necessity.[50]

Captain John Benson was his own final witness. He testified that he had been in the steamboating trade since 1848, running from New Orleans to St. Louis, Louisville, Cincinnati, Vicksburg, and Carolina Landing.[51] Most recently, Benson stated that he was running the *John Kilgour* and the *Governor Allen* in the "packet trade," which means that the "boat has a regular day and a regular hour for leaving." Benson readily admitted that his policy was to segregate colored and White passengers, and that it was pursuant to this policy that he refused to provide Madame Decuir with a room in the ladies' cabin. He insisted that this was the universal custom on the river and that his facilities for colored passengers were equal in every way to those for White passengers.[52]

When asked by Egan why segregation was the custom, Benson replied that

it is to protect a man in his business. I hold that if a man started on a steamboat out of this port or any other port and allowed negroes to occupy rooms in the main cabin and stay in the main cabin, I don't think he would carry many other people. I don't think he would. I don't think there are many white people who would travel on a boat of that kind. . . . It is to protect the owners of the vessel against sustain damage and loss by losing their business [and it is f]or the accommodation of the passengers generally, the white people.[53]

Although the economic necessity of segregation was insisted upon by all of the defense witnesses, there is reason to doubt both that it was the real reason for Southerners' determination to retain segregation and that abandonment of the custom would really have had the dire economic consequences they predicted. On the first point, there is no question that an important impetus for segregation was the perceived threat of racial mixing to the sanctity of White womanhood. That this well-known concern among Southerners went virtually unmentioned by the witnesses suggests that they were being less than forthcoming in their testimony on this point. When Captain Baranco was asked about the reasons for the custom of separating the races on riverboats, he attributed it to the unwillingness of White men to have their ladies travel together with colored people: "You cannot get no man to travel on a boat with ladies where you would set them alongside of colored people. They wouldn't stand it. The business would be ruined as far as passengers are concerned."[54] On the second point, it may be that the volume of travel was adversely affected by adherence to segregation because it suppressed Black travel, and Captain Benson and his colleagues may have viewed the protection of White womanhood as worth the economic cost. Racial boundaries in common carriers and other public accommodations were fluid and uncertain in the immediate post–Civil War period, and it is at least uncertain that segregation was an economic necessity for the business of transportation.[55]

In addition to the suggestion that Whites would not want to occupy a stateroom that had previously been slept in by colored passengers, the strongest taboo discussed in the testimony seems to have been against Whites and colored people eating together. Thus, even when high-status colored travelers were provided with rooms in the area normally reserved for Whites, they were strictly prohibited from eating at the table with Whites.

There were also hints of the taboo, honored throughout early US history only in the breach, against sexual relations across racial lines. On cross-examination, Egan cryptically suggested that the relationship between Washington and Madame Decuir was more than simply lawyer-client. Perhaps Egan was aware of Washington's personal history, with lengthy divorce proceedings and accusations of bigamy, incest, adultery, and impotence leveled back and forth. Egan asked Washington whether he and Madame Decuir had arrived at the boat together, whether he booked her passage, and why they were traveling—possibly trying to suggest a more intimate connection between Washington and Madame Decuir in order to discredit or embarrass them. Egan asked numerous questions about why Washington had to go to Pointe Coupée Parish, why Madame Decuir accompanied him, whether Snaer traveled with them, and whether Washington had chosen the *Governor Allen* for Madame Decuir. One exchange, dripping with innuendo about the relationship between Washington and Madame Decuir, went like this

EGAN: She went up for the purpose of accompanying you?
WASHINGTON: For the purpose of seeing I was accommodated and knew where to go when I got up there.
EGAN: Then you knew she was going up the same evening as you went?
WASHINGTON: No.[56]

There was also significant discussion at various points in the testimony concerning racial identity and the appearance of various people. The attention to the racial characteristics of Madame Decuir and others lacked relevance to the law governing the case. Whether she was colored or White, under both Louisiana's Constitution and statutes, and the underlying common law, Madame Decuir had been wronged by Captain Benson. Based on the responses that questions about skin and hair color provoked, this line of questioning may have been seen as offensive to its subjects then as it would certainly be today. After Washington testified that he did not realize at first that Madame Decuir was a woman of color, Egan pursued the matter. When Egan asked Washington whether Madame Decuir was "a colored person," his response was: "So reputed." Egan pressed Washington on her appearance, asking whether she was "about the color of a new law book," to which Washington replied, "I do not think quite so dark as that. The colors of new law books are various. I did not suspect her to be a colored person. She was not as dark as that." Washington then stated that she was not as dark as one of his witnesses, P. G. Deslonde.[57]

Washington's answer, that Madame Decuir was "reputed" to be a woman of color, is consistent with the way many people in the nineteenth century viewed the determination of race—as a matter of reputation rather than physical attribute. Although science and "the performance of race" became more important to legal determinations of racial identity during the nineteenth century, Ariela Gross has explained: "Just as often, trials turned on the testimony of lay witnesses giving reputation evidence."[58] A person's racial identity would thus be determined not by biology but by the community's feeling about the person. In this light, it is not surprising that when Snaer questioned Duconge about his race, he began by simply asking, "Are you a reputed colored man?" The question wasn't whether a person is or is not a certain race; it is how that person was thought of and treated by the community. Duconge replied, "They have always known me and taken me to be a colored person; I mean that the people have."[59]

Egan was not satisfied with Duconge's answers, and he pressed him by asking, "You are very white, are you not?" to which Duconge answered, "My complexion is white, but I claim to be a colored man." Leaving no stone unturned, Egan then asked Duconge about his hair, whether his hair is straight, and whether he has the hair of a White man. Duconge was clearly uncomfortable with these questions. He tried to put an end to it with the following answer: "I will answer you this question in this way: I know thousands of white men who have more curley [sic] hair than I have, and then some, of course, straighter. I mean that there are many reputed to be white men have more curley [sic] hair than I have." He was unhappy to have been required to justify his racial identity and to be questioned about the color of his skin and the texture of his hair.[60]

Frustrated at not getting anywhere with his questions about Duconge's hair, Egan then went at the issue more directly, asking Dugone whether he has "any of the features of a negro," to which Duconge answered, "I don't know. I am reputed to be a colored man, and have always been known as a colored man, and I cannot enjoy the same privileges as those reputed to be white. I don't know that I can pass better for a white man than a colored man, but I know I do not enjoy the same privileges as those reputed to be white men." Egan kept pressing, but Duconge would not answer Egan's query: "What are the most prominent features in a colored person's face?" Duconge avoided the question, replying, "That is a question quite delicate. I cannot answer you. I can hardly tell you, because the reputation of a man being colored makes them call him colored."[61]

Egan then asked Duconge about Madame Decuir's color, to which Duconge answered, "About yellow." They then established that she was not as dark as a law book pointed out by Egan, but that she was dark enough that she would not be mistaken for a White woman. Going back to Duconge, Egan asked him whether he might be mistaken for a White man, to which Duconge answered, "Not if he has got native's intuition to know that I am a colored man." Asked again about what features made him a colored man, Duconge stated, "I don't know. There must be some difference, because I am recognized and known as a colored man, and called a colored man. I cannot state in what the difference consists."[62]

Duconge's answers show how differently he and Egan thought about race. The colored people of Louisiana, like Madame Decuir, Sheriff Sauvinet, and Duconge, considered being colored a matter of community convention rather than a biological or physiological fact. Egan considered race a biological fact about a person, evidenced in appearance. Duconge knew he was colored because of how he was treated and how his family self-identified, not because of anything he saw in the mirror or in the faces or essential attributes of his family and friends. Ultimately, Egan's view prevailed, at least as a legal matter, when Southern states in the twentieth century adopted the "one drop rule," under which persons with any African ancestors were considered Black under laws making racial classifications.[63]

Egan also pressed P. G. Deslonde on his racial identity, and Deslonde was willing to point to physical features that made him a colored man. After some discussion of Deslonde's social standing and wealth (he was secretary of state of Louisiana but had apparently lost his fortune during the Civil War), Egan asked Deslonde, "Are you a colored man?" to which he replied, "Yes[.] I show it in my face and all over." Washington steered things back in the direction of reputation, asking Deslonde whether Madame Decuir is "reputed to be a colored person," to which Deslonde answered, "She is known to be so." He added that "she is very much of a lady and always has been." This testimony was taken in open court, and Judge Collum chimed in, asking whether Deslonde had seen White people in the bureau, to which Duconge answered, "I did not."[64]

Washington also queried Baranco on Madame Decuir's appearance and racial identity, asking whether she could have been mistaken for a White person. Baranco answered, "No sir, I think not. She is a yellow woman. Anyone could see that she is a colored woman by looking at her."[65] Egan took up the issue with Baranco as well, asking first about the race of Madame Decuir's husband, to which Baranco answered, "Colored," and then asking about Madame Decuir's race. Baranco replied that "she is a yellow woman—the color of that book there (pointing to a book on a desk) . . . she is what we call a mulatto." When asked if she was "a bright mulatto or a dark one?" he answered, "Well, she is just a medium—neither dark nor bright. . . . There might be some law book—that one—lighter than that. She is about the color of that law-book." This line of questioning continued:

EGAN: There was no difficulty in distinguishing her color from that of a white person?
BARANCO: None in the world.
EGAN: Had she the features of a colored person also?
BARANCO: Well, I couldn't say that she had them very strongly marked, sir.

Washington and then Snaer interjected:

By Mr. Washington:
    Q. Have you ever seen white persons as dark as Madame Decuir in color?
    A. I don't think I have, sir, to the best of my recollections.
By Mr. Snaer:
    Q. Have you not seen some people darker than Madame Decuir claiming to be white?
    A. No sir, I don't think I have.
    Q. Do you know Mr. Sauvinet, of this city?
    A. No sir, I do not.[66]

What relevance any of this had to the legal aspects of Madame Decuir's case is a mystery. There is no indication that Madame Decuir was claiming that she was excluded from the ladies' cabin in error (i.e., that she was actually White). This was not a case where racial identity would have been relevant, such as an attempt to enforce a miscegenation law or a pre–Civil War case about whether someone was a slave.[67] As far as the attention paid to her skin color, nothing in the statute under which Madame Decuir had brought suit distinguished between darker- and lighter-skinned people of color. There was no doubt that Madame Decuir's treatment was based on race. Perhaps the subject was unavoidable simply because Madame Decuir's case brought the race issue into the room. Perhaps the lawyers were exploring racial identity as part of the adjustment to post–Civil War realities, where efforts to preserve racial hierarchy were complicated by legal reform. Maybe it was just an attempt to further humiliate her and her supporters. Regardless, it is difficult to understand why the issue of racial identity came up during the testimony, except perhaps to clarify why Duconge was treated as a White man on one of his trips on the Mississippi. In any case, the questioning may have seemed routine to the White lawyers but was experienced as highly offensive to the witnesses whose physical characteristics were bandied about during the proceedings.[68]

At the conclusion of the evidence, Judge Collum gave the parties one month to file briefs. Egan filed a brief, most likely sometime during April 1873, but unfortunately, the record does not contain a copy of it or a transcript of any legal arguments made orally. It does not appear that Washington filed a brief on behalf of Madame Decuir. Judge Collum decided the case rather quickly, announcing his decision on June 14, 1873.

Madame Decuir's journey and resulting lawsuit was a microcosm of the post–Civil War experience in the South for her group of French-speaking mixed-race Louisianans and a reflection of the hardening of racial attitudes that affected all non-White Americans. Madame Decuir's case against Captain Benson was a minitrial of the fate of Madame Decuir's people, the French-speaking mixed-race population of Louisiana, whether they would lose their prewar privileged status as a middle caste between Whites and enslaved Blacks.

Madame Decuir has been characterized by some as an early Rosa Parks, refusing to submit to racial segregation. On at least three occasions, Madame

Decuir refused to abide by the rule of segregation in place on virtually all riverboats in Louisiana. It is not particularly important whether Madame Decuir was motivated by a general rejection of segregation, as it appears was the case with Rosa Parks when she refused to sit in the back of a bus in Montgomery, Alabama, in 1955, or whether it was more personal, wishing to be treated like a White lady as she was in Paris, and hoping end the humiliation she experienced every time she traveled by boat. Madame Decuir's case represented her effort to establish her right to be afforded the dignity of a citizen of the United States and a woman of culture and morals. Even if Madame Decuir's sense of racial solidarity had been limited to those mixed-race French-speaking people like her, the consequences of her refusal would be felt throughout Louisiana's non-White population.

5

Judge Collum Decides

On June 14, 1873, Judge E. North Collum rendered judgment in favor of Madame Decuir in the amount of $1,000. Madame Decuir may have been gratified that her legal argument was accepted and the injury to her dignity recognized, but she was likely disappointed that the damages award was not larger. Although $1,000 in 1873 has the buying power of nearly $22,000 today, that amount of money would not have made much of a dent in Madame Decuir's quest to regain her prewar financial standing. At the same time, Captain John Benson and his steamboating colleagues must have been horrified by Judge Collum's decision. The amount of the award was much less important to them than the possibility that they might be forced to integrate their boats, which, in their view, would be disastrous for their businesses and to their desire to preserve segregation as an aspect of White supremacy consistent with their view of proper social relations between the races.

Judge Collum recognized the gravity of his decision. He wrote a detailed opinion on the facts and law of the case, rejecting all of Benson's legal and constitutional defenses but awarding Madame Decuir relatively little in compensatory damages and no punitive damages. The centerpiece of Judge Collum's decision was his firm view that the 1869 statute under which Madame Decuir sued Captain Benson prohibited segregation based on race. There was no hint in the opinion that anyone considered the possibility that the statute's antidiscrimination requirement could be satisfied by equal, but separate, facilities.[1]

Judge Collum's opinion began with a racialized description of

Madame Decuir, tinged with references to her class: "The plaintiff in this case is a lady of color, genteel in her manners, modest in her deportment, neat in her appearance, and quite fair for one of mixed blood." Judge Collum indulged in an attempt to identify Madame Decuir's racial background through her appearance: "Her features are rather delicate, with a nose which indicates a decided preponderance of the Caucasian and Indian blood. The blackness and length of the hair, which is straight, confirm this idea." Judge Collum completed his description of Madame Decuir's identity with a reference to her ancestry: "She was never a slave, nor is she the descendant of a slave. Her ancestors were always free as herself."[2]

Judge Collum next described very briefly what happened to Madame Decuir aboard the *Governor Allen*, that she was traveling to return to "the parish of Pointe Coupée, where she has resided in wedded life for many years," that the *Allen* was "engaged in the business of common carrier of passengers and freight, and plying between [New Orleans] and the city of Vicksburg," that she "applied for and was refused a cabin passage," that "a cabin . . . was offered her in what is called and known as the 'bureau' which, on the Governor Allen, is situated below the berths and floor assigned to the white passengers," that "this bureau is kept exclusively for people of color, and that there is not so much comfort nor so many facilities for seclusion as on the cabin floor above it; indeed, that it is very uncomfortable for a lady particularly." Although inequality of facilities was not the basis for Judge Collum's decision, this finding apparently rejected one of Captain Benson's main contentions, that the facilities for colored passengers on the *Governor Allen* were equal to those provided for White passengers.[3]

Judge Collum found that Madame Decuir "declined to accept the accommodations offered her, and passed the night during which she was on board sitting in her chair in the rear part of the boat, in what is known as the recess." He also found, contrary to the evidence, that "upon her arrival at the Hermitage, her point of destination, she paid for a first-class cabin passage." Interestingly, even though it was undisputed that the reason Madame Decuir's request for passage in the ladies' cabin was rejected on racial grounds, Judge Collum recited this only as an allegation: "She now institutes this suit, alleging these facts, and saying further that the defendant did on that trip of said boat refuse to her, on account of her race and color, and for that reason only, the equal rights and privileges accorded to the White passengers on the boat." Perhaps Judge Collum was making clear that Madame Decuir alleged racial discrimination because in another case, a different plaintiff's claim under the Louisiana antidiscrimination statute, it was rejected due to the plaintiff's failure to explicitly allege racial discrimination.[4]

Judge Collum also treated the facts relating to Madame Decuir's claims for damages as allegations, not facts established by the testimony. The judge recounted that Madame Decuir alleged that "she suffered for want to rest from inability to sleep, and from exposure. She also alleges that the mortification and mental anguish which she was thus compelled to undergo justly entitle her to exemplary damages in the sum of $75,000."[5]

The legal issues addressed in the trial court's decision can be sorted roughly into three categories. The first category can be characterized as legal technicalities, including whether damages are available for the mental anguish Madame Decuir alleged she suffered, whether the case belonged in the admiralty jurisdiction of the federal courts rather than in the state trial court, whether Madame Decuir had no claim because she did not tender the fare charged to White women, and whether Louisiana's 1869 antidiscrimination statute reached only establishments licensed by the state of Louisiana or some other authority and thus did not apply to the *Governor Allen*. The second category involved the importance of the custom of segregation and the rules of the boat, and whether a custom or rule requiring segregation could prevail over a statute that might be construed to prohibit segregation. The third category of issues involved whether the state of Louisiana had the power to regulate the practices on the *Governor Allen* or whether that power was exclusively the federal government's under Congress's commerce power. The discussion of all of these issues was infused with Judge Collum's views on the definition of discrimination under the Louisiana statute and constitutional provision at issue in the case.

The first category of issues addressed in Judge Collum's opinion did not implicate the main issue of the legality of the practice of separating White and colored passengers on the boat. One of the first issues addressed in Judge Collum's opinion was the defense's argument that the court could not award damages for mental anguish. Judge Collum dismissed this argument with little analysis: "It will suffice to say that the supreme court of this State, in the days of Judge Martin, has declared that the 'law gives compensation for mental suffering occasioned by acts of wanton injustice.'"[6] Although Judge Collum did not cite the authority from which he drew the quote, it came from an 1833 opinion of the Louisiana Supreme Court in a case involving a sea captain who, among other alleged indignities, referred to the plaintiff's wife in front of his crew as the plaintiff's mistress or prostitute, and placed the plaintiff and his wife in fear of being "assassinated" at any time during their fourteen-day trip. This implies, of course, that Judge Collum viewed Captain Benson's treatment of Madame Decuir as a case of "wanton injustice," constituting a vindication of her claim to the dignity recognized in Louisiana law.[7]

The second somewhat technical issue addressed was the defendant's claim that the case belonged in the federal admiralty jurisdiction since it involved the conduct of the captain of a steamboat on the river. Although many cases can be heard in either state or federal court, federal admiralty jurisdiction is exclusive. Typical admiralty cases involve accidents between boats on navigable waters, injuries to workers on such boats, crimes on the high seas involving US citizens, and contracts relating to the operation of a boat on navigable water. If a case arises under federal admiralty law, it must be heard in a federal court. Judge Collum concluded that "the United States courts in admiralty have nothing to do with this case" because "a contract between a passenger and the master of a vessel for the passage is a personal one not cognizable in the Admiralty."[8]

The next legal argument addressed by Judge Collum's opinion was whether Madame Decuir had no claim of discrimination because she had not tendered the fare charged to White women for passage in the ladies' cabin. As revealed in the testimony, it was a widespread custom on the river to charge colored passengers about 25 percent less than White passengers. Madame Decuir paid five dollars for her passage, while White women traveling in the ladies' cabin were charged seven dollars. Egan apparently pressed this point in his brief, which unfortunately is not included in the record of the case. Judge Collum stated in his opinion: "Counsel has furnished a lengthy brief in which he endeavors to show that if the plaintiff was not treated as the white ladies were, she cannot complain, because she did not make a tender in advance of the amount of money which white ladies paid." Judge Collum had a two-pronged response to this argument. First, he characterized it as "a mere technicality, which cannot be permitted to defeat a legal right." He added that tendering the fare would have been "useless" since the defendant made it plain that they would not provide her with a room in the ladies' cabin. Second, Judge Collum relied on the statute under which Madame Decuir brought her case. As Judge Collum noted, the statute allows the common carrier to deny service "when such person shall, on demand, refuse or neglect to pay the customary fare." From this language, Judge Collum concluded that "it was therefore the duty of the defendant to first make the demand of the customary fare before he could, under the law, deny to her the rights and privileges accorded to white ladies on board his boat."[9]

The defendant also argued that the laws under which Madame Decuir sued "extend only to cases in which a State or other license is paid, and that as steamboats do not pay a license, the law does not affect them." Although the argument is not elaborated, it appears that Egan was arguing that when the 1869 statute refers to "common carriers," it means only state-licensed establishments. While this argument would strip unlicensed steamboats of the rights detailed in the 1869 statute, presumably they would then be governed by the common law, which would provide all of the rights included in the statute without subjecting them to the antidiscrimination norm imposed by the 1869 act. In any case, Judge Collum rejected this argument on the simple ground that neither article 13 of the Louisiana Constitution nor the Act of 1869 makes "mention . . . of a license to be paid by such public conveyance as a prerequisite to its obligation to afford equal rights and privileges."[10]

The next set of issues addressed a central aspect of the testimony, the importance of the custom of segregation on the river and the related rules of the *Governor Allen* confining colored cabin passengers to the bureau. Judge Collum rejected Egan's efforts to persuade him that a custom or a rule of a boat could displace a validly enacted state statute. Significantly, Judge Collum seems to have had no doubt that the 1869 statute's requirement that common carriers "make no discrimination on account of race or color" prohibited segregation even if the facilities were equal. It did not appear to cross Judge Collum's mind that "separate but equal" and "no discrimination" could be consistent. We do not have Egan's brief, so we do not know if he argued the point, but from the pleadings and the testimony, it appears that Egan did not. Had he, it seems likely that Judge Collum would have addressed it in his detailed opinion. Judge Collum clearly read the statute's prohibition of discrimination to require integration. This casts doubt on one scholar's claim that when Radical Republicans legislated for racial equality, they did not intend to outlaw racial segregation.[11]

Rather than argue for separate but equal, Egan apparently argued that somehow, the well-established custom of segregation should prevail over the law's prohibition of racial discrimination. The notion that a custom could supersede a statute was contrary to Judge Collum's understanding of the rule of law and the role of the judge. As this was Egan's central point, Judge Collum addressed it in several different parts of his opinion. Although today it may seem obvious that the law supersedes customs to the contrary, Judge Collum felt that he was making an important point here, because apparently the relative strength of statute law and custom was not so clear in 1870s Louisiana. As he put it: "I have thought it prudent to collate authorities on this point to a greater extent than is ordinarily deemed necessary, by reason of the generally prevailing impression concerning some personal rights that customs are laws, legislation to the contrary notwithstanding." Judge Collum portrayed the obligation to enforce the law in the face of a contrary custom as a constitutional obligation on the part of the courts, integral to the separation of powers: "With what reason or propriety can the courts, which are but the creatures of the law, refuse to yield obedience to the requirement of that constitutional power upon which alone they must depend for existence, and without which they would possess no authority whatever."[12]

Judge Collum put the point quite simply when he stated, "When called upon to interpret an express and positive law, it is a matter of very little importance what existing customs are, if they plainly contravene both the letter and spirit of the law." He added that "no association of men whatever can create or establish a custom for their convenience, and vitalize it with a power paramount to the authority of an express and positive statutory enactment." Judge Collum thus must have concluded that segregation was plainly inconsistent with the statute's "no discrimination" language. He allowed that in cases of ambiguous statutes, "courts from time immemorial have been aided by customs in construing" them, "but their judgments can never be properly influenced by [customs] where the law is plain and easily understood." Again acting on the assumption that the 1869 statute plainly prohibited segregation, Judge Collum found that

the constitution is the only limitation to legislative power, and I am not aware that customs have, in any country, been deemed of such high authority as to supersede the behest of even the common law. . . . Illegal customs can't have . . . weight and courts cannot recognize them, however long they have been established. . . . They are obligatory on parties only when the law does not provide for the case, and when they are opposed to the provisions of a statute they are not binding.[13]

Judge Collum gave short shrift to the defendant's key argument, that the custom and rule of segregation was necessary to the economic viability of his business, finding that as a judge he was bound to apply the law as written regardless of the economic consequences. He also opined that the law may, at times, injure some for the benefit of society at large, stating that "the rule established by law may give rise to personal or private injuries, and it will no doubt do so in this case, but whilst it is the duty of the Government to protect the right of each individual, however humble or obscure he may be, private interests are never insuperably set up as a barrier [to] public necessity." In rejecting the relevance of policy considerations to this task, Judge Collum stated: "Whether laws are adapted to the present state of society or not is an important matter, it is true, but it is one with which the courts have nothing to do." Later in the opinion, Judge Collum reiterated this point:

Whatever may be thought of the wisdom, propriety, or policy of the foregoing constitutional and legislative provisions, one thing is clear to my mind, it is that they are laws, and that the courts of this State must recognize and declare them to be such. If they operate injuriously to private interests, it is to be regretted, but if experience should successfully prove that they promote the general prosperity and the welfare of the public, then, according to the well recognized and wholesome principles of government, they should be respected.

Judge Collum thus swept aside the suggestion that he should take into account the argument that integration would destroy the riverboating industry.[14]

Judge Collum also rejected the related argument that Madame Decuir had no right to complain because she knew of the custom of segregation, and the rules of the *Governor Allen*, before she boarded the boat. The court's answer to this argument depended once again on Judge Collum's firm conviction that segregation constituted discrimination. He said,

It is equally true that Captain Benson knew of the existence of the laws whose authority had superseded those rules and regulations. If, then, it is fair to argue that plaintiff should have been governed by those rules and regulations when they had been swept away by legislation, it is far more just to insist that he should have been guided by the imperative requirements of the law. A systematic disregard of them furnishes no argument to excuse their violation but on the contrary, should admonish courts to vindicate their authority the more promptly—the more impartially.[15]

In the Civil Rights Act of 1871, the United States Congress recognized that local authorities may disregard people's constitutional rights in deference to local custom, providing that state and local officials may be held liable for constitutional violations committed, inter alia, under color of "custom or usage, of any State or Territory."[16]

Judge Collum also rejected Egan's arguments that depended on common carriers' rights to enforce their own rules. Egan argued that while a common carrier may have an obligation to carry all passengers willing to pay the fare, such carriage is subject to reasonable rules and regulations. Egan cited *Jencks v. Coleman*, in which Joseph Story, as circuit justice for the US Circuit Court for the District of Massachusetts, charged a jury that "the right of passengers to a passage on board of a steamboat is not an unlimited right. But it is subject to such reasonable regulations as the proprietors may prescribe, for the due accommodation of passengers and for the due arrangements of their business."[17]

It may seem frivolous to argue that the rules of a boat could displace statutory law, but the issue is not so simple. Traditionally, owners of common carriers had wide discretion to establish rules and regulations, exercising a quasi-sovereign power to govern their businesses. As noted above, this was recognized in the statute of 1869, with the proviso that the rules could not discriminate on the basis of race. The court's answer to this argument depended, once again, on its unwavering conviction that the 1869 statute prohibited segregation. Judge Collum asked rhetorically whether "a rule or regulation can be judicially declared reasonable which supersedes express law, and bids defiance to its authority? Can courts say that rules are reasonable which are contrary to and subversive of positive law? It is not pretended that boats may not establish regulations, but they are prohibited from making discriminations on account of race or color."[18]

In response to Egan's argument that "any interference by a State with the rules and regulations of vessels is in substance an attempt to regulate commerce," Judge Collum wrote a miniessay on federalism, addressing the distribution of powers between the federal and state governments. Owing to the expansion of federal power over civil rights at the conclusion of the Civil

War, this was a propitious time in the history of the relationship between the states and the federal government, and Judge Collum carefully considered this part of his analysis.[19] He began by stating the traditional view of the powers of the federal government, that

the Government of the United States is one of enumerated powers. These powers are expressly delegated by the Constitution, and the Government can rightfully claim none which are not granted by it. . . . The tenth amendment to the Constitution of the United States provides that the powers not delegated to the United States by the Constitution, nor prohibited by it to the States, are reserved to the States, respectively, or to the people.[20]

Judge Collum also adopted the traditional view of the reach of the federal power to regulate interstate commerce, which favored state control. Judge Collum quoted chancellor James Kent for the point that "the power was restricted to that commerce which concerned more States than one, and the completely internal commerce of a State was reserved for the State itself." After listing quarantine laws and inspection laws regarding articles to be exported as within state power, Judge Collum relied upon the *Slaughter-House Cases* for the proposition that "the Supreme Court of the United States expressly recognized the fact that notwithstanding the convulsions that have shaken and endangered the permanency of the fabric of American Union, and despite the amendments added to its Constitution, the States still have certain sovereign rights which they may lawfully exercise."[21] This is in keeping with the view that at the time, the *Slaughter-House Cases* were significant not for narrowing the scope of Fourteenth Amendment rights but rather for recognizing the continued vitality of the state police power in the face of a challenge based on the recently enacted Fourteenth Amendment.

Despite his reliance on traditional federalism principles, Judge Collum also adopted language acknowledging that the balance of power between the states and the federal government had changed after the Civil War. Judge Collum relied upon two grounds for holding that enforcement of the 1869 act would not intrude on Congress's commerce power: first, that Madame Decuir's trip was wholly within Louisiana, and second, that the cases Egan relied upon "antedate all the recent changes in the Constitution of the United States establishing and providing for the regulation of the states of the colored race in America." The reasoning behind the first ground is obvious, but the second ground is not so clear. It seems that Judge Collum was saying that the Reconstruction-era constitutional amendments expanded state power to legislatively protect the rights of colored people. How did they do that? Judge Collum did not really say, except to disparage Egan's pre–Civil War citations by stating, "As well might he invoke the decision in the *Dred Scott* case as authority for the denial of the black man's citizenship. It is useless to dwell at greater length on these questions."[22]

Rather than answering the Commerce Clause argument directly, Judge Collum simply reiterated the basis in Louisiana law for Madame Decuir's claims, apparently because they were founded on his post–Civil War understanding of the states' power to protect Black people from discrimination and legal disabilities. The closest he came to an analysis of the Commerce Clause argument was to list several ways in which Louisiana already regulated steamboats without any question as to its constitutional authority to do so: "It has enacted laws imposing penalties in cases of accidents, for regulating the carrying of gunpowder, to compel the use of iron chains as a substitute for the formerly-used tiller-ropes, for carrying lights and several other matters." He then asked, rhetorically, "Was it ever pretended that this legislation was unlawful interference with commerce, or that it deprived steamboats of the right to make reasonable rules and regulations for the management of their business?" Judge Collum thought that to rule in favor of the defense would be to single out race as a special case immune from state regulation.[23]

Madame Decuir had requested $75,000 in compensatory and punitive damages. Even though the statute provided for them, Judge Collum rejected the claim for punitive damages, citing the novelty of laws prohibiting racial discrimination:

The public in general is not sufficiently apprised of the existence and validity of the laws which govern such cases to be severely punished for their violation. When it shall have become a settled theory in the State's jurisprudence that these laws exist by constitutional authority, and that they will be enforced, and when the people, who have been taught to condemn them as unjust and consequently unwise, shall have learned that there is nothing unconstitutional in them, it will be time enough to inflict punitory damages for withholding the rights and privileges which they are designed to secure.

Notice that Judge Collum did not state that Captain Benson was unaware that he was violating the law. Rather, he seems to be acknowledging that it would be unfair to punish Captain Benson for actions sanctioned by established social custom.[24]

Turning to compensatory damages, Judge Collum engaged in some hand-wringing over how strongly this law should be enforced. Judge Collum decided to award damages sufficient to pay for Madame Decuir's costs of litigation, and no more, apparently believing that the enforcement of the 1869 act was of tremendous value in and of itself. He concluded that

the evidence is positive and conclusive that she was denied those rights and privileges for no other reason than she was a colored woman. She was therefore forced to institute this suit for judicial establishment and vindication of her rights under the laws. She had to employ counsel as a necessary means of having her case properly made up and presented to the court, and I think that whatever sum it may fairly have cost her to do so should be awarded her as damages. I cannot think it just or prudent to do more under all of the circumstances.[25]

Judge Collum's discussion of compensatory damages reveals that he either did not accept or did not fully comprehend the degree of dignitary harm that Madame Decuir had suffered, or the gravity of the harm that segregation inflicted on people of color. He did not specifically address Madame Decuir's claim that she suffered great emotional distress due to her treatment on the *Governor Allen*. While he found a "duty of courts, whether it be pleasant or not, to declare fearlessly what the law is, whether it be wise or not, and to make themselves the impartial mediums through which rights may be enforced and wrongs repressed, . . . they are not . . . to be used as the stepping-stones to fortunes." In other words, judicial remedies should not be a windfall to the victorious plaintiff. Although Judge Collum had ruled in favor of damages for emotional distress, he apparently believed that damages for Madame Decuir's hurt feelings in excess of actual monetary loss would amount to a windfall. Judge Collum simply did not comprehend the harm segregation caused persons like Madame Decuir.[26]

How did Judge Collum arrive at the figure of $1,000? There is no suggestion that Washington presented his bill to the court, or that Madame Decuir actually paid $1,000 for legal services and litigation costs. This was a rough estimate and, apparently not coincidentally, the exact amount awarded by a different judge to Sheriff Sauvinet in his suit over being excluded from the Bank Coffeehouse, and also the amount awarded in a case decided after Madame Decuir's involving exclusion from a theater on account of race. Judge Collum cited Sauvinet's case and also the case of *Bells v. Leathers* as support for the size of the award. One thousand dollars had apparently become the going rate for a violation of the 1869 act.[27]

In the course of his opinion, Judge Collum did not reveal much of his own thoughts on the wisdom of Louisiana's recent antidiscrimination laws. Consistent with his status as a leading Democratic political orator, if anything, he may have been sympathetic to the hostility toward these laws that predominated among Whites. However, he concluded his opinion with an eloquent prayer that patriotism and unity based on US citizenship would transcend racial prejudice:

I cannot conclude without expressing the fond and sincere hope, that the time may speedily come when a fostering government may by wise laws and a mild administration, aided by an independent judiciary, venerable by its gravity, its inflexible integrity, its benign dignity, profound wisdom, and official independence and supported by a willing, patriotic people, inspired by a unity of political purposes, and striving for the general welfare, may submerge and do away with every necessity for investigations of causes like this, and when all distinctions germinating in prejudice, and unsupported by law, may be finally forgotten, and when the essential unity of American citizenship shall stand universally confessed and sincerely acquiesced in by the national family.[28]

This language could be interpreted as a plea for national unity and an end to discrimination based on race, color, or previous condition of servitude. Without more evidence of Judge Collum's views on the subject, it is impossible to know if that was what he meant.

Living up to his reputation for zealous advocacy, two days after Judge Collum announced his decision, Egan requested a new trial, arguing that the verdict was contrary to the law and the evidence, that Madame Decuir "never tendered any passage-money for the accommodation she pretends to have been denied . . . [and] the damages allowed by the court are excessive, and totally unsupported by the evidence found in the record." Judge Collum denied this motion that same day, June 16, 1873.[29]

———————

Judge Collum, the parties, and their associates understood that more than $1,000 was at stake in Madame Decuir's litigation against Captain Benson. To Madame Decuir and her social circle, the question may have been less about segregation and more about categorization—would the French-speaking free people of color in Louisiana maintain their special social status, or would they be lumped together at the bottom of the social hierarchy with the newly freed slaves? Would people like Madame Decuir be afforded the dignity to which they felt they had always been socially entitled and now to which they were legally entitled? Put most simply, Would people of color be recognized as full and equal citizens under the law and social norms? To the defense, this was a challenge to the well-established Southern practice of segregation, which Whites saw as integral to their continued social dominance and Blacks saw as a continuation of the humiliation and degradation of slavery and pre–Civil War subordination. It is thus not surprising that Captain Benson and his allies continued their fight in the Supreme Court of Louisiana.

6

The Louisiana Supreme Court Affirms

Captain John Benson and his attorney Bentinck Egan quickly set
in motion the process of appealing Judge E. North Collum's decision to the Louisiana Supreme Court. Two weeks after Judge Collum awarded Madame Decuir $1,000 in damages against Captain
Benson, Egan filed a motion in the district court for a "suspensive
appeal" in the case. A "suspensive appeal" is an appeal that stays
the execution of the underlying judgment until the appeal is resolved. Judge Collum granted the motion for a suspensive appeal
on the routine condition that Captain Benson provide a bond, in
the amount of $1,500, to guarantee payment of the judgment, plus
interest and costs, should Madame Decuir prevail. The order set
the date of appearance in the Louisiana Supreme Court as "the first
Monday of November, 1873." This ended Judge Collum's involvement in the case.[1]

Captain Benson's appeal bond evidenced the interest of the
steamboating and White commercial community in the case. Just as
Madame Decuir's brother, State Treasurer Antoine Dubuclet, had
promised at the outset of the litigation to be responsible for any
costs assessed against her, Benson's promise to pay the $1,500 if re-
quired was backed by guarantees of nineteen of Benson's colleagues
and business associates, including Captain Thomas Leathers, steamboat agent George D. Hite, and *Slaughter-House* plaintiff William
Fagan. E. K. Washington, Madame Decuir's lawyer, signed the bond
as satisfactory to him, and on that same day, the clerk of the district
court, Thomas Duffy, certified the accuracy and completeness of the
record he was filing with the Louisiana Supreme Court. Those 247

pages contained a copyist's rendering of all of the pleadings, motions, and testimony, as well as Judge Collum's opinion. Unfortunately, other than the pleadings including the complaint and answer, there is no transcription of the legal arguments made either orally or in writing to the trial court.[2]

On November 4, 1873, Washington filed the same motion in the Supreme Court that he had filed in the trial court, asserting his client's right to an expedited hearing under the statute granting preference to cases filed under the 1869 act. In response, on December 1, 1873, the Louisiana Supreme Court ordered that "this cause be fixed for trial with preference." Both parties filed briefs in with the Supreme Court, and on December 15, Washington filed a pleading in the Supreme Court praying "that the judgment of the lower court be affirmed with costs."[3]

The case was argued to the Louisiana Supreme Court on January 20, 1874. Egan argued for Captain Benson and Washington argued for Madame Decuir. S. R. Snaer attended the proceedings but did not argue. Neither the briefs nor any transcript of oral argument is available today.

Due to the turmoil in Louisiana's government, the Court that heard the case was a relatively young institution, having been reconstituted pursuant to the Louisiana Constitutions of 1864 and 1868. In accordance with those documents, the Supreme Court consisted of five justices appointed by the governor and confirmed by the Louisiana Senate. Previously, under the constitution of 1852, Supreme Court justices had been elected by district. The five members of the Court in 1874 were John T. Ludeling, chief justice, and Rufus K. Howell, James G. Taliaferro, William G. Wyly, and Philip H. Morgan, associate justices. All were Union loyalists, appointed by Republican governor Henry Clay Warmoth, a native Illinoisan who had been elected governor in 1868 at the age of twenty-six.[4] (Howell and Taliaferro, who ran against Warmoth for governor, had been initially appointed by Governor James Madison Wells pursuant to the constitution of 1864 and were reappointed by Governor Warmoth under the constitution of 1868.)

Governor Warmoth was thought of by his political opponents as a "carpetbagger" (i.e., a Northerner who came South during or after the Civil War as a political or economic opportunist). He arrived in Louisiana during the Civil War after having practiced law in Missouri. Although Warmoth defeated Taliaferro for governor by capturing the Black vote, he later betrayed his Black constituents by vetoing civil rights legislation, refusing to integrate Lousiana's public schools and endorsing a Democratic ticket for other offices. Impeachment proceedings were brought against him, and Lieutenant Governor P. B. S. Pinchback temporarily assumed the governorship, thereby becoming the first colored governor in the history of Louisiana. (Pinchback was later ostracized by Black political leaders in Louisiana after he supported segregating public schools, establishing a segregated university for Black students, and a new constitution that, inter alia, repealed the 1868 constitution's antidiscrimination provisions.)[5]

On April 6, 1874, less than two months after argument, the Louisiana Supreme Court issued an opinion affirming the lower court's judgment. Chief Justice Ludeling wrote the Court's opinion with Justice Wyly dissenting. Chief Justice Ludeling's opinion was shorter and more to the point than Judge Collum's trial court opinion, but it contained some expansive language recognizing a broad right to equality for Black people based in the Fourteenth Amendment. Justice Wyly's dissenting opinion was a bit longer than that of the majority, and no other justice joined it.[6]

Chief Justice Ludeling was sympathetic to the cause of racial equality but he was not a Radical Republican, and in 1860, he owned fourteen slaves.[7] In the parlance of the time, he was a scalawag.[8] He opposed secession and, unlike his two brothers, he did not join the Confederate army during the Civil War. He was a member of the 1868 constitutional convention, although ultimately he refused to sign the constitution after having voted in the minority on many issues with the more conservative wing of the Republican Party.[9] In particular, he argued at the convention against "social rights" for Blacks and expressed concern over the proposed constitution's shift of power toward Black politicians and their constituents.[10] Ludeling served on the Supreme Court until 1877 when, after a disputed election, supporters of one of the candidates claiming to be governor, Francis Nicholls, forced the incumbent justices to vacate the courthouse.[11] This did not save him or his family from the hostility of Louisiana's White Democrats. After he left the Supreme Court and returned to his plantation in Monroe, Louisiana, he had to stay out of sight during an 1879 political campaign "to escape assassination."[12] In 1881, his son was murdered, apparently for hiring Black laborers away from a neighboring plantation, which violated the conventions of the time, prohibiting hiring Black laborers away from their employers or former owners without permission.[13]

The Court's Opinion

Chief Justice Ludeling's opinion for the Court began with a short and sweet recitation of the facts as alleged by Madame Decuir, including her request for $25,000 in compensatory damages and $50,000 in punitive damages, which, in her complaint, was lumped together as a single request for $75,000. Chief Justice Ludeling then recited Benson's defenses, including the lack of jurisdiction; the fact that the *Governor Allen* was licensed under federal law and engaged in interstate commerce; that Benson had the right to make regulations for the passengers on the *Governor Allen*; that the segregation regulation is well-established, reasonable, and well known to Madame Decuir; that Madame Decuir was offered the appropriate accommodations in the bureau; and that she knew the rule when she came on board and paid only five dollars, the rate for colored passengers, and not the seven dollars charged to "other passengers."[14]

After making short shrift of Benson's state law defenses, the Louisiana Supreme Court ruled for Madame Decuir on the facts and law. On the facts, Chief Justice Ludeling's opinion found that "the evidence sustains the material allegations of the petition." The opinion stated that the defendant's own testimony established that Captain Benson refused to accommodate Madame Decuir in the ladies' cabin due to her race, and not due to the unavailability of a room. The opinion quoted Benson's testimony: "'I would not have given her a room if they had not all been taken.' . . . When asked if the reason for refusing to give her a berth in the cabin was on account of her being a colored person, he answered: 'Yes, sir, as being contrary to the rules of the boat.'" This alone was sufficient to sustain the judgment.[15]

The Louisiana court's main focus was on Egan's assertion that applying the Louisiana antidiscrimination statute to Madame Decuir's case would violate Captain Benson's federal constitutional rights. Justice Ludeling boiled the federal issues down to two: "Is the act of 1869, No. 38, in conflict with article 1, section 8 of the constitution of the United States [as an interference with Congress's power to regulate interstate commerce]? Is it in conflict with article 14, section 1, of said constitution [as depriving Captain Benson of his property without due process of law]?"[16]

In 1874, the jurisprudence governing if and when a state law would violate Congress's power over interstate commerce was undeveloped. The US Supreme Court had hinted for decades that state laws might be void if they interfered with interstate commerce, but it had not struck down a statute on those grounds until 1872, while Madame Decuir's case was pending. That case involved a state law that explicitly taxed interstate commerce.[17] Chief Justice Ludeling's principal conclusion was that, as an antidiscrimination provision, the law did not regulate commerce:

The first section forbids those engaged in the business of common carriers of passengers from discriminating against the passengers on account of race or color, and that is the substance of the section so far as it is applicable to this case. It was enacted solely to protect the newly enfranchised citizens of the United States, within the limits of Louisiana, from the effects of prejudice against them. It does not, in any manner, affect the commercial interest of any State or foreign nation or of the citizens thereof.

Basically, Chief Justice Ludeling's point was that a noneconomic law like Louisiana's antidiscrimination law did not regulate business transactions and thus could not interfere with Congress's power over interstate commerce.[18]

Throughout the history of the United States, subjects of government regulation have argued that regulation of the use of their property is inconsistent with the Constitution's protection of property rights. This argument almost never succeeds, and in this case, the Louisiana Supreme Court found that the defense's argument that the Louisiana antidiscrimination requirement deprived Benson of his property without due process of law bordered on frivolous:

The objection that the act No. 38 violates section 1 of article 14 is utterly untenable. No one is deprived of life, liberty or property, without due process of law by said statute. The position that because one's property can not be taken without due process of law, therefore a common carrier can conduct his business as he chooses, without reference to the rights of the public, is so illogical that it is only necessary to state it to expose its fallacy.[19]

Ludeling might have added a citation to the *Slaughter-House Cases*, which in the prior year upheld Louisiana's power to regulate private businesses against a Fourteenth Amendment challenge. Instead, he continued by describing the traditional legal obligations of common carriers to establish that they did not possess unlimited legal rights to do business as they see fit. He quoted from a Louisiana decision that stressed the less tangible obligations owed to passengers:

It is a stipulation not for toleration merely, but for respectful treatment, for the decency of demeanor, which constitutes the charm of social life, for that attention which mitigates evils without reluctance, and that promptitude which administers aid to distress. In respect to females it proceeds yet further; it includes an implied stipulation against general obscenity, that immodesty of approach which borders on lasciviousness, and against that wanton disregard of the feelings, which aggravates every evil, and endeavors by the excitement of terrors and cool malignancy of conduct to inflict torture on susceptible minds.[20]

Apparently appreciating the harm to Madame Decuir's dignity, Chief Justice Ludeling found Captain Benson's conduct toward Madame Decuir so improper that he said he would have held Benson liable for breaching the obligations of a common carrier toward passengers, regardless of the existence of the antidiscrimination provisions. "In truth the right of the plaintiff to sue the defendant for damages would be the same, whether act No. 38 existed or not; but the act is in perfect accord with the constitution of the United States." It is not clear whether Justice Ludeling's outrage was provoked by the discriminatory aspects of Madame Decuir's treatment or by the fact that she was left overnight in the semipublic area behind the ladies' cabin. It is, clear, however, that Ludeling thought that Madame Decuir's newly created right to equality under law was violated by Benson's policy and practice of segregation. The opinion was adamant on this point:

It is settled, in this State at least, that colored persons now have all the civil and political rights which White persons enjoy. See succession of *Caballero and Hoss & Elder v. Hart et al.* 25 An.

Mrs. Decuir was denied the right to go into the ladies' cabin. She was compelled to remain in a small compartment back of the ladies' cabin, or to go into the "Colored Bureau," and to take her meals there also. If she had been a white lady, it will not be denied that she would have had just cause for complaint. Under the constitution and laws of the United States and of this State, she was entitled to the same rights and privileges, while upon the defendant's boat, which were possessed and exercised by white persons. In a recent case, Chief Justice Beck, of Iowa, held the following language, which we adopt: "These rights and

privileges rest upon the equality of all before the law, the very foundation principle of our government. If the negro must submit to different treatment, to
accommodations inferior to those given to the white man, when transported by
public carriers, he is deprived of the benefits of this very equality. His contract
would not secure him the same privileges and the same rights that a like contract
made with the same party, by his white fellow citizen, would bestow upon the
latter." *Cager v. Northwestern Union Packet Company*, American Law Register
for March, 1874.[21]

Notice that this quotation does not rule out equal-but-separate treatment as
proper. Although Chief Justice Ludeling condemns segregation, this citation
provides at least a hint that inequality was more problematic than separation.
However, Chief Justice Ludeling also firmly rejected the argument that as a
common carrier, Captain Benson had the right, under the power to make
reasonable rules and regulations for his passengers, to require racial segregation: "That the common carrier may make reasonable rules and regulations
for the government of the passengers on board his boat or vessel is admitted,
but it can not be pretended that a regulation, which is founded on prejudice
and which is in violation of law, is reasonable."

Chief Justice Ludeling concluded his opinion by hinting that had she
asked, he might have increased Madame Decuir's damages beyond the
$1,000 awarded by the trial court: "The appellee has not asked for an increase
of the judgment. It is therefore ordered and adjudged that the judgment of
the district court be affirmed, with costs of appeal."[22]

The Dissent

Justice William G. Wyly, a wealthy cotton planter, former slave owner, and
supporter of the Union, dissented in an opinion that apparently was filed on
April 17, 1874, nearly two weeks after the majority opinion was announced.[23]
Justice Wyly's opinion made two points: first that the 1869 act's prohibition
on discrimination, as applied to travel on the Mississippi River between two
states, violated the Commerce Clause, and second, that because the custom
of segregation was well-established, even if the act was unconstitutional,
Madame Decuir had no breach-of-contract claim that might make Captain
Benson liable.

Justice Wyly began his dissent by finding that Louisiana had "encroach[ed] upon the power conferred by the Constitution of the United States upon Congress, to regulate commerce among the States." His main reason was that with regard to a boat traveling between states, two states might make inconsistent laws on the subject. He asked rhetorically,

If Louisiana can require the passengers to be mixed . . . why may not Mississippi require the white and the colored passengers to have separate apartments, and make it a penal offense for them to be mixed in the same cabin? . . . The result would be that the boat could carry no passengers. . . . If States have the authority to pass conflicting laws which in effect would prohibit the transportation of passengers on steamboats from one State to the other, why may they not enact similar laws in regard to freight? . . . Are they not, in effect, regulating commerce among the States, in contravention of the Constitution of the United States?[24]

Justice Wyly denied that Louisiana's antidiscrimination law was a proper exercise of the police power, primarily because of the interstate context. ("The police power" is shorthand for a government's power to provide for health, safety, and good order. In the United States, the states, and not the federal government, have the police power.) As Justice Wyly put it, "They are in no sense enactments springing from the police power; because the police power of a State cannot extend beyond its own limits. It cannot be brought into activity to regulate commerce between the States; to prescribe how freight shall be carried or passengers accommodated upon steamboats running from one State to another."[25]

In addition to finding that Louisiana's antidiscrimination provisions could not be constitutionally applied to travel on the Mississippi River, Justice Wyly concluded that segregation was a reasonable rule, within the ordinary power of the operator of a common carrier to impose. To Wyly, the only possible claim Madame Decuir might have against Captain Benson was for breach of contract, either express or implied, for carriage in the ladies' cabin. To establish that there could be no such implied contract, Justice Wyly recounted in detail the testimony of Captains Leathers, John W. Cannon, and Benson, establishing the universal custom of segregation on riverboats. For Wyly, this established that "the contract was made in reference to the custom of that boat and all others carrying white and colored passengers. Entering that boat as a colored passenger, in view of the well-known regulation referred to, the plaintiff tacitly consented to take accommodation in the colored cabin." In affirming the reasonableness of the custom and rule requiring segregation, Justice Wyly found that Captain Benson was required to provide White and colored passengers with equal facilities, which he found that Captain Benson did.

Justice Wyly found that

the obligation of the defendant was to furnish her as good a room and as good fare, in that apartment, as he gave to any passenger on the boat. . . . Now, the complaint is not that the accommodation in the colored cabin was not as good as it was in the white cabin (and the proof is, there was no difference in the comforts of the two apartments). . . . It was the duty of the defendant . . . to provide suitable accommodations and to make each cabin equally comfortable; and this he is shown to have done.[26]

Justice Wyly thus endorsed the legal concept of separate but equal.[27] Interestingly, however, Justice Wyly raised the possibility that the federal government might, in the future, prohibit segregation under its power over interstate commerce. He noted that "Congress, which alone has authority to regulate commerce among the several States, has not seen proper to enact a law making this custom or regulation unlawful, although the subject in the shape of the civil rights bill has been lately under its consideration."[28] Here he was likely referring to what ultimately became the Civil Rights Act of 1875, which was invalidated by the US Supreme Court in 1883.[29] As we shall see in chapter 10, unlike Justice Wyly, the US Supreme Court of the time apparently did not believe that the Commerce Clause gave Congress the power to require integration, although to be fair, the Court's attention was not drawn to the particular case of segregation in interstate travel.

On April 15, 1874, after the majority's opinion was issued but before Justice Wyly filed his dissent, Captain Benson asked the Louisiana Supreme Court for a rehearing. During this period of the Court's history, petitions for rehearing were common, both because the legal community had lost a degree of confidence in the Court and because the Court faced numerous novel issues arising out of the end of slavery and the provisions of the new constitution of Louisiana.[30] Perhaps sensing the need for reinforcements, Egan was joined by attorney Robert H. Marr, who would later take the case to the US Supreme Court. In this motion, Egan and Marr raised what may have been a new argument, that the 1869 statute required only that the defendant admit Madame Decuir to his boat, which he did, and not unreasonably expel Madame Decuir from the boat, which he did not.[31] This was not an argument for separate but equal, but rather an argument that Louisiana law prohibited complete exclusion based on race, nothing more. We do not know if this argument was raised in Egan's brief to the Louisiana Supreme Court since we do not have it, so it may have been argued for the first time in the motion for a rehearing. The Court denied the request for a rehearing on April 22, 1874, and this fact was noted at the conclusion of the published version of Justice Wyly's dissent.

———————

The Louisiana Supreme Court understood *Decuir v. Benson* as a case about the proper treatment of the newly freed slaves and other colored people of Louisiana. Chief Justice Ludeling viewed Louisiana's antidiscrimination provisions as consistent with the recent amendments to the Constitution of the United States and the direction of US law as rejecting race-based treatment. It does not appear that he seriously considered the possibility that segregation into equal accommodations could satisfy the Louisiana requirements. Because he was focused on the social institution of segregation, he did not view the Louisiana law as potentially interfering with interstate commerce, or commerce of any kind. Justice Wyly, in dissent, accepted the defense's argument that as applied, Louisiana law was an unconstitutional attempt to regulate interstate commerce and could not stand. To Benson and his fellow sea captains, the decision presented the potential to upend the social order and, they claimed, for economic disaster. They quickly took the necessary steps to present their case to the Supreme Court of the United States.

7

Captain Benson Takes His Case to the US Supreme Court

The defense, including Bentinck Egan and newly engaged cocounsel R. H. Marr, wasted no time in seeking review of the Louisiana Supreme Court's decision in favor of Madame Decuir in the US Supreme Court. Under the law in effect at the time, they had grounds for an appeal in the mandatory jurisdiction of the US Supreme Court, that a state statute had been sustained against a challenge to its validity under the Constitution of the United States. On April 23, 1874, the day after the Louisiana court denied the request for a rehearing, Marr and Egan took four steps necessary to perfect their federal appeal. First, the defense filed a bond in which Captain John Benson and three others—Captains John W. Tobin, John W. Cannon, and Thomas Leathers—promised to pay any damages and costs of litigation. Second, they made sure that the record was certified by the clerk of the Louisiana Supreme Court. Third, they procured an order directing the Louisiana Supreme Court to send the record to the US Supreme Court in Washington, DC, for hearing on the "second Monday of October next." Fourth, they issued a summons requiring Madame Decuir to appear in Washington to defend the appeal. The summons was received by the sheriff of Orleans Parish on May 11, 1874, and was served on E. K. Washington on May 14, with return of service on May 16, sworn to by Deputy Sheriff Henry Benit.[1]

The addition of Marr to the defense team was a big step, likely initiated by the group of steamboat captains who were concerned with the future of their businesses and their cherished practice of segregation as an element of the social order of White supremacy.

If there was one lawyer among those who worked on the litigation in *Hall v. Decuir* who today would be thought of as a "cause lawyer," it was Marr.[2]

R. H. Marr

Marr, of Scottish and English descent, was born in Clarksville, Tennessee, on October 29, 1819. He studied at the University of Nashville, but then began practicing law in Kentucky. The bulk of his career was spent as a lawyer and a judge in New Orleans. He married in 1850, and he and his wife (and cousin) Jane Marr had seven children, one of whom, Robert H. Marr Jr., went on to have a distinguished career as a lawyer, legal scholar, and judge, including service as district attorney for Orleans Parish.[3] The elder Marr was a leader among the White establishment and may have been interested in the case out of political commitment to the cause of segregation and White supremacy.[4] He supported the Confederacy and, after receiving a pardon from President Andrew Johnson for his rebellious activities, he petitioned the Supreme Court to readmit him to practice law before the federal courts. Congress had statutorily barred rebels like Marr from federal court practice, but on a petition from Marr and another attorney named Augustus Hill Garland, the Supreme Court held the statute unconstitutional as retroactive punishment and restored their right to appear in federal courts.[5]

Marr, described as a "staunch Democrat," was at the forefront of the movement to "redeem" the Louisiana government by expelling Republicans and reinstating White rule. As one writer put it, "Marr had one talent Louisiana's white supremacists desperately needed: a silver tongue. He had a knack for recasting their most regressive racial ideas and aggressive political demands in honeyed terms of state sovereignty and constitutional traditionalism."[6] When a group of New Orleans elites issued a manifesto urging unity among White and non-White citizens, Marr decried the group's proposals for an end to racial segregation as "an invasion of the rights of other citizens."[7] He was a politically active and distinguished lawyer who litigated more than once in the US Supreme Court, including participation as the leader of the defense team in *United States v. Cruikshank,* in which the Supreme Court invalidated indictments of Marr's White clients arising out of their alleged participation in the execution of Black prisoners taken in a violent clash over control of the Grant Parish government seated in Colfax, Louisiana (later

called the Colfax massacre), after a contested election.[8] Historian Eric Foner
has characterized the Colfax massacre as "the bloodiest single instance of
racial carnage in the Reconstruction era."[9]

Marr's most direct involvement in post–Civil War insurrection was as
a prime instigator of 1874's Battle of Liberty Place, in which rioting Whites
attempting to remove the (disputed) elected government of Louisiana killed
nearly a dozen metropolitan police officers and took control of the city of
New Orleans until federal troops arrived to restore order. At the prebattle
rally, Marr's fiery speech worked the crowd into such a frenzy that they began shouting "Hang Kellogg," referring to the "carpetbagger" Republican
governor of Louisiana William Kellogg, who first traveled to Louisiana as
President Lincoln's April 1865 appointee to the position of customs collector
for New Orleans. Marr urged his White followers to "go home and get their
arms," and eighteen hundred men reported with weapons to do battle with
what they considered an illegitimate government. Marr personally informed
Governor Kellogg that his life and property would be spared if he resigned.
When White Democrats finally seized control of the Louisiana government,
Marr was among those who accompanied the newly installed governor on a
triumphant carriage ride to the statehouse.[10]

In 1875, a congressional committee held hearings in New Orleans to investigate the political situation in Louisiana and the 1873 events in Colfax.
Marr testified before the committee on February 3, 1875. He defended the
violent White attack on the colored group that had taken control of the Colfax courthouse as justified by basic principles of the Republican form of government, which guarantees free choice in elections. He claimed that "not
one-tenth of the thinking people believe the present Government to be otherwise than illegal, imposed against their will." As far as purely racial issues
were concerned, he claimed that there was no "strict color line" in Louisiana
politics, and that colored men had been placed on the Conservative Party
ticket and had voted for the Conservatives in the election. He acknowledged
that an anti-Kellogg manifesto his group issued included the words, "We the
white men and all others opposed to the Kellogg government," but he noted
that the proposed name "White Men's Party" had been voted down in favor
of "Conservative Democratic Party." In his view, there was no intent to exclude non-Whites and that "whites had no disposition to take away from the
negro his rights or any of them."[11]

On the killings at Colfax, Marr testified that the violence was instigated by the Black men claiming to have been rightfully elected. According to Marr, it was only after the killing of one of the members of the White crowd that had assembled to take over the parish courthouse that "the killing, which went beyond measure" began. By describing the killing as "beyond measure," Marr did not deny that a massacre occurred, which included the execution of fifty men who had been taken prisoner after the shooting died down.[12]

Marr's reward for his leadership in the transition back to a White supremacist government was appointment to the Louisiana Supreme Court by Democratic governor Francis Nicholls, which occurred in early 1877 while the Decuir case was still pending at the US Supreme Court. When the US Supreme Court reversed the Louisiana Supreme Court's decision, the case was remanded to the Louisiana Supreme Court and, as far as can be discerned from the papers in the case, Judge Marr participated in the Louisiana Supreme Court's decision, ordering the state district court to reverse Madame Decuir's judgment in accord with the decision of the US Supreme Court despite the fact that he had served as a lawyer for one of the parties.[13]

After only a few years on the Louisiana Supreme Court, Judge Marr lost his position in 1880 when a new constitution took effect in Louisiana.[14] Marr's consolation prize was appointment eight years later as a district judge on the state criminal court, when Nicholls again became governor. Meanwhile, Marr went back to the private practice of law. In the reported appellate cases in which he served as counsel, Marr litigated a wide variety of personal and commercial disputes, some of them involving substantial amounts of money. His status as a leading lawyer in 1880s New Orleans is reflected by several cases in which he represented parties against the city of New Orleans, who were resisting the payment of taxes and license fees to the city. Some cases involved constitutional issues. In one such case, Marr won a judgment at trial invalidating a city tax only to have that verdict reversed by the Louisiana Supreme Court in heavy reliance on an opinion Marr himself had written for that court.[15] In another case, the Louisiana Supreme Court referred to Marr as "able counsel of defendant" in the course of rejecting his argument that increased city license fees did not apply retroactively to licenses awarded before the new fee schedule was imposed.[16] In perhaps the most interesting case against the city in this period, Marr represented a group of taxpayers challenging the city's refusal to accept city-issued scrip (issued as evidence of city indebtedness when the city could not pay its bills) as payment for interest on delinquent taxes. At this time, due to economic difficulties in the postwar period, delinquent taxes were the norm. As the Court described it, "In consequence of epidemics which had devastated the city, of short crops, of decreased confidence in public affairs, and of other causes, the prosperity of the city had been suddenly checked, and business had gradually stagnated, until real estate had almost become a burden to its owners." The trial court held that only principal (the taxes themselves) but not interest could be paid in city-issued scrip. The Louisiana Supreme Court reversed, accepting Marr's argument that once assessed, interest has the same status as the underlying unpaid taxes and therefore the city must accept its scrip in payment. The only element of the debt that could not be paid in scrip, according to the Court, was court costs, because those did not arise out of any debt to the city.[17]

The end of Marr's life was a national news event. On April 19, 1892, Marr went missing, never to be seen or heard from again. He apparently disappeared while taking a walk along the river in New Orleans. A *New York Times* report on Marr's disappearance speculated that the seventy-three-year-old judge, in "feeble health," wandered off, "perhaps to his death" due to a temporary "unsettle[ing of] his reason" resulting from "his arduous duties, the excitement of the election and his recent sitting on the Board of Pardons and resisting the pressure brought to bear to save the lives of Murderers Deschamps and Baker."[18] The river was swollen with spring rains, and Marr's love of the river may have led him to get too close to the rushing water. Although Marr was never heard from again, on July 30, 1892, a ransom note was received by the New Orleans chief of police from "the Mafia," signed by "P. J. Nunnez," claiming to have Judge Marr. The letter offered to deliver Judge Marr for $500 or simply set him free for $100. In somewhat confusing language, the letter writer offered to prove he had Judge Marr by sending his old clothes or his right ear and promised that if anything improper was done, Marr's body would be "riddled with shot." The ransom note was viewed as a fraud, and after several months, Marr was declared dead.[19]

After Marr was declared dead, Southern Presbyterian leader Dr. Rev. Benjamin Morgan Palmer published an ebullient tribute to him in the *Southwestern Presbyterian* newsletter, which was reprinted in the New Orleans *Picayune*. Palmer's tribute described Marr as "the soul of honor" and characterized Marr's disappearance as "so tragic that it pierced the heart of this community." If nothing else, Palmer's deep respect and affection for Marr illustrates the degree to which White supremacist beliefs were ingrained in the

Southern psyche of the time. Palmer expressed the view that Marr was not temperamentally suited to be a criminal court judge: "His sensitive nature made his part of his judicial life in no small degree a constant martyrdom." According to Palmer, Marr shied away from the limelight and did not seek office but rather acceded to others' requests that he serve. Palmer obviously had a great deal of personal affection for Marr, stating that "the friend who dropped in at the cheerful fireside went away refreshed from the capacious stores of a mind filled with various and discursive reading."[20]

Palmer was the pastor of the Presbyterian Church in New Orleans from 1856 until 1902 when he died after being run over by a streetcar he was trying to board.[21] A recent biography of Palmer states, "He was a pastor to the entire South, encouraging the hopes of a rising Confederacy, providing comfort after it collapsed, and working to resurrect what he believed to be its enduring principles."[22] On Thanksgiving Day, 1860, after Abraham Lincoln was elected president, Palmer gave a widely read and highly influential sermon defending slavery on religious grounds and urging Louisiana to secede from the Union.[23] During the Civil War, after Southern Presbyterians left their national organization over the secession issue, Palmer served as moderator of the Presbyterian Church of the Confederate States.[24] After the Civil War, under Palmer's leadership, Southern Presbyterian churches were officially segregated by race. Although he was a segregationist, Palmer favored education for Black people so that they could improve their own situation, and he had good relations with the Jewish community of New Orleans, expressing solidarity with them over mistreatment of their brethren in Russia.[25] He apparently never changed his views on slavery, race, and secession.[26]

Marr was replaced on the criminal court by John Ferguson, who later presided over Homer Plessy's prosecution for disobeying a Louisiana statute requiring segregation on railroad cars within the state.[27]

The case of *Benson v. Decuir* was filed in the US Supreme Court on October 6, 1874, as case number 552 on the docket for the Court's October term, 1874, but Captain Benson's appeal was not decided until nearly four years later, on January 14, 1878, as case number 17 on the docket for the Court's October term, 1877. This delay was due not only to the US Supreme Court's crushing caseload at the time but also due to Captain Benson's death on November 12, 1875.[28] Just nine days before he died, Benson married Eliza Jane Hall, who was already a widow at the time of the marriage.[29] A year after Benson's death, and more than two years after the case was filed,

Marr telegraphed D. W. Middleton, clerk of the US Supreme Court, asking whether Benson's death had been "suggested" to the Court. After receiving an answer in the negative, on November 14, 1876, Marr asked that proceedings in the case be suspended, and then he filed a motion in the US Supreme Court asking that Hall be substituted as plaintiff in error in her role as administratrix of Captain Benson's estate. In January 1877, Marr provided the US Supreme Court with a certificate from the Second District Court for the Parish of Orleans showing that on December 16, 1875, Hall had been appointed administratrix. Subsequently, a request was filed to return the case to the US Supreme Court's "call" so it would be heard in due time. Thus the case was off the Court's active docket for at least fourteen months.[30]

There was also a significant delay in briefing the case. Some correspondence indicates that E. K. Washington intended to file a motion to dismiss the appeal, but there is no record that any such motion was actually filed. Marr wrote to the clerk of the US Supreme Court on December 3, 1875, acknowledging receipt of the record in the case, asking when it would be heard and indicating that he might wish to argue it orally. Marr also informed the clerk that Benson had died "a few weeks since" and that he would soon act to have his administratrix made a party. The clerk replied that the case "will hardly be reached before the latter part of April." On December 19, 1876, Marr filed twenty-one copies of his brief, and on that same day that he filed his motion to substitute Hall as plaintiff in error.[31] Washington's brief was filed sometime after Marr's. There is also some incomplete correspondence indicating that Bentinck Egan, ever the zealous advocate, may have submitted a brief to the US Supreme Court that was not accepted by the clerk. Egan's brief may have arrived after the case had already been submitted to the Court for decision. Marr wrote to the clerk that "I have embodied in my Brief in the De Cuir case the substance of Mr. Egan's Brief, and it is [illegible] to attempt to obtain any consent to file his Brief."

The Supreme Court Briefs

While there is no record of Washington having litigated any other case in the US Supreme Court, Marr had many, mainly commercial and shipping, cases arising in New Orleans but that also included *Cruikshank*, the 1875 ruling that limited the reach of federal civil rights law.[32] Their relative experience is reflected in the quality of the briefs they filed. Marr's was much better, both in form and substance. Washington's brief contained some potentially persuasive reasons for affirming the Louisiana Supreme Court's decision, but it was nowhere near as well written or well organized as Marr's. In fact, it was so poorly written and so disorganized that it raises suspicion that S. R. Snaer wrote Madame Decuir's complaint, since that document exhibited none of the defects of the Supreme Court brief. There is also no indication in the historical record that Washington considered bringing in a more experienced cocounsel, such as his professional colleague Simeon Belden, and Madame Decuir's financial situation may have precluded it anyway.

Marr began by identifying the parties, Benson as master and owner of the "Governor Allen," and Madame Decuir "a colored woman, of African descent." By not mentioning Captain Benson's race and by using Madame Decuir's race as her primary identifying characteristic, Marr was portraying her as "other," a person who is in some sense outside the social system occupied by White society. Marr's description of the events that led to the litigation freely admitted that race was the only reason why Madame Decuir was not provided a room in the ladies' cabin, stating that "she could be accommodated in the bureau, a part of the boat specially provided and set apart for colored passengers."[33]

Marr's brief identified the state and federal legal bases for the Louisiana Supreme Court's judgment in favor of Madame Decuir and included extended arguments concerning the rights of masters of boats and what it would mean to attempt to mix the races, illustrating that the defense understood that the legality of segregation writ large was being litigated.[34] The defendant argued that equality means that each passenger should receive what was contracted for, "but there is no law which requires the master of a boat to put in the same apartments persons who would be disagreeable to each other or to seat, at the same table, those who would be repulsive, the one to the other."[35] In possible response to the trial court's plea that US citizenship transcend racial distinctions, the brief argued that "it is no purpose to say that the unwillingness of most white people to occupy the same apartments with colored people, and to eat at the same table with them . . . is a prejudice. We must deal with things as they are, not as we may imagine they ought to be. Laws cannot change human nature. This feeling exists; it is almost universal; it is natural[.]" The defense concluded this argument with the statement that to require integration would destroy the steamboat business on the Mississippi.[36]

The brief's extended discussion of common carriers mixed arguments about the rights and duties of common carriers with arguments defending the reasonableness of rules requiring racial segregation. The core idea, as first argued in the motion for a rehearing in the Louisiana Supreme Court, was that the common carrier's duty to accept all paying customers does not deprive the carrier with the power to make reasonable regulations, and that separating the races is a reasonable regulation. Marr's brief quoted opinions containing statements justifying racial segregation as natural, ordained by God, and necessary for the preservation of order and the businesses involved.[37]

In defending the legality of segregation, Marr had case law on this side, which he deployed effectively. His brief cited several decisions from various courts to support the view that the law should not act against racial segregation. These were all cases in which racial segregation was judicially approved, such as segregation in the Ohio public schools, the New York public schools, the Boston public schools, and the Nevada public schools, pointing out that segregated schools were held unlawful only in Michigan, where they were contrary to a state statute "which declares that all residents of any district shall have an equal right to attend any school therein."[38] The brief contained an extended discussion of the litigation in *Roberts v. City of Boston*, in which the Massachusetts Supreme Judicial Court upheld segregated schooling in Boston, including a quotation from future senator Charles Sumner's arguments for the plaintiff and Chief Justice Lemeul Shaw's opinion, who both stated that the law could not eradicate the prejudice that motivated the city to separate Black and White school children.[39] The brief also pointed to the judicial approval of an Indiana miscegenation law challenged as violating the Fourteenth Amendment and the Civil Rights Act of 1866. The Indiana Supreme Court held that marriage is the exclusive domain of the states and thus neither the Fourteenth Amendment nor the federal Civil Rights Act overrode Indiana's decision to prohibit marriage between White persons and those having one-eighth or more of "Negro blood." The message Marr conveyed was that, in general, courts all over the United States had approved segregation.[40]

In addition to summarizing the general legal approval of segregation, the brief contained its own invocation of the necessity of segregation. In fact, it was a plea for complete separation of the races. The argument may seem specious in light of the large number of children born to mixed-race couples throughout the South, and especially in Louisiana where such relationships were much more socially accepted than elsewhere, but it was consistent with the ideology of the White supremacist movement that "redeemed" the Southern states after Reconstruction. There was also an apocalyptic flavor to the argument, reflecting the Southern concern over White racial purity:

All the repulsion, all that keeps the colored and the white races apart in the United States, is the effect, the consequence of that natural instinct, that pride of race, without which no people can ever become truly great; without which degrading illicit connections, or marriages scarcely less degrading, would soon fill the land with a degenerate progeny, possessing neither the best physical qualities of the black race, nor the best moral and intellectual qualities of the white race; and whatever tends to bring the two races, so clearly distinguished, so really distinct, into such intimate association as would facilitate and encourage amalgamation, would soon prove destructive of the best interests of society, and would be most disastrous to prosterity [sic].

God made the white and black races distinct; and He separated them geographically, as plainly as He has done by instincts, habits, color and physiognomy. This great law of separation cannot be violated with impunity; and the attempt to abrogate it, if persisted in, may have the story of its failure told in mournful characters, and in the expulsion or extermination of the weaker race.[41]

Marr's brief made it clear that the key to protecting the divine plan of racial purity was the sanctity of White womanhood: "If a negro take his seat beside a white man, or his wife or daughter, the law cannot repress the anger, or conquer the aversion which some will feel."[42]

Marr's brief also attacked the Louisiana court's conclusion that separating the races violated Louisiana law. He argued, as he had in his petition for rehearing in the Louisiana court, that all Louisiana law required was that Captain Benson offer Madame Decuir passage somewhere on the boat. He also claimed that she did not deny that the accommodations she was offered were "equal in comfort to those afforded in the ladies' cabin." Although a logical implication of this argument may be that at most she was entitled to equal accommodations, not integrated accommodations, it is important to note that his brief did not suggest directly that equal but segregated accommodations would satisfy Louisiana's requirements. This entire line of argument was probably beyond the scope of the authority of the US Supreme Court. The rights and duties of common carriers, and the proper interpretation of the Louisiana constitution and statutes, are matters of state law, not federal law. State courts have final say on the meaning of a state statute, and their conclusions would apply even in federal court. Further, without a well-established federal rule allowing common carriers to segregate their customers based on race, the US Supreme Court was very likely to respect the views of the Louisiana Supreme Court on that issue. Thus, it is unclear whether Marr had any expectation that the US Supreme Court would rule in favor of the defendant on this issue. Perhaps Marr was simply adding to the atmospherics of error on the part of the state courts.[43]

Although he struggled against the implications of the Louisiana constitutional and statutory provisions involved in the case, Marr had no choice but to acknowledge that the Louisiana Supreme Court had decided that state law prohibited segregation, and his basis for review in the US Supreme Court were his arguments that this violated the federal constitution and federal law. Marr's federal arguments were based on two legal theories: first, that regulating the practices of a steamboat on the Mississippi River interfered with Congress's exclusive power to regulate interstate commerce, and second, that regulating the practices on the steamboat deprived Captain Benson of his property without due process of law, in violation of the Fourteenth Amendment.[44]

The Fourteenth Amendment argument, which the Louisiana court found to be virtually frivolous, was made only briefly but still was presented in a much more sophisticated manner by Marr than it had been by Egan in the Louisiana courts. Marr grounded the argument on both Benson's ownership of the *Governor Allen* and his property interest in the federal license the *Governor Allen* had to carry passengers and freight on the Mississippi River. Marr argued that the provisions of Louisiana law,

in so far as they forbid the carrier to prescribe reasonable rules . . . attempt to deprive him of his property without due process of law. The right to use his property, in the only business for which it is adapted . . . is as much his property, and is as valuable to him as the thing which he so uses. . . . The license confers the right to use the boat in accordance with its terms; and the right thus conferred is as much the property of the owner as the boat itself. When any state attempts . . . to deprive the owner of the full, free and perfect enjoyment of this right, or to

abridge it by subjecting it to terms and conditions, such attempt is in violation
of Section 1, Article 14, of the Amendments to the Constitution.

Insofar as Marr's argument relied on the *Governor Allen*'s federal license as
a species of property, it was ahead of its time, as the US Supreme Court did
not recognize property interests in government licenses and the like until the
early 1970s.[45]

Marr's main federal argument was what today would be called a Negative
or Dormant Commerce Clause challenge. The Commerce Clause provides
that "the Congress shall have power . . . to regulate commerce with foreign
nations, and among the several states, and with the Indian tribes." The essence of a Dormant Commerce Clause argument is that even though nothing in the Constitution explicitly prohibits state regulation, on some matters
the federal Constitution has implicitly granted Congress exclusive regulatory
powers. As Marr put it, "The power granted to Congress is exclusive; and the
whole subject has been placed beyond the reach and control of the States, so
far as those vessels are concerned of which the Government requires, and to
which it grants enrollment and license for the coasting trade." At bottom,
this argument holds that Louisiana could not regulate Captain Benson's
practices because the *Governor Allen* was engaged in interstate commerce
on its route between New Orleans and Vicksburg, Mississippi, on the Mississippi River.[46]

There is an irony to this line of argument coming from a Southerner in
opposition to a state civil rights law. One of the rallying cries long associated with the secessionist movement and Southern opposition to federal civil
rights laws is "state's rights." Here, by contrast, we see a Southern White
supremacist arguing that federal authority supersedes state power over the
rights of state citizens. Of course, the other side's arguments are similarly
flipped, with the side advancing a civil rights claim arguing for limitations on
federal authority in deference to state power.

At the time that *Hall v. Decuir* was decided, the US Supreme Court had
found Dormant Commerce Clause violations only twice: first in 1849, when,
based on the Foreign Commerce Clause, the Court struck down state fees on
the landing of passengers from overseas; and second in 1872, based on the
Interstate Commerce Clause, when the Court invalidated a Pennsylvania tax
on all freight carried by railroads in the state, including freight that was only
passing through on the way to another state.[47] Dormant Commerce Clause

doctrine is controversial because it is not based on the text of the Constitution and is inconsistent with the Constitution's structure. The text of the Commerce Clause does not support Dormant Commerce Clause arguments because it is phrased as a power of Congress, not a limitation on the states, and there is no textual hint of exclusivity. Further, because several other of the Constitution's provisions, including the prohibition on state laws that impair the obligation of contracts and state laws that constitute treaties or alliances with foreign powers, are phrased as limitations on the power of the states, there are strong structural reasons for questioning the fidelity of Dormant Commerce Clause jurisprudence to the Constitution. However, the Dormant Commerce Clause has since become a well-established element of US constitutional law.

Marr divided his Commerce Clause discussion into several elements. The first element was based on the need for uniformity that was central to Louisiana Supreme Court Justice Wyly's dissent in that court: different states might prescribe conflicting rules, and it would be difficult or even impossible for boats to comply with them all. The brief here nearly paraphrased Justice Wyly:

If one of the States, Louisiana, can give colored passengers on a steamboat, plying between different States, the right to recover vindictive damages for being separated from the white passengers, any other state might give the white passengers, on the same voyage, the right to recover like damages for being forced into association and contact with the colored passengers. No business could live under such conditions; and uniformity in the regulation of inter-State commerce is an absolute necessity.[48]

This suggests, anticipating *Plessy v. Ferguson*, that states would be allowed to require segregation, at least when it did not interfere with interstate commerce.[49]

The second element of Marr's Commerce Clause argument was that all business activity on navigable waters, including paid travel, constitutes interstate commerce and thus is subject to regulation by the federal government alone. Marr wrote: "The Constitution . . . subjects the commerce which is carried on by means of steam vessels navigating wholly within a State, on the public waters of the United States, which are, in whole or in part, the highways of inter-State and foreign commerce, to the rules and regulations without which that commerce might be interfered with or endangered."[50]

The third element of Marr's Commerce Clause argument relied on a federal statute passed in 1871 regulating the safety of vessels operated on the navigable waters of the United States, even if the vessel, or the navigable water, did not cross state lines. Marr argued that the existence of this federal statute was evidence that transportation on navigable waters was commerce subject to Congress's control, even on waters wholly within a single state.[51]

The fourth element of Marr's Commerce Clause argument was a relatively undeveloped argument that federal law displaced (or preempted, as it would be phrased today) all state regulation of steamboats subject to it. The brief referred to numerous federal requirements for the operation of steamships on navigable waters, including

rules relating to inspections, qualification and license of officers, signals, lights, boats, axes [etc.] and by requiring and granting a license for the coasting trade, which cannot be obtained until all the requirements of the laws of the United States have been complied with. . . . These requirements constitute the terms and conditions which the Government of the United States has chosen to impose upon the business, the coasting trade; and the license is the evidence that these terms and conditions have been fully complied with, and of the right and title of the owner of the boat to employ his boat in the specified trade. . . . The supreme law of the land gives the right to pursue the coasting trade, on the terms and conditions which it has seen fit to prescribe; and no State can interfere with this right, either to abridge or to enlarge it, or to subject it to any terms whatsoever.

This is an argument for what today would be characterized as "field preemption," which means that federal law is so detailed and comprehensive that there is no room for state law, even if it is not logically inconsistent with federal law.[52]

Marr's brief also addressed the federal Civil Rights Act of 1875, pointing out once again that it could not apply to Madame Decuir's case because it was passed almost three years after the case arose. He questioned whether the 1875 act was an unconstitutional invasion of private property rights, but as to common carriers, he conceded that "it is an assertion, by Congress, of the right to regulate commerce." He went on to argue that even so, it should not be construed to prohibit segregation, although "it does require equality of comforts in accommodations on public conveyances." We thus have another

undeveloped pre–*Plessy* pronouncement that equal-but-separate accommodations do not violate legal prohibitions on race discrimination.[53]

Washington's brief for Madame Decuir, written without acknowledged
help from Snaer, was much shorter than Marr's—twenty-two pages versus
fifty-five—and it was much less polished. In fact, some of it is nearly incom-
prehensible. Although neither brief was organized around doctrinal themes
in the way a brief would be today, the plaintiff's brief wandered among
themes much more than the defendant's, opening with a puzzling rhetorical
flourish: "The basis-misconception into which plaintiff in error has fallen in
his writ of error to your Honorable Court—is this: That the law respects the
rights of property more than it does the rights of man."[54]

The brief contained a confusing and imprecise discussion of the source
of the rights that Madame Decuir claimed were violated. The essence of the
argument, as best as it can be discerned, was that the Louisiana laws at issue
enforced the Fourteenth and Fifteenth Amendments to the United States
Constitution, and thus there could be no violation of the Commerce Clause
lest the US Constitution be viewed as "naturally self-repugnant and contra-
dictory." This was an odd idea, that Louisiana law was enforcing federal constitutional amendments that were, at bottom, restrictions on state authority,
but it reflects an interesting theme, that Louisiana law was consistent with
the federal Constitution because it was moving in the same direction, that of
eradicating racial discrimination.[55]

Washington's brief based Madame Decuir's personal rights firmly on her
status as a citizen of the United States, arguing that Louisiana law had merely
recognized those rights and was not inconsistent with any legally protected
interest of the defendant. This is an argument for an expansive understanding of the effects of the post–Civil War amendments, for a general reorien-
tation of the law toward racial justice, and equality based on US citizenship.

Washington argued that the commerce power should be understood
in light of the Constitution's new provisions creating citizenship and legal equality for colored persons. He may have been arguing that the Court
should not act in the absence of Commerce Clause-based legislation, but if
that's what he meant to say, he did not say it very clearly:

If even the act of the General Assembly of the State of Louisiana . . . were repugnant to section 8, article 1st of the Constitution of the United States, then the said
constitution is repugnant to itself in its 1st section, article 14th and its 15th article,

section 1st—which cannot be admitted; for the organic basis of the government of a country cannot be held by your court to involve absurdity and incongruity. But there is no such collision. Congress may regulate commerce between the States. The constitution, by an irrevocable fiat, has fixed the rights of persons. Madame Decuir asserts a violation of personal rights of equality before the law as a citizen of the State of Louisiana, and of the United States.[56]

Washington made a couple of poorly phrased arguments based on the fact that Madame Decuir's trip did not cross state lines and therefore was not interstate commerce. He argued that the Commerce Clause does not "detach Captain Benson . . . from all immunity [he probably meant 'liability' rather than 'immunity'] from a State penalty for infringing the personal rights of a passenger in a contract for a passage, commencing and ending within the bounds of the State of Louisiana," that "the words 'commerce between the States,' do not extend to that commerce which is completely internal and carried on between different parts of the same State," and that "'commerce' generally refers to the exchanging of commodities between different countries or States," not to an intrastate trip on a steamboat.[57]

Washington also attacked the jurisdiction of the US Supreme Court on the ground that the controversy concerned the operation of a steamboat wholly within Louisiana: "The record does not present such a case as gives your court jurisdiction, since . . . it is nothing more than a question of passage from one port within a State to another." It appears that Washington did not understand the basis for US Supreme Court jurisdiction, that the highest court of a state had denied a claim that a state statute was repugnant to the federal Constitution. He was conflating the Court's jurisdiction with Congress's authority to regulate only interstate commerce.[58]

In addition to arguments concerning the reach of the Commerce Clause, Washington's brief contained several appeals to the justice of the cause of racial equality; none as direct, however, as the defendant's appeal to the natural or even religious requirement of segregation. The brief referred to Madame Decuir as a "humble citizen of the United States" and stated that

various attempts have been made to protect these citizens of the United States in their mere citizen rights. The constitution of the United States, in its 14th and 15th amendments has tried to do something. The State of Louisiana . . . has tried to do something. The Supreme Court of Louisiana, in this case and in the case of

Sauvenet vs. Walker, before your court, has tried to do something. . . . It remains now to see whether your honorable court can do anything in the premises.

Washington also relied on the Magna Carta, the Declaration of Independence, the US Constitution, and Louisiana law for the proposition that "if a human being be anything else than a slave, he has a solemn and omnipotent residuum of right inherent in him as an equal man[.] To discriminate against any one on account of his color, is to attack the basis-condition of his being and nature: for color is neither a moral nor a legal fault."[59]

Washington appealed to the history of Southern slavery as heightening the importance of sustaining Madame Decuir's right to be free from discrimination. This weird passage is all the more interesting coming from Washington, a former Confederate lieutenant who, during the testimony in the case, boasted of being "more of a Confederate" than others while working together with a mixed-race lawyer representing a mixed-race woman in a discrimination case:

A state law inhibiting its special citizens from discriminating against the common citizens both of it and the general government cannot be repugnant to the latter, unless the latter has made such discrimination. And it is incumbent upon the plaintiff in error to prove such antagonism, and when such discrepancy is proved, he has extracted the manhood out of man, and emasculated the constitution of all meaning. It more especially devolves on us who are of the Old South—who have been and are now the rebels to all sectional administrations of the affairs of the nation, who originated this nation and its salient ideas—to *give* to these people on broad, general and magnanimous grounds their mere rights under the law. And having supported them for two centuries: having paid three thousand million of dollars for them, and having lost it, and having once subjugated swamps—now slowly re-seeking their aboriginal desolation to throw into the vortex, as *discordia semina rerum* of the new creation—the metaphysical rights of the Anglo Saxon race, which have coerced in all climates, ameliorations and sciences for twelve centuries!

Although the passage is not altogether clear, and even the Latin phrase appears to have been ill-used, it seems that Washington was arguing that the US people owed something to the former slaves and the free colored residents of the South—even, apparently, former slave owners like Madame Decuir.[60]

Washington's brief responded to Marr's argument that imposing the antidiscrimination norm deprived the defendant of his property without due process, simply that "all rights are limited by the laws, or general good of all. The right to control his property is not absolute, unlimited and destructive to the rights of other persons." Basically, Washington argued that the boat owner's property rights are subject to the police power and that as a property owner, the boat owner does not have the right to damage the rights of passengers, just as he does not have the right to set his boat on fire and impose risks on neighboring boats. Washington acknowledged that absent state legislation, the captain might have the power to "[direct] colored cabin passengers into the Colored Bureau, an inferior and badly ventilated series of rooms, underneath the ladies' cabin, and refuse them the ordinary rooms and places at table. . . . But when the State comes in, and from a regard to the welfare, comfort and safety of all its citizens" requires that "all must be treated equally," the State's exercise of its police power supersedes the rights of the captain. Along these lines, Washington argued that the US Supreme Court should resolve all doubts in favor of the constitutionality of state law. The brief purported to quote from US Supreme Court statements that "the incompatibility must not be speculative . . . it must be clear," and that with regard to any law, the Court should "presume in favor of its validity, until its violation of the constitution is proved beyond all reasonable doubt."[61]

Washington argued that the most recent US Supreme Court precedent on state power to regulate steamboats supported his argument in favor of allowing Louisiana to require integration. Washington quoted the following passage from the Supreme Court's 1873 opinion in *Railroad Co. v. Fuller*, which rejected a challenge to a state requirement that interstate railroads post their rates and adhere to them until new rates are posted:

No discrimination is made between local and interstate freights and no attempt is made to control the rates that may be charged. The public welfare is promoted without wrong or injury to the company. The statute was doubtless deemed to be called for by the interests of the community to be affected by it, and it rests upon a solid foundation of reason and justice. It is not, in the sense of the Constitution, in any wise a regulation of commerce. It is a police regulation, and as such forms a portion of the immense mass of legislation which embraces everything within the Territory of a state not surrendered to the general government, all which can be most advantageously exercised by the states themselves.[62]

Washington argued, in reliance on this passage, that "the above reasoning fully covers the case. . . . The power it exercises is one that may be exercised, if not exclusively by the State, at least concurrently with Congress, or exclusively till Congress shall legislate on the subject, and till then the exercise of the power is valid, and both can stand together afterwards."[63] Without coming out and saying so, Washington was attacking the existence of a Dormant Commerce Clause—arguing that state power is not displaced until Congress exercises its power under that clause.

Washington's argument based on *Fuller* was not as strong as he portrayed it, because the state law in *Fuller* did not impose substantive obligations on boats engaged in interstate commerce. Rather, it required them only to post rates and adhere to them, a common form of price regulation known as "tariffing." The Supreme Court in *Fuller* specifically noted that state law did not attempt to control the rates charged, even for intrastate trips. Washington needed to demonstrate that the distinction between posting and substantive regulation should not be viewed as determinative. Without such an argument, it was open for the justices to distinguish the statute in *Fuller*. They could have noted that an analogous statute in *Decuir* would have required steamboats to post and adhere to their policies regarding the treatment of racial groups on their boats.

Washington's brief concluded with a federalism argument and another plea to reject Captain Benson's claim that Louisiana's antidiscrimination requirements violated his property rights. The brief argued that Congress's commerce power should not be construed to extend to the issue of racial discrimination on steamboats in Louisiana, and that Congress should not legislate on the subject because that would be an attack on "the reserved rights of the thirty-eight States of this Republic . . . monopolizing for partisan purposes the essential rights of said States" and would attack "the organic theory of this republic, which is a general government, with special enumerated powers, and State governments, with all powers not thus enumerated."[64]

On Benson's property rights, Washington argued that "Capt. Benson, in his liberty to manage his own property, has no right to entrench on the personal rights of Madame Decuir as a citizen, and discriminate against her because she is colored." The brief noted that the defendant's own evidence established that he violated Louisiana law, and there was no sound basis to find that the Louisiana statute was "repugnant to the constitution of the United States."[65]

Madame Decuir's lawyer E. K. Washington was clearly outgunned by the more experienced US Supreme Court advocate Marr. Still, the briefs presented a fundamental disagreement over the soul of the law and its relationship to the future of Southern society. Washington's brief looked to the law as the protector of human dignity and the citizenship rights of a disadvantaged racial and social class. Marr's brief portrayed the law as protector of property and privilege.

Once the briefs were submitted, all the parties could do was wait for the Court's decision, which was made public on January 14, 1878.

8

Louisiana (and the Entire South) Redeemed

The decade of the 1870s began with the promise of equality and full citizenship for Louisianans of color, guaranteed by federal law and by Louisiana's constitution as implemented by Louisiana statutes. The years during which Madame Decuir's case against Captain John Benson worked its way through the courts were pivotal ones in the journey from emancipation to Jim Crow, from the promise of equality to the reality of *Plessy v. Ferguson*. When Madame Decuir embarked on her travels on July 29, 1872, Louisiana was controlled by a Republican government that included substantial numbers of people of color in its ranks. Many people of color held office in Louisiana from 1868 through 1874. At the federal level, congressional Reconstruction supported the hopes of Black people across the country that their rights as citizens might be recognized.[1] Madame Decuir's brother Antoine Dubuclet was state treasurer. Louisiana's 1868 constitution prohibited racial discrimination, and an 1869 Louisiana statute forbade segregation in transportation.

The political environment was, however, highly unstable, with strong opposition to Congress's Reconstruction policies and accusations by Democrats that the Republican Party had been corrupted. In fact, corruption was a central issue in the 1876 Louisiana elections. More troubling than any perceived or actual corruption, conservative Whites witnessed the new, unprecedented access by people of color to political and social institutions from which they had long been excluded, with dismay. As one author put it:

When Negro slavery ended, mistresses and masters discovered several dismaying truths: the extent to which they had never really known of their so-familiar human chattels at all; the attachment they had developed to the exercise of dominion over others; and the jealousy they felt when outsiders related to Negroes in roles traditionally reserved for white Southerners. Class divisions among Caucasians blurred into insignificance next to the imperatives of White supremacy.[2]

White supremacy in Louisiana, as in the entire South, was soon reestablished by force and violence directed at Republican governmental and political institutions and at colored Louisianans who tried to exercise their legal rights. By 1877, none of the three branches of the federal government would act to protect the rights of African Americans. After the disputed 1876 presidential election, Republicans agreed to end federal supervision of the Southern states and to let full control over colored populations return to state and local governments in exchange for Democratic acquiescence in the election of Republican Rutherford B. Hayes as president. (Democratic cooperation was necessary due to the party's control of the House of Representatives where the electoral votes were counted.) Democratic control of the House precluded congressional action, and Hayes himself did not share President Ulysses S. Grant's commitment to civil rights.

By 1878, when the US Supreme Court decided Captain Benson's challenge to the state court rulings in Madame Decuir's favor, the Louisiana government was firmly in the hands of White Democrats, and Jim Crow was beginning to take hold. Soon after, the new Louisiana Constitution of 1879 replaced the 1868 constitution, eliminating the 1868 antidiscrimination provisions. While the 1879 constitution prohibited racial tests for voting and office holding, it established a poll tax that was employed to prevent poor Black men from voting.[3] On the judicial side, a series of decisions by the US Supreme Court, culminating in *Plessy v. Ferguson*, explicitly ratified Jim Crow, rendering federal law ineffective to protect the rights of freed slaves and other citizens of color.[4]

Louisiana in the 1870s and "Redemption"

Much has been written about the history of "redemption" of the South, in which White Democrats took control of Southern governments, expelled

Republican officials they viewed as corrupt or carpetbaggers or both, passed laws that prevented virtually all people of color from voting and required segregation in virtually all public places. As the Louisiana Historical Society proclaimed in 1938, "White supremacy was established as a cardinal principle of a wise, stable, and practical government" in April 1877. Less appreciated today is the leading role that violence played in this process throughout the South, including Louisiana.[5]

The earliest notorious incident of postwar racial violence in Louisiana was known as the Opelousas massacre, as it happened in Opelousas in St. Landry Parish. In late September 1868, an estimated two hundred to three hundred Black people were killed by Whites set on excluding them from political participation. The political environment in St. Landry Parish at this time was strange. After a narrow election loss in the state elections of 1868, the local Democratic Party realized that if Blacks were allowed to vote, it would have to woo them to prevail in future elections, including the November presidential election. By day, White Democrats courted Black voters, inviting them to political meetings and barbecues and forming colored Democratic organizations. By night, Whites terrorized the Black population, using violence and threats of violence to re-establish White supremacy. After a first round of rioting in the parish ended, the White mob executed more than two dozen Black prisoners who were being held in the local jail. The violence, including more killings, continued for weeks after the executions, until the Black population was basically subdued in fear. An illustration of the success of the violence is that in November, not a single Republican vote was cast in the presidential election in the parish, even though the Republican candidate for governor had won a majority less than seven months earlier. It was violence and threats of violence that convinced Black voters in St. Landry Parish to support the Democratic Party.[6]

These incidents, and many others, were brought before Congress in the late 1860s and early 1870s as it considered civil rights legislation. Congress was told that in 1868 in Louisiana, 297 persons were killed by racial violence, and a White supremacist organization was credited with "driving thousands of men from the polls." In 1870, election-related violence claimed the life of Joseph L. Official, a newly elected member of the Louisiana legislature.[7] Instances of racial violence throughout the South, including in Louisiana, led Congress to pass the Civil Rights Act of 1871, also known as the Ku Klux Klan Act.

Perhaps most important to Madame Decuir, the historical distinction between the treatment of mixed-race people such as herself and other Black people was also breaking down, as illustrated most famously by the 1871 refusal of the Bank Coffeehouse in New Orleans to serve Charles Sauvinet, the mixed-race sheriff of Orleans Parish. Sauvinet's exclusion indicated a hardening of racial lines in New Orleans where, in earlier times, light-skinned people like him might be tolerated in predominantly White social institutions. In the words of Daniel Sharfstein, "In slavery's absence . . . preserving white privilege seemed to require new, less flexible rules about race and constant, aggressive action to enforce them."[8] In this new world, Madame Decuir's social position was becoming increasingly precarious.

The Supreme Court and Civil Rights in the 1870s

The US Supreme Court actively abetted the "redemption" of the South by the White racist establishment. In numerous cases involving race relations before the Court, the White establishment prevailed. Decision after decision limited the scope of civil rights laws and Congress's power to legislate in that field. Many of these decisions were legal landmarks. They set the framework for Jim Crow laws that lasted until the civil rights movement of the 1950s and 1960s. In effect, the Supreme Court had its own plan for Reconstruction, and it was much closer to that of President Andrew Johnson than to Congress's.

The legal march to Jim Crow did not begin immediately after the Civil War. Three early Supreme Court decisions affecting race relations, including two from Louisiana, were won by the progressive side, although there was one significant defeat for the rights of Blacks during this early period. The first was the landmark *Slaughter-House Cases*, known today mainly for narrowly construing the Privileges or Immunities Clause of the Fourteenth Amendment, but at the time was understood as a victory for the progressive Republican government in Louisiana.[9] The second was a rarely cited case concerning segregation on railroads running through the nation's capital. The third was the little-known case involving Sheriff Sauvinet, in which the court upheld a procedural aspect, added in 1871, to the antidiscrimination statute that Louisiana's Republican legislature enacted in the late 1860s under which both Sheriff Sauvinet and Madame Decuir brought suit.

The *Slaughter-House Cases*, decided in 1873, involved a controversy over economic regulation that the challengers framed as an individual rights case. Butchers challenged a Louisiana statute regulating slaughterhouses in New Orleans that the Republican legislature had passed in 1869 and the Louisiana Supreme Court had upheld, making it unlawful to keep or slaughter animals in the city of New Orleans on the east bank of the Mississippi River. The law, intended to protect the health and safety of New Orleans residents from the ill effects of butchery, also established a new corporation to which it awarded a monopoly over slaughterhouse operations in three Louisiana parishes. The legislature may have also been concerned with race discrimination in the business since it was well known that Blacks found it difficult if not impossible to have their livestock slaughtered after the war.

Incumbent slaughterhouse operators and butchers challenged the law, claiming it violated the Thirteenth and Fourteenth Amendments. They characterized it as creating an involuntary servitude, which abridged their privileges and immunities as citizens of the United States, denied them equal protection, and deprived them of property without due process of law. The main claim was that the statute deprived butchers in New Orleans "of the right to exercise their trade."[10]

The Court's decision upholding the statute took an expansive view of the regulatory powers of state and local governments and a narrow view of the scope of the Privileges or Immunities Clause of the Fourteenth Amendment. On governmental power, the Court stated, "It is both the right and the duty of the legislative body—the supreme power of the State or municipality—to prescribe and determine the localities where the business of slaughtering for a great city may be conducted." The Court noted that government-granted monopolies can be contrary to the public interest and have been condemned in Europe, but it found that representative bodies, such as those in the United States, should be presumed to be acting in the public interest and so could grant them without the degree of suspicion inherent in those granted by unelected monarchs.[11]

The Court also found ample justification for the law in the health and safety problems that had been generated by the location of slaughterhouses throughout the city. As Michael Ross has described the legislative record:

The abattoirs were bloody, filthy, and unregulated. Burly butchers killed the animals with hammers or knives, then skinned, gutted, and hung their fly-covered carcasses on hooks to dangle unrefrigerated for hours, even days. The mass of gory waste generated by these squalid businesses was then thrown directly into either the streets or the Mississippi River. A New Orleans doctor testified to a legislative committee: "Barrels filled with entrails, liver, blood, urine, dung, and other refuse, portions in an advanced stage of decomposition, are constantly being thrown into the river . . . poisoning the air with offensive smells and necessarily contaminating the water near the bank for miles." Much of the rotting refuse from the slaughterhouses and stock landings collected in the river around the giant suction pipes from which New Orleans drew its water supply. "When the river is low," the president of the New Orleans Board of Health testified, "it is not uncommon to see intestines and portions of putrefied animal matter lodged immediately around the pipes. The liquid portion of this putrefied matter is sucked into the reservoir." Pilings designed to stop the bulk waste matter from entering the pipes proved inefficient, and the pumping system repeatedly clogged.[12]

Finding that the law fell within the traditional powers of state and local governments, the Court turned next to whether any provision of the newly adopted amendments to the US Constitution had been violated. The amendments' primary purpose, the Court said, was to protect the newly freed slaves and other racial minorities—not to interfere with existing state regulatory power over businesses such as slaughterhouses. The Court refused to read the Privileges or Immunities Clause as creating extensive federal power superseding that of the states. It merely prohibited discrimination against persons from other states and guaranteed a limited range of rights implicit in federal citizenship, like the right to bring claims against the government and to access outlets of foreign commerce. The Court also found no violation of due process or equal protection, saying that to read those clauses to invalidate the Louisiana slaughterhouse statutes would work a radical redistribution of government power away from the states and toward the federal government.[13] (A few decades later, during the so-called Lochner era, named for *Lochner v. New York*, the Supreme Court would read the Due Process Clauses of the Fifth and Fourteenth Amendments to protect property and contract rights and invalidate all kinds of economic regulation.[14])

The *Slaughter-House Cases'* narrow construction of the Privileges or Immunities Clause has long been lamented as a defeat for the cause of progressive change. Civil rights advocates believe that the Court could have used the clause as a tool to protect Black people against Jim Crow laws that restricted voting, property, and other rights. But at the time, it was understood that the *Slaughter-House* plaintiffs were mounting a conservative challenge to state regulatory power with the aim of preserving White economic and racial domination in the business of slaughterhouses. Given the convulsive changes throughout US constitutional law that have occurred since 1873, the Court's narrow reading of the Privileges or Immunities Clause in that one decision cannot explain why the Court has never read the clause more broadly in other contexts.[15]

The Court's second postwar progressive decision on race was also handed down in 1873, and it involved segregation of passengers on a Virginia railroad that, with permission of Congress, passed through the District of Columbia. In 1863, when the Alexandria and Washington Railroad Company applied for permission to alter its route in the District of Columbia, Congress agreed on the condition that "no person shall be excluded from the cars on account of color." By 1868, the railroad's successor, the Washington, Alexandria, and Georgetown Railroad Company, had established a rule or practice of providing separate cars for colored passengers and barred Catharine Brown, a woman of color, from the car reserved for "white ladies." The railroad's defense to her suit over this was that she was offered a seat in a car reserved for colored ladies, which was equal, in all respects, to the White ladies' car. The Supreme Court, in an opinion by Justice David Davis, rejected the railroad's argument, pointing out that the phrase "excluded from the cars" must be understood to require integration since complete exclusion was never practiced by railroads. This supports the general sense that segregation was not understood at the time as consistent with a requirement of equal treatment.[16]

The Court's third major decision on race, 1875's *Walker v. Sauvinet,* marked the culmination of the litigation over the owner of the Bank Coffeehouse's refusal to serve longtime customer Sheriff Charles Sauvinet.[17] When the jury deadlocked, the trial judge, pursuant to a recently enacted Louisiana statute, decided in favor of Sauvinet. Walker claimed that this procedure deprived him of his privileges and immunities as a citizen of the United States, under *Slaughter-House,* and that it was contrary to due process. In an opinion by Chief Justice Morrison Waite, the Court rejected both arguments. It found that there is no federal right to trial by jury in state court civil (non-criminal) actions, and that the principal requirement of due process as understood at that time—that process be followed "according to the law of the land"—was satisfied, since the Louisiana court had followed Louisiana law. Justices David Dudley Field and Nathan Clifford dissented without opinion.[18]

Around the same time as the decision in Sheriff Sauvinet's case, the Court began to lay the groundwork for a narrower view of the reach of federal civil rights law. In *United States v. Reese*, the Court invalidated a federal statute imposing criminal penalties on state election officials who wrongfully denied citizens the right to vote. Two Kentucky election inspectors refused to allow William Garner, "a citizen of the United States of African descent," to vote.[19] The federal statute involved, the Enforcement Act of 1870, provided for the punishment of state officials and others who fail to allow citizens to perform acts necessary to qualify to vote or who "by force, bribery, threats, intimidation, or other unlawful means, hinder, delay, &c., or shall combine with others to hinder, delay, prevent, or obstruct, any citizen from doing any act required to be done to qualify him to vote, or from voting, at any election."[20] The Court, in an opinion also written by Chief Justice Waite, found that the law was too broad to be supported by the Fifteenth Amendment because it made no reference to race as the motivation for the denial of the right to vote. The Court refused to read a requirement of racial motivation into the statute, viewing that as a "new law" that only Congress has the power to enact. Although it must have been frustrating to prosecutors, *Reese* was a relatively minor decision because it did not disable Congress from redrafting the statute to include a racial motivation and thus criminalize the racially motivated interference with the right to vote.[21]

Meanwhile, the White struggle to regain dominance over people of color in the 1870s in Louisiana continued to erupt into violence until, by the time Madame Decuir's case was finally decided by the Supreme Court, Whites had finally regained complete control. In addition to legal measures, Whites throughout the South used violence and threats of violence to prevent Black men from voting and to generally intimidate them into accepting their social and economic subjugation.[22] The violence escalated in Louisiana to the point that in 1876, so many Blacks and other Republicans were prevented from voting, or voted Democratic for self-preservation, that Democrats' claim that the state went for the Democrat Samuel Tilden in that year's presidential election was actually credible. A report commissioned by President Grant in 1875 reported that 2,141 Black people had been killed in Louisiana, 2,115 had been injured, and that no one had been punished for any of these crimes.[23]

The most well-known post-1872 incidents of racial violence in Louisiana were the Colfax massacre and the Battle of Liberty Place. The Colfax massacre of April 1873, discussed also in chapter 7, occurred when Whites assaulted the Grant Parish courthouse to retake it from an occupation by elected Black officials and their supporters after the former sheriff refused to cede power.[24] Although they later claimed that they began their assault only after one of theirs, James Hadnot, a leader of the effort to take the courthouse, was shot dead, the attack was premeditated and initiated by the White mob. The White attackers killed dozens of Blacks, including prisoners who were summarily executed behind the courthouse. They then reinstalled the former sheriff who, in 1871, had led a mob to set fire to a home harboring Black officeholders, then shot them as they fled the flames. The three Whites who died in the fighting—Hadnot, Stephen Parish, and Sidney Harris—were honored in 1921 with a monument erected "In loving remembrance . . . of the heroes, who fell in the Colfax Riot fighting for white supremacy, April 13, 1873."[25] A 1950 monument on the site of the riot proclaims that "three white men and 150 negroes were slain" and that the "event . . . marked the end of carpetbag misrule in the South."[26]

In response to this massacre, federal authorities prosecuted more than one hundred of the White participants in the riot. After some of the cases were dismissed by a federal circuit court, the United States government took the case to the US Supreme Court where the defendants were represented by a distinguished group of lawyers, including R. H. Marr, Captain Benson's Supreme Court lawyer. The resulting decision, rendered the next year, was a major victory for the White supremacist redemption movement. *Cruikshank* was an early test of the boundary between state and federal criminal jurisdiction involving civil rights. The prosecutions were brought under a provision of the Enforcement Act of 1870 that made it criminal for "two or more persons" to "injure, oppress, threaten, or intimidate any citizen, with intent to prevent or hinder his free exercise and enjoyment of any right or privilege granted or secured to him by the constitution or laws of the United States, or because of his having exercised the same." The rights that the indictment invoked included the right to peaceably assemble, the right not to be deprived of life or liberty without due process of law, and the right to bear arms. In an opinion by Chief Justice Waite, the Court found that the indictments failed to properly allege violations of any right guaranteed by the United States Constitution.[27]

The Court's analysis in *Cruikshank* was a mixture of broad, principled statements on the reach of federal law and a technical discussion of defects in the indictments. The Court outlined principles of federalism, under which the states remain the primary protectors of individual rights, even after the adoption of the post–Civil War constitutional amendments explicitly limiting state power. The decision became an early landmark in the law on the scope of the recently adopted Fourteenth Amendment, establishing the principle that while the Fourteenth Amendment applied certain rights contained in the Bill of Rights to the states, including the right to free assembly and the right to petition the government, these applied only against state action and thus could not have been violated by the private mob at Colfax.[28] Relying on the developing state-action doctrine, the Court concluded that "the case as presented amounts to nothing more than that the defendants conspired to prevent certain citizens of the United States, being within the State of Louisiana, from enjoying the equal protection of the laws of the State and of the United States," and equal protection applied only to governmental action, not to the behavior of one citizen toward another.[29] The Court observed that to rule otherwise would bring all cases of murder or false imprisonment within federal criminal jurisdiction. To preserve the traditional federalist structure of the United States, the Court said federal jurisdiction must be limited.[30]

The Court also noted an additional reason to reject the charges based on the right to assemble; namely, that it was a First Amendment right that applied only against the federal government, not against the states.[31] The Court found that the counts involving life and liberty were defective because, although the victims were identified as "of African descent," the indictment did not specifically allege that "that this was done because of the race or color of the persons conspired against."[32] This must have been frustrating to the federal prosecutors because everyone knew that what happened in Colfax was a race-based conflict. As far as alleged violations of the victims' Second Amendment right to bear arms were concerned, the Court stated that "the right to bear arms is not granted by the Constitution; neither is it in any manner dependent upon that instrument for its existence. The Second Amendment means no more than that it shall not be infringed by Congress, and has no other effect than to restrict the powers of the National Government."[33] This understanding of the Second Amendment as not applying to action by state or local governments survived for 134 years, until 2010, when the US Supreme Court reversed itself and held that the Second Amendment restricts state and local gun control laws.[34]

Foreshadowing its opinion in *Hall v. Decuir,* the *Cruikshank* Court virtually ignored the race issue and the case's social importance. The Colfax massacre had been covered widely in newspapers and prompted hearings in Congress, with the general understanding that it was a particularly striking example of racially motivated violence. The opinion by contrast is largely a technical discussion of the requirements of federal criminal jurisdiction under the Enforcement Act. Its rhetorical flourishes were confined to stressing the importance of maintaining state control over state criminal law. Chief Justice Waite characteristically avoided expressing concern over the social problem of racial discrimination. The decision was unanimous, save for a Justice Clifford opinion, styled as a dissent but that agreed with the Court's result, though for different reasons. He thought the indictments were too "vague and indefinite" and thus did not meet the traditional requirements for certainty and fair notice in criminal prosecutions.[35] That had also been Justice Joseph P. Bradley's view when he heard the case while riding circuit in Louisiana. The *Cruikshank* decision inspired Whites to increase their violent efforts to re-establish White rule in Louisiana and throughout the South.

The Battle of Liberty Place occurred in 1874 and was a battle for control of the state government, after the Colfax massacre but before the US Supreme Court's *Cruikshank* decision. It had its roots in Louisiana's election of 1872, in which both Democrat John McEnery and Republican William Kellogg claimed victory in the Louisiana governor's race. Outgoing Republican governor Henry Clay Warmoth's appointed election board declared McEnery the winner, but the Republican legislature impeached and removed Warmoth, which resulted in colored Lieutenant Governor P. B. S. Pinchback serving as governor for the last month of Warmoth's term and a decision that Kellogg had been elected governor. As controversy over the legal government in Louisiana raged, the battle was instigated in part by Captain Benson's Supreme Court lawyer R. H. Marr, who called on members of the White League to take to the streets with arms to install the Democrat as governor.[36] The battle broke out when Democratic Party loyalists and members of the White League, a White supremacist paramilitary organization associated with the Democratic Party, attacked the lawful authorities and occupied the statehouse for three days, retreating only in the face of the imminent arrival of federal troops.[37] Ultimately, the federal government certified Kellogg as the winner of the election, temporarily continuing Republican rule in postwar Louisiana.

Following the *Cruikshank* decision, Congress enacted its final

Reconstruction-era civil rights statute, the Civil Rights Act of 1875. This statute, passed in the waning days of Reconstruction, was a public accommodations law, prohibiting businesses like inns, theaters, and transportation providers from discriminating on the basis of race. Because this statute was adopted three years after her journey, it did not apply to Madame Decuir's case. It was drafted in 1870 by Massachusetts senator Charles Sumner and John Mercer Langston, an early African American lawyer and one of the founders of Howard University Law School who was later elected to the United States House of Representatives from Virginia. Sumner had introduced it every year, and it was finally enacted the year after his 1874 death. This statute, if enforced, might have stopped the movement toward separate but equal dead in its tracks. Soon after it passed, the Grant administration brought many cases to enforce it, an effort that was halted, as we shall see, by a US Supreme Court decision in 1883 holding it unconstitutional.

After the passage of the Civil Rights Act of 1875, Congress fell silent on the race issue, largely because the balance of power had already begun to shift away from Radical Republican control. A key event in the restoration of White supremacist rule in the South that occurred while Madame Decuir's case awaited decision in the US Supreme Court was the close presidential election of 1876. The result turned on the vote in three hotly contested Southern states: Florida, Louisiana, and South Carolina. In each state, separate certificates were produced by competing government entities proclaiming Democrat Samuel J. Tilden and Republican Rutherford B. Hayes as the victor. There were numerous allegations of vote fraud and intimidation. Ultimately, Congress created a commission to resolve the dispute, composed of ten members of Congress and five Supreme Court justices. Republicans feared that Supreme Court Justice David Davis, a conservative Republican, would vote with Democrats, so Illinois Republicans had Davis named senator, which made him ineligible for service on the commission. He was replaced by Justice Joseph Bradley, also a Republican, and with Republican votes now outnumbering Democratic votes 8–7, the commission accepted the Republican certificates in all of the disputed states.[38]

Once the commission ruled in favor of the Republicans, Congress, with Democratic cooperation, still had to tally the electoral votes and proclaim Hayes as president. The Democratic Party retained control of the House of Representatives in the 1876 congressional elections, and one of the Democrats' conditions for accepting the electoral for Hayes was withdrawal of all federal troops from Louisiana, South Carolina, and Florida. This spelled doom for Republicans and non-White voters in those states. Without federal troops to protect them, they would be unable to resist the violence and the political turmoil that was leading inexorably to the Democratic, and therefore White supremacist, takeover of all Southern state governments.

The 1877 inauguration of Rutherford B. Hayes marked the end of Reconstruction and paved the way for Whites' final "redemption" of the South. Politically, significant federal support for the rights of Black Southerners was over. In relatively short order, White supremacists regained control over governments throughout the South. The only remaining question was whether the Jim Crow laws—imposing segregation, exclusion, and disenfranchisement of virtually all people of color—would survive legal challenges based on the constitutional amendments and statutes enacted during the second founding. It was against this background that the US Supreme Court finally reached the merits of the appeal in *Hall v. Decuir.*

The Supreme Court Decides

When the US Supreme Court finally decided Eliza Hall's appeal of her late husband's loss to Madame Decuir in the Louisiana Supreme Court, it was presided over by Morrison Waite, who had been sworn in as the seventh chief justice of the US Supreme Court on March 4, 1874. Chief Justice Waite was an Ohio Republican and was not President Ulysses S. Grant's first choice to fill the vacancy left by the death of Chief Justice Salmon Chase. By some reports, he was Grant's seventh.[1] Waite was a moderate, and as expected based on his reputation, he excelled in minimizing disagreement at the Court and maintained good personal relations with Justices with whom he differed on legal outcomes. He was known for integrity and accomplishment as a lawyer and public servant, although his loyalty to Republican Party principles was questioned by some.[2] Radical Republicans, such as Charles Sumner, were alarmed by Grant's choice, noting that Waite had run for Congress "as a conservative supporter of Lincoln against James Ashley, a Radical Republican and close associate of Charles Sumner," although a leading biography of Sumner attributes his opposition to concerns over Waite's lack of distinction as a jurist rather than his conservative outlook.[3] Waite's confirmation vote was 63–0, with Sumner abstaining. It turned out that Sumner's fears were warranted, as Waite presided over the Court's dismantling of much of the Radical Republican civil rights program, with Waite leading a Court majority to narrow or strike down civil rights laws, including a number of those discussed in previous chapters.

Hall v. Decuir was originally docketed during the Court's October term 1874, and then was carried over to the terms of 1875, 1876, and 1877. The November 1875 death of Captain John Benson delayed the case until Benson's widow Eliza Jane Hall was appointed administratrix and lawyer R. H. Marr provided documentation sufficient to convince the Court to substitute her as plaintiff-in-error. This did not happen until early 1877, and on April 5, 1877, E. K. Washington and Bentinck Egan filed a joint motion to have the case restored to the Court's calendar. Egan had reassumed the lead role representing Captain Benson's estate because Marr became an associate justice of the Louisiana Supreme Court in January 1877. Both Washington and Marr had consented to the Supreme Court deciding the appeal without oral argument, although Marr had said that if he was in Washington, DC, when the case was reached, he would like to argue.[4]

After the case was restored to the Court's docket in 1877, the Court made its preliminary decision on October 26, 1877, voting 5–3 to reverse the Louisiana Supreme Court's ruling in favor of Madame Decuir, without hearing oral argument.[5] There were only eight justices at the time because Associate Justice David Davis had resigned in January 1877, after being selected United States senator by the Illinois legislature to prevent him from serving on the commission formed to resolve the disputed election of 1876. His replacement was John Marshall Harlan, a former Kentucky slave owner and opponent (at the time) of Lincoln's Emancipation Proclamation, who later became the nineteenth-century Court's most outspoken advocate for the legal rights of Black people.[6] Harlan was nominated ten days before the Court's conference in *Hall v. Decuir*, but he was not confirmed by the Senate until November 29, 1877, did not take the judicial oath until December, and thus did not participate in the decision in *Hall v. Decuir*. In early January 1878, he corresponded from his home in Louisville with Chief Justice Waite about how he would vote on some other pending cases, but there was no mention of *Hall v. Decuir*.[7]

Justice Harlan was a Kentucky native who had vehemently opposed secession. He served as a colonel in the Union army and was credited with helping drive the rebels from the Kentucky hills. His family included a colored half brother, Robert, who was apparently the product of a relationship between Harlan's father and one of Harlan's uncle's slaves. Harlan suffered from serious financial difficulties his entire professional life, although he was also known to be generous to relatives and friends alike, and he was observed handing out apples to other passengers on the streetcar he rode with his fellow justices to the Supreme Court's courtroom in the basement of the capitol building, cutting off a generous slice for his colleague Justice Joseph McKenna.[8]

The 5–3 vote to reverse the Louisiana Supreme Court's decision in *Decuir v. Benson*, recorded in the Chief Justice Morrison Waite's notebook, had Chief Justice Waite and Associate Justices Joseph P. Bradley, David Dudley Field, Noah Swayne, and Nathan Clifford voting to reverse and Associate Justices Ward Hunt, William Strong, and Samuel Freeman Miller voting to affirm. Chief Justice Waite assigned the opinion to himself. Given Waite's reputation as seeking to minimize conflict on the Court, it is not surprising that he assigned what, at the time of voting, appeared to be a controversial case to himself. Had any justice in the majority changed his mind and voted to affirm, the decision of the Louisiana Supreme Court would have been affirmed by an equally divided court.[9]

Waite may have also sensed that the dissenters were not strongly committed to their votes and hoped to draft a narrow opinion that might bring them along. If so, he got his wish. When his opinion was circulated to the other justices, as far as can be discerned from the Court's files, no dissenting views were expressed, and no dissenting votes were noted when the decision was made public. Maybe Chief Justice Waite's opinion convinced the dissenters to go along.[10] Justice Nathan Clifford of Maine, notoriously independent in his legal views, filed a lengthy concurring opinion. When the decision in *Hall v. Decuir* was announced on January 14, 1878, it represented the unanimous conclusion of the US Supreme Court that Louisiana could not apply its antidiscrimination provisions to a steamboat on the Mississippi River.[11] Just a few years later, the Court would not prevent Louisiana and other states from requiring segregation in similar, although nominally intrastate, circumstances.

The Supreme Court's Opinion

Chief Justice Waite's opinion for the Court overturning the judgment of the Louisiana courts was an emotionless application of general legal principles to state regulation of transportation on navigable waters. There is only the slightest hint in the opinion that racial segregation was a pressing social issue—the opinion could just have easily been about regulation of the price of a steamboat ticket or the strength of crew members' beer. Madame Decuir was not even mentioned in the Court's opinion, either by name or some other designation such as plaintiff or defendant-in-error, and the opinion included none of the facts of the case or any discussion of the concerns that might have led Louisiana to include the antidiscrimination provisions in its Reconstruction constitution and statutory law, much less the social context of the violent "redemption" of the South. Rather, the case was presented as raising an abstract issue of the proper distribution of authority between the state and federal legislatures.[12] It was the sort of bloodless judicial decision-making that the late Judge John Noonan criticized in his book *Persons and the Masks of the Law*.[13]

Chief Justice Waite's seven paragraph opinion rejected Marr's argument that the statute at issue required only that common carriers do not exclude or expel persons based on race. Waite stated that the Court was bound to treat the act of 1869 as requiring integration on the boat because "such was the construction given to that act in the courts below, and it is conclusive upon us as the construction of a State law by the State courts." Chief Justice Waite foreshadowed the Court's reasoning by stating that the Louisiana courts had determined that integration was required by "those engaged in inter-state commerce," although in fact the Louisiana Supreme Court had expressly denied that the statute regulated commerce at all.[14]

Despite the fact that the Constitution does not use language suggesting exclusivity, Chief Justice Waite characterized Congress's power to regulate interstate commerce as an "exclusive power [that] has been conferred upon Congress." He noted, however, that stating this principle was much simpler than drawing the line between state and federal power, since, as he acknowledged, state law often affects interstate commerce without constituting regulation thereof. He recited the age-old refrain of judges when they find it difficult to construct a clear governing legal rule, that the court must instead engage in case by case decision-making, governed by judgment concerning legal principles rather than clear legal rules:

The line which separates the powers of the States from this exclusive power of Congress is not always distinctly marked, and oftentimes it is not easy to determine on which side a particular case belongs. Judges not unfrequently differ in their reasons for a decision in which they concur. Under such circumstances it would be a useless task to undertake to fix an arbitrary rule by which the line must in all cases be settled in each case upon a view of the particular rights involved.[15]

The Court recognized that state law often affects interstate commerce, noting several cases in which it had upheld state laws that undeniably imposed burdens on interstate commerce. Unlike these other state laws, the Court found that the Louisiana antidiscrimination law imposed a direct burden on interstate commerce because it required integration on Louisiana's portion of the Mississippi River when segregation might be required in one of the other nine states through which the river passes.

Chief Justice Waite then stated his conclusion that applying the act of 1869, even to the intrastate portion of the *Governor Allen*'s trip (between New Orleans and Hermitage Landing), was a direct burden on interstate commerce and thus unconstitutional:

State legislation which seeks to impose a direct burden upon inter-state commerce, or to interfere directly with its freedom, does encroach upon the exclusive power of Congress. The statute now under consideration, in our opinion, occupies that position. It does not act upon the business through the local instruments to be employed after coming within the State, but directly upon the business as it comes into the State from without or goes out from within. While it purports only to control the carrier when engaged within the State, it must necessarily influence his conduct to some extent in the management of his business throughout his entire voyage. His disposition of passengers taken up and put down within the State, or taken up within to be carried without, cannot but affect in a greater or less degree those taken up without and brought within, and sometimes those taken up and put down without. A passenger in the cabin set apart for the use of whites without the State must, when the boat comes within, share the accommodations of that cabin with such colored persons as may come on board afterwards, if the law is enforced.

Although some of this is difficult to comprehend (what does "It does not act upon the business through the local instruments to be employed after coming within the State, but directly upon the business as it comes into the State from without or goes out from within" mean?), the crux of Chief Justice Waite's analysis seems to be that Captain Benson's obedience to the act of 1869 with regard to intrastate passengers would necessarily affect his treatment of interstate passengers.[16]

The only mention of racial segregation in the opinion shows the attitude that prevailed at the time—Waite stated that the Louisiana law would require "a passenger in the cabin set apart for the use of whites [to] share the accommodations of that cabin with such colored persons as may come on board[.]" The same is of course true for passengers in the cabin set apart for Black people—they would be forced to share their cabin with Whites. The effects of the law were examined from the perspective of Whites only.[17] As the late Robert Cover would so eloquently describe it, with words lacking any true indication of what was at stake for her, the Court destroyed Madame Decuir's "normative world" and replaced it with the perspective of the White majority seeking to repress her vision.[18]

Chief Justice Waite's analysis depended primarily on the fact that the *Governor Allen*'s route included stops in more than one state, but he also placed some importance on the special geography of a navigable river that touches more than one state at the same time. As Chief Justice Waite put it:

The river Mississippi passes through or along the borders of ten different States, and its tributaries reach many more. . . . On one side of the river or its tributaries he might be required to observe one set of rules, and on the other another. Commerce cannot flourish in the midst of such embarrassments. No carrier of passengers can conduct his business with satisfaction to himself, or comfort to those employing him, if on one side of a State line his passengers, both white and colored, must be permitted to occupy the same cabin, and on the other be kept separate.

To Waite, the Commerce Power was designed precisely to grant Congress the exclusive power to regulate when uniformity is necessary. (Notice also that Waite's analysis, like Marr's brief, anticipates that despite the Equal Protection Clause, states have the power to require segregation, which, of course, became reality less than twenty years later in *Plessy v. Ferguson*.)[19]

Chief Justice Waite still had to explain why it was appropriate for the Court to act in the absence of congressional legislation. Although the Court had long threatened to strike down state legislation for encroaching on interstate commerce, it was not until 1872, the year of Madame Decuir's trip on the *Governor Allen*, that the Court actually struck down state legislation as infringing on Congress's power to regulate commerce among the states.[20] To some, judicial application of the Commerce Clause in the absence of federal legislation is arguably contrary to the fundamental structure of the United States under which the states retain their police powers, including the power to regulate commercial activity, unless the Constitution or a valid statute explicitly displaces state authority. This understanding may be more faithful than Dormant Commerce Clause jurisprudence to the text of the Commerce Clause, which is phrased as a power of Congress, and to the early understanding of the relationship between the federal government and the states, as reflected in the Tenth Amendment, which preserves state power in the absence of valid federal law.[21]

Waite's solution to the absence of federal regulation explicitly displacing state authority over segregation on riverboats was to justify the Court's action as consistent with Congress's intent, expressed through silence:

By refraining from action, Congress, in effect, adopts as its own regulations those which the common law or the civil law, where that prevails, has provided for the government of such business, and those which the States, in the regulation of their domestic concerns, have established affecting commerce, but not regulating it within the meaning of the Constitution. . . . Applying that principle left Benson at liberty to adopt such reasonable rules and regulations for the disposition of passengers upon his boat.[22]

This analysis in effect bestows a quasi-constitutional status to traditional state common law and civil law rules when interstate commerce is involved, shielding them from state legislative alteration. Further, it assumes a degree of uniformity of state common-law principles, which may have been the prevailing view in the nineteenth century but has since been abandoned in favor of the realization that each state supreme court promulgates common law based on its own views of law and policy.[23]

Chief Justice Waite's opinion implicitly rejected E. K. Washington's argument that the weight of the Constitution was with Madame Decuir and her right as a citizen to equal treatment regardless of race. By deciding that Benson had the right to segregate his passengers by race, Waite obviously did not find that Madame Decuir's rights had been violated. Waite did not even seem to notice that she had suffered a dignitary harm that weighed in favor of enforcing Louisiana's antidiscrimination law. The failure to appreciate the importance or even the existence of these interests may go a long way toward explaining the Supreme Court's failure to protect Madame Decuir's legal rights and the rights of others in similar circumstances. Waite even left open the possibility that the statute might be void, even with regard to purely intrastate transportation. Marr had argued that the 1869 act violated the property rights of ship owners who would lose control over the management of their property. Waite's opinion concluded that "we confine our decision to the statute in its effect upon foreign and inter-state commerce, expressing no opinion, as to its validity in any other respect."[24]

The Dormant Commerce Clause

Although nothing in the text of the constitution prohibits states from enacting laws that interfere with interstate commerce, the Court had, as far back as 1829, threatened to strike down state laws that, in its judgment, interfered too much with that commerce. Despite these threats, Madame Decuir's case was only the third time that the Supreme Court had actually invalidated a state law under the Commerce Clause in the absence of inconsistent federal regulation, one of which involved international, not interstate, commerce. Thus, one striking feature of *Hall v. Decuir* is that the Court employed this novel and unsettled doctrine to prevent a Southern state from prohibiting segregation.

Throughout the history of Dormant Commerce Clause jurisprudence, the Court's decisions have seemed to point in conflicting directions, making it difficult to predict the outcome of any particular case. When Madame Decuir's case reached the US Supreme Court, the Court's most recent pronouncement gave E. K. Washington hope that Louisiana's antidiscrimination statute would survive Supreme Court review. In *Railroad Co. v. Fuller*, decided in 1873, the railroad challenged an 1862 Iowa statute that required railroads to set passenger and freight rates for the coming year each September and post a printed copy of their rate schedules at every station and depot in the state. This is very similar to modern day tariff-filing requirements that apply to many businesses. Any railroad failing to post rates as required, or charging rates higher than those posted during the year for which they were effective, was subject to statutory damages of between $100 and $200, to be awarded to "any person injured thereby and suing therefor." After the plaintiff won a judgment against the railroad in the Iowa courts, the railroad took the case to the Supreme Court, arguing that the Iowa statute intruded on Congress's exclusive authority over interstate commerce (i.e., it violated the Dormant Commerce Clause).[25]

The Supreme Court, in a relatively brief opinion by Justice Noah Swayne, unanimously rejected the railroad's challenge. The Court found that the rate posting requirement was a "police regulation," well within traditional state powers and barely burdening interstate commerce. In language that Washington seized upon in his brief for Madame Decuir, the Court stated:

No discrimination is made between local and interstate freights, and no attempt is made to control the rates that may be charged. It is only required that the rates shall be fixed, made public, and honestly adhered to. In this there is nothing unreasonable or onerous. The public welfare is promoted without wrong or injury to the company. The statute was doubtless deemed to be called for by the interests of the community to be affected by it, and it rests upon a solid foundation of reason and justice.[26]

As noted, after quoting this passage in his brief, Washington proclaimed, "The above reasoning fully covers the case," apparently believing, or at least arguing, that if a state can require interstate railroads to post their rates and adhere to them for an entire year, a state can surely prohibit racial discrimination on interstate riverboats.[27]

The Court's forgiving attitude toward state regulation in *Fuller* was completely absent from Chief Justice Waite's opinion in *Hall v. Decuir*, as was any reference to the *Fuller* opinion.

To evaluate the Supreme Court's basis for overturning the Louisiana courts' decisions in favor of Madame Decuir, it would be necessary to take an extended detour into the origins and details of Dormant Commerce Clause jurisprudence. To avoid unduly distracting the reader from Madame Decuir's case and its civil rights context, this analysis is contained in an appendix to this volume.

Justice Clifford's Concurring Opinion

Justice Nathan Clifford's concurring opinion was twice as long as Waite's opinion for the Court and contained a longer and more detailed examination of the distribution of regulatory power between the state and federal governments than Waite's. At the time of the decision, Clifford was the longest serving member of the Supreme Court, having been appointed by

President James Buchanan in 1858. A New Hampshire native, Clifford settled in Maine to practice law, was friendly and outgoing, and was known more for hard work and determination than for a brilliant intellect.[28] He was a Jacksonian Democrat and served as attorney general of the United States under President James Polk. At the Court, he was a hard worker, writing more opinions than many if not most of his colleagues, and while he was praised for the diplomatic skills he displayed while presiding over the commission that resolved the 1876 election dispute, on the Waite court, he gained a reputation for being obstinate, and his opinions were often ponderous and confusing. Before Chief Justice Waite was appointed, as the senior associate justice, Clifford presided over the Court and even suggested when Waite arrived that he continue to do so until Waite learned the ropes.[29]

Justice Clifford never explained why he did not join the majority opinion or why he found it necessary to write separately. His concurring opinion focused mainly on federal power over the navigable waters of the United States. Like the majority opinion, Justice Clifford's opinion did not mention Madame Decuir by name, but he did refer to her as "plaintiff" and included a brief discussion of the facts of the case and the procedural background. In addition to his view that the federal government had exclusive power over activities on navigable waters, he also focused on the existence of federal regulation of steamboats, both of which may be viewed as narrower, or at least more precise, than the majority's less specific Dormant Commerce Clause reasoning. But Justice Clifford did not point to any aspect of the majority's reasoning as a basis for disagreement. One might speculate that he had been assigned the majority opinion and could not get the other justices to sign on, but the chief justice's notebook indicates otherwise. Thus, it seems that Justice Clifford took it upon himself to write a comprehensive opinion in the case, and he simply may not have paid any mind to Chief Justice Waite's efforts.[30]

Justice Clifford drew extensively from Marr's brief for Captain Benson. Clifford noted, as Marr had described, that Congress had passed statutes licensing and regulating steamboats on navigable waters. Clifford also stated that it was undisputed that the *Governor Allen* was licensed and enrolled under federal law. He concluded that "Congress has prescribed the conditions which entitle ships and vessels belonging to the national marine to pursue the coasting trade without being subjected to burdensome and inconsistent State regulations," and that "enrolled and licensed vessels have

the constitutional right to pursue the coasting trade on the terms and conditions which Congress has seen fit to prescribe and no State legislature can
interfere with that right, either to abridge or enlarge it, or to subject it to any
terms and conditions whatsoever." This is a very strong statement of what
today would be understood as an argument for field preemption, that the
existence of a comprehensive federal statutory scheme leaves no room for
contrary or even supplementary state law. Justice Clifford then brought the
point home with the uniformity problem raised by Justice Wyly's dissent
and Marr's brief, that while Louisiana might require integration, Mississippi
might require segregation, which would put the boat owner in an untenable
position.[31]

Justice Clifford seemed especially interested in establishing exclusive federal regulatory power over ships engaged in commerce on navigable waters,
mainly to avoid the inconvenience of compliance with disparate regulatory
regimes as ships moved from one state's jurisdiction to another's. He recognized that the Constitution did not explicitly grant exclusive power to the
federal government, but he found it only natural that the federal government's regulatory power over navigable waters could not be shared with the
states: "Whenever the terms in which a power is granted to Congress, or the
nature of the power, requires that it should be exercised exclusively by Congress, the subject is as completely taken from the State legislatures as if they
had been expressly forbidden to exercise the power." To Justice Clifford, the
nature of regulatory power over ships moving in interstate commerce upon
navigable waters required exclusive federal power. Thus, Louisiana's constitutional and statutory provisions prohibiting segregation in transportation
were unconstitutional, at least as applied to boats operating on navigable
waters such as the Mississippi River.[32]

Unlike Chief Justice Waite, Justice Clifford exhibited an understanding
that the social phenomenon of race discrimination was a central issue in
the case. In passages that have been characterized as Clifford going "out of
his way" to endorse the reasonableness of racial segregation, he commented
extensively on cases from various courts approving racial segregation, here
drawing largely on the citations in Marr's brief. He embraced the notion that
equality under the law does not mean identity, paralleling Louisiana Justice
Wyly's proto-separate-but-equal argument. Although Justice Clifford did
not embrace the religiously based segregationist views espoused by Marr,
he was sympathetic to the difficulty some would find in racial integration:

"Passengers are entitled to proper diet and lodging; but the laws of the United States do not require the master of a steamer to put persons in the same apartment who would be repulsive or disagreeable to each other."[33]

Postdecision Proceedings

As noted, the US Supreme Court issued its opinion in *Hall v. Decuir* on January 14, 1878, after having had the case on its docket for nearly three and one-half years. On that same day, the Court issued an order directed to the Louisiana Supreme Court, informing it that its judgment was "reversed with costs" in the amount of "Two Hundred & four dollars & one cent." The order also "remanded [the case] to the said Supreme Court with instructions to reverse the judgment of the district court." The order broke down the costs as $184.01 for the "Clerk" and $20 for the "Attorney." An itemized bill in the case file shows that the single largest item in the costs was $119 for printing the record, which was presumably done by the Supreme Court clerk pursuant to the Court's recently adopted rule that twenty copies of each case be printed for the Court. The clerk, D. W. Middleton, in correspondence contained in the file, seemed very anxious to collect his costs, which raises the possibility that he may have personally incurred some of the costs, such as printing the record, and then charged them to the parties at a profit, as was common practice among federal government officials at the time.[34]

The ever-diligent Egan set out to help Middleton collect the costs of litigation, even though as counsel to the prevailing party he was under no obligation to do so. Shortly after the opinion and order were issued, Egan wrote Middleton requesting a copy of the opinion and promising to "endeavor to collect any costs that may be due to you." Egan also informed Middleton that he was taking over for Marr because Marr had recently become a "Judge of our Supreme Court, and therefore unable to attend to the matter any more." He also stated, "I think Mrs. Decuir is well off and if I am not misled she would pay as soon as I get the mandate." In one letter Egan stated that Madame Decuir "has more money than god." On March 8, 1878, Egan wrote Middleton again, thanking him for the copy of the opinion and his bill for costs. He let Middleton know that he had presented the bill to George Hite, one of Benson's guarantors, and he promised to show it to "Mr. John Janney, who was at the time agent of the Governor Allen [*sic*] belonging to Capt.

Benson and is still said to have in his possession some money belonging to Benson." After stating that he thought he should leave them to consult over the bill for a few days, he added that "Mr. Washington has informed me that his client Madame Decuir is insolvent." On April 13, 1878, Egan wrote Middleton again, that "I fear that the prospect of collecting your bill for costs in the case of Benson vs. Decuir is very bad." Egan reported that George Hite said that he is "broke" and that John Janney refuses to pay. He concluded, "I might collect the claim from Mrs. Decuir but I am told the prospect of doing so is bad." Egan seemed eager to please the Supreme Court clerk, and there is evidence in the file suggesting that someone on his side of the litigation paid the clerk his costs with hopes of being ultimately reimbursed by Madame Decuir.

Meanwhile, the Louisiana Supreme Court took up the case on remand from the US Supreme. On April 30, 1878, on Egan's motion, the Louisiana court remanded the case to the district court with instructions to dismiss it. As far as one can tell from the order of the court, Judge Marr, who had litigated the case on behalf of Benson and his administratrix, ruled along with his colleagues in favor of Egan's motion, something that today would be viewed as highly irregular. The Louisiana Supreme Court also specified that Madame Decuir was required to pay Benson's costs in both state courts, and the court also ordered Madame Decuir to pay the other side $204.01, representing the costs assessed by the US Supreme Court.

Washington was probably correct that Madame Decuir was insolvent by the end of the case. The property she and her husband owned together was insufficient to satisfy all of the creditors with claims against his estate. Her plantation in Pointe Coupée Parish was gone, and she lived the rest of her life in New Orleans with her daughter Rosa. The city directory listed Rosa as a "seamstress" and Madame Decuir as simply "widow, Antoine." Madame Decuir died in 1891. Her burial location is unknown, although her remains may be in the Dubuclet family tomb in St. Louis Cemetery No. 2 in New Orleans.

The Reaction to the Decision

The Supreme Court's decision in *Hall v. Decuir* was viewed as a signal defeat for Black people's claims to equal civil or public rights in the post–Civil War period. Newspapers at the time recognized that it was an "important civil rights case," with one paper reporting on it under the headline "A Civil Rights Law Exploded."[35] One early book advocating civil rights for Black people, *Justice and Jurisprudence,* mentioned *Hall v. Decuir* at least one hundred times and criticized the decision as "license" of a "spirit of tyranny" by letting federal courts nullify state antidiscrimination laws, and that it "judicially determines that there is an unlimited power to oppress and wound color." The authors further characterized the "opinion in *Hall v. Decuir*" as "pro-slavery," asking, "Can anything be more justly due to the vain show and weakness of the Fourteenth Amendment than laughter? What can be more absurd than that 'a colored fellow,' 'coon,' 'darky,' 'domestic,' should be manufactured into a citizen of the United States, with all the privileges and immunities of the superior race, by the mere parchment of the Fourteenth Amendment?"[36] Most simply, the decision allowed providers of interstate transportation to segregate their passengers by race, which would almost certainly lead to inferior accommodations for non-Whites. The authors of *Justice and Jurisprudence* recognized the connection between the decision and the doctrine of separate but (un)equal, stating that the "actual effect of the doctrine of *Hall v. Decuir,* that 'Equality is not identity,' was the authorization of the public servant to observe the letter but to defeat the spirit of the Fourteenth Amendment while ostensibly conforming thereto."[37]

The effect of the Supreme Court's decision in *Hall v. Decuir* was not simply to disable Louisiana from enforcing its antidiscrimination law. Unless the Civil Rights Act of 1875 remained in effect, owners of interstate common carriers, such as steamboats and railroads, were free to make and enforce their own rules regarding racial segregation. In the South, this meant segregation in all interstate transportation by their owners even before state governments enacted laws requiring segregation of local transportation. This is how the lower courts interpreted and applied the decision, and it was the governing understanding of *Hall v. Decuir* as late as 1952.[38]

In *Hall v. Decuir,* the Supreme Court, for the first time after the Civil War, embraced racial segregation as an acceptable practice in interstate travel. If nothing more, *Hall v. Decuir* set the tone for the Supreme Court's treatment of claims involving racial discrimination for decades. Although the majority opinion did not hint at it, it is difficult to believe that the justices were unaware of the social significance of *Hall v. Decuir.* Or maybe they thought that their decision actually meant very little, either because the Civil Rights

Act of 1875 applied to new cases like Madame Decuir's or because the federal government had, after the Compromise of 1877, basically abandoned the freed slaves and other persons of color to their fate at the hands of the states. By the time of the decision, political change throughout the South would have muted the effects of a ruling in favor of Madame Decuir. In a very short time, Southern states would institute Jim Crow and would become much more likely to prohibit integration than require it. The Supreme Court would cooperate in this effort, issuing ruling after ruling, narrowing the scope of federal civil rights protections enacted during Radical Reconstruction. In succeeding decades, *Hall v. Decuir* was a significant precedent on the distribution of regulatory power between the states and the federal government, but its importance as a symbol of racial injustice faded over time, so that by the time that the law began to turn away from segregation, more than seventy years later, it was virtually forgotten by all but a handful of historians specializing in that period.

10

The Completion of the Law's Journey to "Equal, but Separate"

The US Supreme Court's decision in *Hall v. Decuir* was a harbinger of things to come. Over the two decades following Madame Decuir's loss, the Court would dismantle Congress's efforts to protect the civil rights of African Americans and mute the effects of the Reconstruction-era constitutional amendments and statutes that had held so much promise in the years following the end of the Civil War. The Court's slash-and-burn expedition through Congress's Reconstruction program did not end with the infamous decision in *Plessy v. Ferguson,* but *Plessy* was a culmination of sorts in that it left no doubt over which side US law would take in African Americans' quest for dignity and racial justice.

The continuation of the pattern revealed in *Hall v. Decuir* began in 1883, with a pair of the most significant civil rights cases decided by the US Supreme Court under Chief Justice Morrison Waite. In these cases, the Court struck down two federal civil rights statutes: a portion of the Civil Rights Act of 1871, and the entire Civil Rights act of 1875.

The first case, *United States v. Harris,* involved a criminal provision of the Civil Rights Act of 1871 aimed at the Ku Klux Klan and similar White-supremacist organizations.[1] The statute provided:

If two or more persons in any state or territory conspire or go in disguise upon the highway or on the premises of another for the purpose of depriving, either directly or indirectly, any person or class of persons of the equal protection of the laws, or of equal privileges or immunities under the laws, or for the purpose of preventing or hindering the constituted authorities of any state or territory from giving or securing to all persons within such state or territory the equal protection of the laws, each of said persons shall be punished by a fine of not less than $500 nor more than $5,000, or by imprisonment, with or without hard labor, not less than six months nor more than six years, or by both such fine and imprisonment.[2]

The *Harris* case arose out of a lynching. An armed mob, including, incredibly, County Sheriff R. G. Harris, raided the Crockett County, Tennessee, jail to seize and assault four Black prisoners. Despite the efforts of a deputy, William A. Tucker, to stop them, the mob removed the four Black prisoners from the jail and beat all four, killing one. The perpetrators, including Sheriff Harris, were prosecuted by federal authorities. The indictments charged that the beatings and killing arose from a conspiracy among the defendants to deprive the victims of their rights, privileges, and immunities under federal law, and that the conspiracy aimed to prevent the local authorities, including Deputy Sheriff Tucker, from protecting the victims' federal rights.[3]

It is obvious from the language of the statute ("conspire or go in disguise") that Congress was referring to groups like the Ku Klux Klan, then terrorizing Blacks and Republican advocates of equal rights all over the South. In its early days, the criminal provision of this statute had been incredibly successful. In 1871 alone, federal prosecutors, led by President Ulysses S. Grant's Attorney General Amos Akerman, head of the newly established US Department of Justice, brought thousands of prosecutions against the Klan and similar gangs, and, with 1,143 convictions, succeeded in temporarily restoring peace and security to large areas of the South. The Klan was crippled, and as Akerman noted, Black people could once again sleep in their own homes without fear. President Grant viewed the passage and enforcement of the 1871 Civil Rights Act as one of the great achievements of his presidency.[4]

The issue before the Supreme Court, which the lower court divided on, was whether Congress had the power to enact this provision. The government argued for four sources of constitutional power; the Thirteenth, Fourteenth, and Fifteenth Amendments and the Privileges and Immunities Clause of the original Constitution. After dismissing the Fifteenth Amendment as concerned solely with the right to vote, the Court turned its attention to section 1 of the Fourteenth Amendment, finding that it could not support the statute because, by its terms, it was aimed only at official governmental action, not private conduct. It found it perfectly clear, from the language of the first section, that its purpose . . . was to place a restraint upon the action of the states. . . . The section of the law under consideration is directed exclusively against the action of private persons, without reference to the laws of the states, or their administration by the officers of the state, we are clear in the opinion that it is not warranted by any clause in the fourteenth amendment to the constitution.

That Harris, as county sheriff, had been acting under color of state law was not considered.[5]

The Court also found that the Thirteenth Amendment did not authorize Congress to pass the Civil Rights Act of 1871 because the act went beyond prohibiting conduct related to slavery to matters that were, in its view, the exclusive preserve of the states:

A law under which two or more free white private citizens could be punished for conspiring or going in disguise for the purpose of depriving another free white citizen of a right accorded by the law of the state to all classes of persons,—as, for instance, the right to make a contract, bring a suit, or give evidence,—clearly cannot be authorized by the amendment which simply prohibits slavery and involuntary servitude.[6]

Citing his opinion in the *Reese* case, discussed in the previous chapter, Chief Justice Waite drew a line between what was the state's business and what was the federal government's and refused to read the newly enacted amendments as giving Congress the power to stamp out race discrimination, which must remain a state preserve.[7] Waite did not appear to be conscious of the tension between this observation and his determination in *Hall v. Decuir* that the application of state antidiscrimination law interfered with federal authority.

The Court also held that the Privileges and Immunities Clause of article 4, section 2, did not give the federal government the power to interfere with matters of private behavior governed by state law: "This section, like the fourteenth amendment, is directed against state action," not personal behavior, said the Court. Prosecuting racial violence was left to the states. Unfortunately, at this juncture in history, disempowering federal enforcement essentially ensured the restoration of mob rule and lynch law in the Southern states.[8]

The Civil Rights Act of 1871 also contained a civil remedy designed to provide a damages action against the perpetrators of Klan violence. Its constitutionality was not directly addressed in *Harris*, but the logic of the decision seemed also to apply to it. Because of this, the civil remedy lay dormant for decades. It was assumed that if Congress lacked power to create a criminal remedy against private racially motivated violence, it similarly lacked power to create a damages remedy for the same conduct. Today, the Court reads the civil provision to apply only when the violation is motivated by race and only when the conspiracy involves a constitutional right that is capable of being violated by private individuals, such as the right to be free of involuntary servitude and the right to engage in interstate travel, which means that most Klan violence cannot give rise to a civil claim under the 1871 act.[9]

The *Civil Rights Cases*

Eight months after the *Harris* decision, the Waite Court decided the *Civil Rights Cases*, striking down the Civil Rights Act of 1875.[10] The Civil Rights Act of 1875 was a public-accommodations law prohibiting racial discrimination in specified businesses that served the general public, including the *Governor Allen* and all other steamboats plying the navigable waters of the United States. In it, Congress declared that "all persons within the jurisdiction of the United States shall be entitled to the full and equal enjoyment of the accommodations, advantages, facilities, and privileges of inns, public conveyances on land or water, theaters, and other places of public amusement; subject only to the conditions and limitations established by law, and applicable alike to citizens of every race and color, regardless of any previous condition of servitude."[11] Did "full and equal" include prohibiting segregation? If so, this provision would have changed the result in cases like *Hall v. Decuir*, as Justice Nathan Clifford anticipated in his concurring opinion.

As noted, the original proposal that led to the Civil Rights Act of 1875 was drafted in 1870 by Senator Charles Sumner of Massachusetts and John Mercer Langston, a successful lawyer, public servant, and diplomat, and one of the founders of Howard University Law School. Langston was also (sort-of) related to Supreme Court Justice John Marshall Harlan; he was the maternal great-grandfather of Robert Jackson Harlan, a descendant of Justice Harlan's mixed-race half-brother Robert Harlan.[12] Based on his 1855 election as township clerk in Brownhelm, Ohio, Langston was the third Black American to be elected to public office. Later, Langston served as a member of the United States House of Representatives from Virginia after a contested election that had to be resolved by a vote of the House.[13]

Sumner introduced their civil rights bill each year until his death in 1874. Originally, the bill included provisions requiring school desegregation and attacking discrimination in jury selection, but those aspects of the proposal were dropped, leaving only the public-accommodations provision.[14] Sumner was the leading champion in the Senate for civil rights for African Americans in the United States. In 1856, he delivered a fiery antislavery speech, which included passages insulting Senator Andrew Butler and his state of South Carolina. The next day, South Carolina Representative Preston Brooks, Butler's cousin, went into the Senate chamber and beat Sumner severely with his cane. To some, this ugly episode signaled the inevitability of civil war.[15] Reportedly, among Sumner's last words before he died in 1874 were "take care of the civil rights bill."[16] When it was passed and signed into law by President Grant in 1875, the national tide had already begun to turn against protecting Blacks from discrimination, and the law may have seemed more like a memorial to Sumner than a serious attempt at reform.

The *Civil Rights Cases* consisted of five consolidated cases from Kansas, Missouri, California, New York, and Tennessee prosecuting operators of various businesses for violating the 1875 act. They dealt with the broad swath of the act's coverage, including denials of accommodations to Black people in a hotel, a theater, an opera house, and a railroad. The central purpose of the act, said the Court, was "to declare that, in the enjoyment of the accommodations and privileges of inns, public conveyances, theaters, and other places of public amusement, no distinction shall be made between citizens of different race or color, or between those who have, and those who have not, been slaves." The only issue the Court addressed in the cases before it was whether Congress had the power to enact it.[17]

Most of the cases were straightforward applications of the act to simple racial segregation or exclusion, but in the Tennessee case, Sallie Robinson, a woman "of African descent," had been denied a seat in the ladies' car on the Memphis & Charleston Railway Co.'s train due to the fact that "the conductor had reason to suspect that the plaintiff, the wife, was an improper person, because she was in company with a young man whom he supposed to be a white man, and on that account inferred that there was some improper connection between them." In other words, she was suspected of breaking the taboo against publicly revealed interracial, intimate relationships. Although common carriers were expected to serve anyone willing to pay the fare, traditionally they could exclude "improper persons" and others violating the carrier's rules. The circuit court charged the jury that if this was the conductor's reason for excluding Mrs. Robinson from the car, they could take it into account in determining whether the railroad should be held liable. Apparently, a woman of color in the company of a White man might be considered an improper person.[18]

Justice Joseph P. Bradley, a Republican who had previously been a successful lawyer practicing in Newark, New Jersey, wrote the opinion for the Court. Almost offhandedly, at the outset, his opinion considered and dismissed anything other than the enforcement clauses of the Thirteenth and Fourteenth Amendments as sources of power for the 1875 act: "Of course, no one will contend that the power to pass it was contained in the Constitution before the adoption of the last three amendments."[19] At least as applied to interstate modes of transportation, this statement would seem to be in direct conflict with the Court's determination in *Hall v. Decuir* that Congress had exclusive power to regulate the terms of interstate travel.

Because it dismissed the Commerce Clause so easily, the Court's opinion in the *Civil Rights Cases* focused on the enforcement clauses of the Thirteenth and Fourteenth Amendments. As for the Fourteenth Amendment, Justice Bradley's analysis expanded on *Harris*. As in *Harris*, which struck down a provision of the 1871 act, the Court held that the federal government could not regulate private discrimination because the Fourteenth Amendment reached only state action:

Until some State law has been passed, or some State action through its officers or agents has been taken, adverse to the rights of citizens sought to be protected by the Fourteenth Amendment, no legislation of the United States under said amendment, nor any proceeding under such legislation, can be called into activity, for the prohibitions of the amendment are against State laws and acts done under State authority.[20]

The "state action" theme has become familiar in disputes over the scope of federal civil rights authority. The fear is that without a state-action limitation, the federal government would have the power to displace the traditional police powers of the states. As the Court stated, "If this legislation is appropriate for enforcing the prohibitions of the amendment, it is difficult to see where it is to stop. Why may not Congress, with equal show of authority, enact a code of laws for the enforcement and vindication of all rights of life, liberty, and property?" After speculating that Congress might attempt to exercise exclusive power over private relations, the Court concluded that this would be "repugnant to the Tenth Amendment of the Constitution, which declares that powers not delegated to the United States by the Constitution, nor prohibited by it to the States, are reserved to the States respectively or to the people."[21]

The Court's analysis of the Thirteenth Amendment was more complex, for, in abolishing the private relationship of master and slave, that amendment clearly regulates purely private conduct. The Court assumed, as the government argued, that "the power vested in Congress to enforce the article by appropriate legislation clothes Congress with power to pass all laws necessary and proper for abolishing all *badges and incidents* of slavery in the United States."[22] The Court then stated the heart of the issue: "Upon this assumption it is claimed that this is sufficient authority for declaring by law that all persons shall have equal accommodations and privileges in all inns, public conveyances, and places of public amusement; the argument being that the denial of such equal accommodations and privileges is in itself a subjection to a species of servitude within the meaning of the amendment."[23] This was what these cases were all about. Should not all racial discrimination, public or private, be considered a continuation of the slave system? African Americans surely experienced it that way at the time. Or was private discrimination a wholly separate social phenomenon and the exclusive province of the states?

Conceding that Congress has the power under the Thirteenth Amendment to abolish the badges and incidents of slavery, the Court then needed to explain why, in its view, private exclusion from public accommodations was not a badge or incident of slavery. The Court began by detailing the legal features of slavery:

Compulsory service of the slave for the benefit of the master, restraint of his movements except by the master's will, disability to hold property, to make contracts, to have a standing in court, to be a witness against a white person, and such like burdens and incapacities were the inseparable incidents of the institution. Severer punishments for crimes were imposed on the slave than on free persons guilty of the same offenses.[24]

While the Thirteenth Amendment gave Congress the power to legislate against these features of slavery, as it had done in the Civil Rights Acts of 1866 and 1870, the Court asked if refusing to provide service to a person of a certain race was a badge or incident of slavery federally enforceable under the Thirteenth Amendment (in the types of businesses addressed in the Civil Rights Act of 1875). Here, the Court's analysis was conclusory, stating only,

After giving to these questions all the consideration which their importance demands, we are forced to the conclusion that such an act of refusal has nothing to do with slavery or involuntary servitude[.] It would be running the slavery argument into the ground to make it apply to every act of discrimination which a person may see fit to make as to the guests he will entertain, or as to the people he will take into his coach or cab or car, or admit to his concert or theater, or deal with in other matters of intercourse or business.[25]

If nothing else, the lack of a basis in legal precedent or legal principle for the Court's judgment that segregation "has nothing to do with slavery or involuntary servitude" demonstrates that when it limited Congress's power to legislate racial equality, the Court was making a purely normative determination. There was no legal barrier to a contrary determination, that segregation and exclusion based on race were "badges and incidents of slavery" that Congress was empowered to act against by the Thirteenth Amendment. The subjugation of the Black race after the Civil War did not materialize out of thin air. Rather, it was a continuation of the social system that embraced slavery and denied personhood, citizenship, and human dignity to slaves and their descendants. And it was a continuation embraced by the Supreme Court, as it imposed crippling limitations on Congress's power to enforce the Thirteenth and Fourteenth Amendments.

The Court did not conclude that the law was powerless to prohibit racial segregation or exclusion. It opined that state law could require the operators of public accommodations to admit all regardless of race: "Innkeepers and public carriers, by the laws of all the States, so far as we are aware, are bound, to the extent of their facilities, to furnish proper accommodation to all unobjectionable persons who in good faith apply for them," and, "If the laws themselves make any unjust discrimination, amenable to the prohibitions of the Fourteenth Amendment, Congress has full power to afford a remedy under that amendment and in accordance with it."[26] The Court appears not to have considered whether the Civil Rights Act of 1875 could be constitutionally applied to cases like Madame Decuir's that arose on interstate transportation where it had previously held states could not act.

African Americans rightly regarded the Supreme Court's invalidation of the Civil Rights Act of 1875 as catastrophic. The title of an 1893 account of the case provides the flavor of this reaction: "The Barbarous Decision of the United States Supreme Court Declaring the Civil Rights Act Unconstitutional and Disrobing the Colored Race of All Civil Protection. The Most Cruel and Inhuman Verdict against a Loyal People in the History of the World."[27] The combination of *Hall v. Decuir* and the *Civil Rights Cases* must have outraged Southern Blacks being told in *Hall* that *only* Congress could address discrimination on riverboats; then, in the next case, that Congress lacked all power to do so. Paired with *Hall v. Decuir*, the message of the *Civil Rights Cases* was simply that the Supreme Court was hostile to any antidiscrimination legislation—whether state or federal.[28]

Justice John Marshall Harlan, the former slaveowner turned judicial champion of civil rights for Black people, wrote a long, impassioned dissent from the decision in the *Civil Rights Cases*, criticizing the Court for being overly technical and ignoring the "soul" of the law, which he thought should control the interpretation of constitutional amendments. To Harlan, the Thirteenth Amendment gave Congress the power "to protect the freedom established, and consequently to secure the enjoyment of such civil rights as were fundamental in freedom." In Harlan's view, the right to equal use of the facilities covered by the Civil Rights Act of 1875 were civil rights fundamental to freedom. Justice Harlan also found ample authority for the act under the Fourteenth Amendment because the institutions regulated were, in his view, public and not strictly private. Common carriers performed a public function. Innkeepers were also engaged in a public service. As Harlan explained, under the common law, innkeepers were generally required to provide service to all travelers while places of more permanent residence, such as boarding houses, were not. With respect to "places of public amusement," Harlan would have limited the applicability of the Act to state and locally licensed establishments. Harlan found these institutions sufficiently public in character to satisfy the state-action requirement of the Fourteenth Amendment.[29]

Harlan also viewed the Commerce Clause as a source of authority for the act—at least for interstate travelers. *Hall v. Decuir* had held that only Congress had the power to regulate the practices of steamboats in interstate commerce. To Harlan, *Hall v. Decuir* provided strong support for federal power to require equal treatment in interstate travel, which would save at least some applications of the Civil Rights Act of 1875.

Morrison Waite still occupied the office of chief justice of the Supreme Court when he died on March 23, 1888. It may be surprising that under the leadership of a reputed moderate Republican like Waite, the Court eagerly dismantled federal and state efforts to protect people of color from discrimination. Whether the federal government had any legitimate role to play in protecting Blacks from racial violence and oppression was a constant political issue during the Waite years, and it has been observed that Waite was concerned that the assertion of federal power over civil rights might pave the way to an oppressive concentration of power in the central government. Regardless, when presented with the choice between expansive and narrow protection of the rights of people of color, the Waite Court consistently chose the narrow path and was willing to limit both state and federal power to do so. Thus, although Waite had a reputation for being deferential to the political branches, this deference does not seem to have carried over to the area of civil rights for Black people.[30]

The first race case to reach the post-Waite Supreme Court was very similar to *Hall v. Decuir* except that it arose on a railroad. Emboldened by *United States v. Harris* and the *Civil Rights Cases,* the Southern states continued to enact Jim Crow laws.[31] A challenge to the constitutionality of one such law reached the Supreme Court in 1890. An 1888 Mississippi statute required that "all railroads carrying passengers in this state, other than street railroads, shall provide *equal, but separate,* accommodation for the white and colored races, by providing two or more passenger-cars for each passenger train, or by dividing the passenger-cars by a partition so as to secure separate accommodations." Railroads usually opposed such rules because they increased their cost of operating. In August 1888, the Louisville, New Orleans & Texas Railway Company was indicted for not providing separate accommodations as required by law. The railroad said it was an interstate operation, carrying passengers from Tennessee to New Orleans, "and other points in the state of Louisiana, and other states in the United States," and that it had always "provided equal but not separate accommodations for passengers of the white and colored races." The railroad also said that it operated only interstate trains through Mississippi and therefore, under *Hall v. Decuir,* the statute could not be constitutionally applied to it.[32]

The Mississippi Supreme Court disagreed. That court interpreted the statute to be valid because by its terms it applied only to passengers whose entire trip was inside Mississippi. It distinguished *Hall v. Decuir* as a case that involved "an interstate carrier, acting under license from the United States, and plying the navigable waters of the same. The state had no control over the way, the boat, or the owner."[33]

In the US Supreme Court, the railroad renewed its argument that the statute interfered unconstitutionally with interstate commerce. Justice David Brewer's opinion for the Supreme Court rejecting the railroad's claim was brief. In *Hall v. Decuir*, it said, inaccurately, that the Louisiana Supreme Court had determined that the statute sought to regulate interstate travelers coming into the state of Louisiana.[34] To the contrary, Chief Justice Waite's opinion for the Supreme Court in *Hall v. Decuir* specifically noted that the Louisiana statute "purports only to control the carrier when engaged within the State." The US Supreme Court, not the state court, determined that applying Louisiana law throughout the *Governor Allen*'s journey within Louisiana would effectively regulate interstate travelers. In finding a burden on interstate commerce, Chief Justice Waite had concluded that even though the statute prohibited segregation only inside Louisiana, the statute "must necessarily influence his conduct to some extent in the management of his business throughout his entire voyage."[35] The same could be said about the Mississippi statute. In fact, the Court recognized that Mississippi's statute would have the same sort of effect on interstate commerce as Louisiana's. The Court noted that although the Mississippi statute's "provisions are fully complied with when to trains within the state is attached a separate car for colored passengers[, t]his may cause an extra expense to the railroad company; but not more so than state statutes requiring certain accommodations at depots, compelling trains to stop at crossings of other railroads, and a multitude of other matters confessedly within the power of the state." Was there any real difference between these two statutes with respect to interstate commerce? There does not seem to be, apart from their diametrically opposite positions on integration.[36]

Plessy v. Ferguson

The next and most notorious decision in the Supreme Court's post–Civil War racial odyssey was *Plessy v. Ferguson*.[37] This landmark, familiar to all who study the history of race law in the United States, presented the Supreme Court with an opportunity to act on the vision of the Fourteenth Amendment it had formulated in the *Civil Rights Cases*: "It nullifies and makes void all State legislation, and State action of every kind, which impairs the privileges and immunities of citizens of the United States, or which injures them in life, liberty, or property without due process of law, or which denies to any of them the equal protection of the laws."[38] In *Plessy*, a Louisiana statute requiring racial segregation on railroad cars, either through separate cars or via a divider, was challenged as violating equal protection. The Louisiana Railway Accommodations Act of 1890, also known as the Separate Car Law, required:

That all railway companies carrying passengers in their coaches in this State, shall provide *equal but separate* accommodations for the white, and colored races, by providing two or more passenger coaches for each passenger train, or by dividing the passenger coaches by a partition so as to secure separate accommodations. . . . No person or persons, shall be permitted to occupy seats in coaches, other than the ones assigned to them on account of the race they belong to.

The statute provided for fines and imprisonment for passengers insisting on riding in the incorrect car, and for fines for railroad employees who refuse to enforce the law. It also required railroads to post a copy of the law in each passenger coach and ticket office. But the key substantive provision of the statute was that railroads must "provide *equal but separate* accommodations for the white, and colored races."

Plessy v. Ferguson was a test case with roots in Black opposition to the act from the day it was introduced into the Louisiana General Assembly (now the Louisiana State Legislature). A newly formed group, the American Citizens' Equal Rights Association, wrote a "memorial" in opposition to the bill, invoking basic US principles, such as that "all men are created equal." Nevertheless, the bill passed and they, together with other opponents of the act, organized quickly to plan a case to challenge it as unconstitutional. It was expected that the railroads would cooperate, since they were opposed to the act on economic grounds.[39]

The test case was planned by a committee that included two of the signers of the memorial, Louis A. Martinet and Rodolphe Desdunes, well known New Orleans men of color, which adopted the name "Citizens Committee" to stress that their claim to equal treatment arose from their status as citizens of Louisiana and the United States.[40] In his later-published pean to his fellow French-speaking people of color, Desdunes characterized the committee's purpose as "to protest the adoption and enforcement of the statutes that established the unjust and humiliating treatment of the black race in Louisiana." The inclusion of "humiliating" in the Desdune's characterization of segregation confirms the primacy of the affront to their dignity that people of color were experiencing at the time.[41]

The coalition that planned the *Plessy* case was notable for its inclusion of lighter- and darker-skinned people of color. Although disagreement and distrust persisted for decades between these groups, this was the clearest indication to date that the higher status and often lighter-skinned people of color understood that their fate was now joined with that of the freedmen.[42] They recruited New Yorker (and Reconstruction-era official in North Carolina) Albion Tourgee to their cause as lead attorney. After some difficulty in finding a local attorney, which they also needed, the group selected James Walker. They decided that their best strategy was for someone to get arrested for violating the act, after which they would use the habeas corpus procedure to secure the quickest possible process for bringing the challenge to court.[43]

The first client they represented in this pursuit was Daniel F. Desdunes, Rodolphe's son, who was arrested in February 1891 for taking a seat in the first-class car reserved for Whites on a train running from New Orleans to Mobile, Alabama. As luck would have it, Desdunes's case was assigned to Judge R. H. Marr, counsel for the defendant in the Supreme Court's proceedings in *Hall v. Decuir*, and a well-known White supremacist.[44] The case was delayed by Judge Marr's disappearance in April, and ultimate presumed death, until Judge Marr was replaced by Judge John Ferguson, a lawyer who was born in Massachusetts and became a loyal Democrat while practicing law in New Orleans.[45] In July, Ferguson threw out the case against Desdunes in part for technical reasons and in part because the Louisiana Supreme Court, in another case, had determined that the Separate Car Act could not be applied to interstate travelers like Desdunes, citing *Hall v. Decuir* as authority for this decision.[46]

While Desdunes's case was still pending, Homer Plessy, a friend of Desdunes's father, was thrown off a train and arrested for violating the act after he insisted on traveling in a car reserved for Whites. Plessy's train operated wholly intrastate, and the assistant district attorney carefully avoided the technical problems that had doomed the case against Desdunes. After Plessy's motion to dismiss the case was denied by Judge Ferguson, his lawyers maneuvered to have the case heard by the Louisiana Supreme Court as quickly as possible by bringing a petition in that court against Judge Ferguson seeking Plessy's acquittal. The Louisiana Supreme Court issued its decision against Plessy on December 19, 1892, and his lawyers immediately brought the case to the US Supreme Court.[47]

Plessy's lawyers claimed that the act violated the Thirteenth and Fourteenth Amendments, but the Supreme Court disagreed, famously determining that "equal, but separate" treatment satisfied the requirement that states refrain from denying any person the equal protection of the law. This was the final legal blow in the effort to resist restoration of White supremacy in the South. The Court's opinion was written by Justice Henry Billings Brown, a Massachusetts native who practiced maritime law in Detroit, Michigan, before serving as a deputy United States marshal, assistant United States attorney, and federal district judge. Brown was appointed to the Supreme Court in 1891 by Republican President Benjamin Harrison of Indiana.[48]

Given the *Civil Rights Cases'* narrow interpretation of the Thirteenth Amendment, Justice Brown had little difficulty dispatching Plessy's argument that the Separate Car Act violated the Thirteenth Amendment. Echoing (and relying upon) the opinion in the *Civil Rights Cases*, Justice Brown stated

that it does not conflict with the thirteenth amendment, which abolished slavery and involuntary servitude, except as a punishment for crime, is too clear for argument. Slavery implies involuntary servitude, a state of bondage; the ownership of mankind as a chattel, or, at least, the control of the labor and services of one man for the benefit of another, and the absence of a legal right to the disposal of his own person, property, and services. . . . Indeed, we do not understand that the thirteenth amendment is strenuously relied upon by the plaintiff in error in this connection.[49]

Justice Brown's analysis of the Fourteenth Amendment question refuted numerous legal and practical arguments Plessy's lawyers made against legally required segregation. It must have been heartbreaking to people of color of the day. The Court began by distinguishing between legal equality and social equality, placing the "public rights" that Rebecca Scott explains were the object of post–Civil War resistance to segregation into the category of social rights: "The object of the amendment was undoubtedly to enforce the absolute equality of the two races before the law, but, in the nature of things, it could not have been intended to abolish distinctions based upon color, or to enforce social, as distinguished from political, equality, or a commingling of the two races upon terms unsatisfactory to either."[50] Justice Brown then rejected the argument that segregation was equivalent to putting a badge of inferiority on non-Whites: "Laws permitting, and even requiring, their separation, in places where they are liable to be brought into contact, do not necessarily imply the inferiority of either race to the other[.]"[51] Concluding this theme, the Court placed the blame for the experience of inferiority on non-Whites: "We consider the underlying fallacy of the plaintiff's argument to consist in the assumption that the enforced separation of the two races stamps the colored race with a badge of inferiority. If this be so, it is not by reason of anything found in the act, but solely because the colored race chooses to put that construction upon it." Blind to the daily affront to their dignity suffered by non-Whites subjected to segregation, the passage also ignored the widespread awareness that colored passengers were generally relegated to inferior railway cars; for example, confined to second-class smoking cars, even if they paid for first-class passage.[52] To people of color, the mark of inferiority could not have been more clear.[53]

Justice Brown's opinion treated segregation as a normal, accepted, and valid exercise of state police power, citing Charles Sumner's unsuccessful challenge to the segregation of Boston's public schools and Congress's establishment of segregated public schools in the District of Columbia. To Justice Brown, laws requiring segregation, and forbidding interracial marriage, did not infringe the right to equality as long as they applied equally to all.[54]

On the day that *Plessy* was argued to the Court, Justice Harlan had released a unanimous opinion allowing the removal of a Mississippi criminal prosecution to the federal district court on the ground that by law, Blacks were excluded from jury service in that state.[55] Perhaps he had hoped that this decision, which obviously was made before the arguments in *Plessy*, signaled a new receptivity by his colleagues to claims of race discrimination. If so, he was disappointed. Justice Harlan was the lone dissenter in *Plessy*. He strongly disputed the argument that segregation does not imply the perceived inferiority of non-Whites:

Every one knows that the statute in question had its origin in the purpose, not so much to exclude white persons from railroad cars occupied by blacks, as to exclude colored people from coaches occupied by or assigned to white persons. . . . The thing to accomplish was, under the guise of giving equal accommodation for whites and blacks, to compel the latter to keep to themselves while traveling in railroad passenger coaches. No one would be so wanting in candor as to assert the contrary.[56]

Justice Harlan likened the Court's decision in *Plessy* to the *Dred Scott* decision, which held that Black people brought into the United States for slavery, and their descendants, could not be citizens of the United States: "In my opinion, the judgment this day rendered will, in time, prove to be quite as pernicious as the decision made by this tribunal in the *Dred Scott* case."[57]

It was Justice Harlan, in this dissent, who first employed the phrase "separate but equal"[58] in a Supreme Court opinion. The *Plessy* majority quoted "equal but separate" from the Louisiana statute at issue but otherwise did not dwell on the requirement of equality.[59] When the Court declared that "the enforced separation of the races" did not infringe any rights, it did not mention equality, and in the decades that followed, separation would be enforced with far more alacrity than equality. Although "separate but equal" became the established understanding of the requirement of equal protection of the laws, between *Plessy* and its undoing in *Brown v. Board of Education*, the phrase appeared only in a single opinion of the Court, in 1914, in a summary of the *Plessy* holding.[60]

Justice Harlan's dissent argued for a constitutional mandate of color-blind treatment: "The constitution of the United States does not, I think, permit any public authority to know the race of those entitled to be protected in the enjoyment of such rights. . . . I deny that any legislative body or judicial tribunal may have regard to the race of citizens when the civil rights of those citizens are involved."[61] This has been interpreted by some to provide a strong argument against all race-conscious government programs, even those designed to provide aid to historically disadvantaged groups. That interpretation, however, does not pay sufficient attention to Justice Harlan's language or to the social context in which he made the statement. Justice Harlan's language is confined to government recognition of "civil rights," not to programs outside that domain, such as the programs administered by the Freedmen's Bureau in the aftermath of the emancipation of the slaves.

Further, at the time, the issue was not whether government could act to make up for socially imposed racial disadvantage; it was whether the government could compound it by aiding White supremacist programs. In short, Justice Harlan's call in 1896 for a color-blind government has limited relevance to those situations in which race might be considered relevant in modern times.

With *Plessy*, the legal journey to separate but equal was now complete.

The Aftermath of *Plessy*

The journey from *Hall v. Decuir* to *Plessy v. Ferguson* took eighteen years. *Plessy* was but the latest in a string of disappointments for African Americans, with the Supreme Court finally accepting the implications of Captain John Benson's defense of segregation on the *Governor Allen*, that the service provided to his non-White female passengers was equal to that provided to the "White ladies." *Plessy* was the culmination of the White Southern effort to resist all legally compelled integration. Everyone in the United States, except apparently the justices of the Supreme Court, seemed to understand that segregation was an element of postslavery White supremacy and part of a program of subjugation of African Americans. The Court had its own idea for Reconstruction, and it did not include recognizing the right to equality for Americans of African descent.

Plessy's acceptance of separate but equal and its absorption into law affected views on the significance of *Hall v. Decuir*, which decided only that Louisiana could not enforce its integration requirement in interstate transportation. Later, *Hall v. Decuir* was wrongly cited more than once by federal courts as if it lent explicit support to the doctrine of separate but equal, which it did not. For example, in 1948, when the United States Court of Appeals in Virginia denied a claim against segregation on an interstate bus line, it cited *Hall* for the proposition that "an interstate carrier has a right to establish rules and regulations which require White and colored passengers to occupy separate accommodations provided there is no discrimination in the arrangement." Somehow, *Hall v. Decuir*, which rejected a state's power to regulate conduct on a navigable water, was interpreted to grant interstate common carriers a right to require racial segregation.[62]

Plessy was not the last Supreme Court decision validating the country's refusal to recognize the full import of the expansion of US citizenship to include those of African descent. Efforts to retain the right to vote, which some people of color had enjoyed for decades in Louisiana and other Southern states, were dashed when the Supreme Court, in 1903, held that the federal courts lacked jurisdiction to intervene on behalf of Black men seeking injunctive relief to force the state of Alabama to register them to vote.[63] The plaintiffs in a similar challenge to Louisiana's restrictions on voting abandoned their case after losing in state court, recognizing that appeal to the US Supreme Court was hopeless.[64] People of color were thus excluded from political participation almost as completely as during slavery. They may have been freed from slavery, but they were not yet free from oppression.[65]

Socially, people of color were excluded from numerous institutions. Segregation became the norm where exclusion was impracticable. For the always-free mixed-race French-speaking people of Louisiana, the situation actually worsened as the color line became less penetrable than it had been before the war.

Whether judicial decisions rejecting segregation would have been enforceable in the postwar, post-Reconstruction environment is unclear. Michael Klarman argues that Supreme Court decisions condemning segregation would have been unenforceable and made little if any difference to social reality anyway, while Paul Finkelman, reviewing Klarman's book, disagrees, insisting that there was sufficient support for equal rights in the post-Reconstruction period that court decisions supporting equality might very well have made a significant difference.[66] In any event, legally, the South was "redeemed" when the Supreme Court frustrated Congress's efforts to legislative racial equality. The fact that President Ulysees S. Grant was so committed to racial justice and yet failed to make significant progress toward that goal in his eight-year presidency supports the notion that social resistance to racial equality and integration was simply too much for the law to overcome. But the Court's decisions rendered Congress virtually impotent in the face of widespread and violent oppression of non-White populations throughout the South. It would be more than half a century before a realistic prospect arose for challenging racial oppression in the United States, and this time, it would be Northern Democrats, not Republicans, who led the fight.

The Acceptance of Jim Crow and the Administration of "Separate but Equal"

The political, social, economic, and legal redemption of the South could not have happened without national tolerance of the racial segregation and exclusion that ultimately prevailed, de jure in the South and de facto in many areas of the North. Why, after the election of 1876, were Republicans willing to abandon non-White Americans to their fate at the hands of White supremacists in the South? Was it simply a price they were willing to pay for the presidency? Was it the product of racism in the North, practiced in a more polite, or less overt, manner?

The presidency and racism were certainly part of it. The presidency is a valuable prize, perhaps second to none in the United States. And without racism lurking in the background, it is difficult to imagine that Republicans, by acquiescing to overt Southern segregation and exclusion, would have so readily traded the welfare of non-White Americans for the presidency. However, the machinations and uncertainty that led to the compromise of 1877 suggest that Republicans' motivations were more complicated.

An important impetus to Northern acquiescence in Southern segregation and exclusion may have been the desire to facilitate national reconciliation. Rightly or wrongly, Northern Republicans may have calculated that the consequences of insistence on complete racial equality, including full political participation and integration of all institutions within government's reach, would have provoked continued Southern resistance and prevented the re-establishment of a united country. Just as approval of slavery was the price for agreement on the Constitution of 1789, Republicans may have seen the subjugation of Americans of color as necessary for national reconciliation in the "second founding" after the bloody and destructive Civil War.

In fact, Northern Republican acquiescence in Southern White supremacist policies began before the 1876 election controversy and the *Plessy* decision. Although Congress tried to outlaw segregation and exclusion in the Civil Rights Act of 1875, there is no record of pre-act intervention into what the record in *Hall v. Decuir* revealed as a well-established custom of segregation on Southern riverboats. Although the Grant administration's civil rights prosecutions met with success in many locations, Southern people of color, especially people from Louisiana and Mississippi, begged the Grant administration for additional help. In 1874 in Mississippi, Grant was inclined to intervene to protect Blacks but ultimately decided not to in fear that it would be politically costly to Republicans in other states, including Ohio.[67]

Consider the game of baseball as an example of the development of the social practices of segregation and exclusion. Interest in baseball among Whites and Blacks throughout the United States exploded in the years immediately following the Civil War. Abolitionist Frederick Douglass, for example, was an honorary member of the Washington Mutuals Base Ball Club and his son Charles was the leader of the Washington Alerts, a successful colored team that played in the nation's capital. Teams sprung up all over the country, including powerhouses such as the New Orleans Lone Stars, the Philadelphia Athletics, and the Washington Nationals. Many Southern teams chose names indicating pride in the Confederacy, such as the Robert E. Lees of New Orleans. In this era in which there were few organized leagues, most games were local affairs, but some teams traveled far and wide, making and accepting challenges.[68]

Racial lines quickly became an issue in baseball—would clubs be integrated? Would games be played between White and colored teams? As Ryan Swanson recounts, the color line in baseball was officially drawn early on, as early as 1867, with Northern cooperation in the hope that baseball might become a nationally unifying force. The Pennsylvania Association of Amateur Base Ball Players, a leading organization, forced a successful Black team to withdraw its application for membership when it became clear that if it forced a vote, the outcome would be unfavorable. Later that same year, the National Association of Base Ball Players let it be known that teams with colored members would not be welcome. In 1871, as baseball became professionalized, a new organization, the similarly named National Association of Professional Base Ball Players (NAPBB) was established and soon became the sport's most important federation. It was understood from the beginning that clubs with colored players were not welcome in the NAPBB.

Even the federal government itself was complicit in the early segregation of baseball. The City of Washington, DC, under Congress's control, generally followed Southern customs regarding segregation and exclusion. In 1869, during the presidency of Ulysses S. Grant, colored teams such as Charles Douglass's Washington Alerts were banned by Washington's director of public works from playing games at the White Lot, a field next to the White House. Exclusive control over the field was granted to a mediocre White team, the Creightons.[69]

Baseball is just one small example of the way that segregation and exclusion became the norm across Southern society. Restaurants and taverns frequented by Whites, by and large, did not serve Black people, or if they did, it was by selling food to Blacks out of the back door or at special tables in an inferior area. Most hotels would not accept Black people as guests. This, coupled with exclusion from restaurants, made it difficult for Blacks, especially families, to travel long distances. State and local laws often required segregation at public places such as theaters, train stations (and, later, bus stations and airports), sporting events, religious services, and even courthouses. Black people were excluded from many places of public entertainment such as amusement parks, and where they were not excluded, such as in theaters, separate sections were allocated to non-White patrons. Separate school systems for Whites and Blacks were established, and state colleges and universities were not integrated.[70]

Of course, for the people subject to mistreatment under Jim Crow, these were bitter pills that they did not willingly swallow. Civil rights agitation did not simply halt after *Plessy* and then magically reappear sometime in the 1950s with the National Association for the Advancement of Colored People's challenge to segregated schools in *Brown v. Board of Education.* The problem was that agitation over segregation and exclusion was difficult and dangerous, especially in the South, where Blacks were not allowed to vote and lynching was a frequent occurrence. People understood that open resistance to segregation and exclusion was at the peril of life and limb. For those who were able to vote, the absence of a secret ballot in the years immediately following redemption and the potential for violence meant that those people of color who could vote would either vote for segregationist Democratic Party candidates or stay home.

Redemption resulted in virtual exclusion of Black people from political participation and public office. Despite the Fifteenth Amendment's prohibition of race-based exclusion from voting, violence, poll taxes, and discriminatory administration of literacy tests meant that as a practical matter, Blacks were not able to vote. Ironically, the freeing of the slaves, resulting in the repeal of the Constitution's provision under which each slave counted as three-fifths of a person for census purposes actually made matters worse for Black people. The relative representation of Southern interests in the United States Congress increased after the slaves were freed because, even though they were not able to vote, they counted as a whole person for redistricting purposes. Four million freed slaves meant that the Southern census count grew by more than one and a half million people who were still prevented from voting on account of their race.[71]

The legal acceptance of segregation must have also contributed to its widespread acceptance among Whites as a social practice. There is at least a chance that if the Supreme Court had condemned racial segregation and exclusion in cases like *Hall v. Decuir* and *Plessy v. Ferguson*, the forces fighting discrimination may have been strengthened and it would have been more difficult for the twin customs of segregation and exclusion to take hold and continue. That's not to say that segregation would have disappeared overnight or that racial prejudice would have quickly faded away. But perhaps if the law had not embraced segregation, society would have followed, just as, for example, social acceptance has increased dramatically since judicial rulings in favor of same-sex marriage.

Hall v. Decuir had freed carriers in interstate commerce from state control over their racially based treatment of passengers. This legal void was filled with common law and customs that allowed carriers to segregate on the condition that accommodations were equal, foreshadowing the Court's interpretation of the Equal Protection Clause in *Plessy*. From the start, there was substantial litigation over the requirement of equality in transportation, mainly in cases brought by people of color complaining that the facilities provided for them were not equal to those provided for Whites. It was widely known that rail cars reserved for Black people were often inferior to those set aside for Whites, and that Black women and men were often allowed only in undesirable smoking cars even if they had paid for first-class travel. If separate cars for Black people were provided, they were often placed at the very front of the train, where smoke and cinders from the engine made it impossible for the cars to be properly ventilated. Either windows were kept closed or passengers had to endure hot cinders and choking smoke. Black travelers were excluded from dining cars, so they either had to bring their own food or grab what they could during stops at restaurants and shops along the route.[72]

Black plaintiffs were victorious in a surprising number of cases claiming that the accommodations set aside for them were unequal. In a riverboat case that proved to be an important precedent in post-*Decuir* litigation, four women of color convinced a Harvard Law School-educated Maryland federal judge, Thomas John Morris, that the cabin for colored women on the steamboat the *Sue*, running interstate on the Potomac River, was significantly inferior to accommodations provided for White women, and he awarded them each $100 in damages. The court noted that it was in *Hall v. Decuir* that the Supreme Court determined that, in the absence of federal regulation, interstate carriers were free to make and enforce rules requiring racial segregation of passengers.[73]

In some of the cases in federal court, judges made comments that indicated disapproval of segregation. For example, in another case presided over by Judge Morris, he charged the jury that "when public sentiment demands a separation of the passengers, it must be gratified to some extent. While this sentiment prevails among the traveling public, although unreasonable and foolish, it cannot be said that the carrier must be compelled to sacrifice his business in order to combat it."[74] In an 1885 case arising in the US Circuit Court for the Eastern District of Tennessee, brought by a Black passenger who alleged he was forced to travel in the smoking car despite having purchased a first-class ticket, Judge David M. Key's charge to the jury included a comment directed at a fellow passenger who forcibly moved the plaintiff to the smoking car. Judge Key was a colonel in the Confederate army during the Civil War and later served as a senator from Tennessee, but was known for his efforts to bring about national reconciliation after the war. Key's hope was that the South would pursue economic progress and leave "divisive racial issues" behind. Before being appointed to the federal bench, he served as US postmaster general, fulfilling President Rutherford B. Hayes's promise to appoint at least one Southerner to his cabinet.[75] In a stinging rebuke to Southern White supremacists, Judge Key told the jury: "My observation has convinced me that those who are most sensitive as to contact with colored people, and whose nerves are most shocked by their presence, have little to be proud of in the way of birth, lineage, or achievement."[76] However, Judge Key went on to present a more conventional portrayal of segregation to the jury:

I believe that where the races are numerous, a railroad may set apart certain cars to be occupied by white people, and certain other cars to be occupied by colored people, so as to avoid complaint and friction; but if the railroads charge the same fare to each race, it must furnish, substantially, like and equal accommodations. The money of one has the same value as that of the other, and should purchase equal accommodations. There is no equality of right, when the money of the white man purchases luxurious accommodations amid elegant company, and the same amount of money purchases for the black man inferior quarters in a smoking car. The law does not tolerate such discrimination on the part of a railroad company. . . . A colored man and woman of genteel appearance, good repute, and good behavior, who have paid for first-class passage, [cannot] be sent to the smoking car simply because they are black.

In this case, the jury awarded the plaintiff $217 in damages against the railroad company and the passenger who moved them to the smoking car but exonerated the individual railroad employees involved.[77]

These comments condemning or criticizing segregation and exclusion illustrate that like the pre–Civil War sectional divide over slavery, US society remained divided over the treatment of Americans of African descent. Race was an important organizing principle of Southern society. Black and White people lived side by side but in parallel social worlds, intersecting only when Whites found it beneficial for them. Southern segregation was viewed unfavorably in the North. It's not that Northern Whites were free of racial prejudice or that Northern institutions did not practice similar, if less overt, racial customs. To Northerners, the South's visible symbols of racial separation fell below standards they could accept.

The federal government was also complicit in perpetuating segregation and racial discrimination in US society. As noted, the Southern customs of segregation and exclusion were followed in Washington, DC, with tacit acceptance if not the active support of Congress and local authorities. Reconstruction-era laws prohibited segregation in restaurants and other public places in Washington, DC, but those laws were not enforced until the 1950s, after a 1953 Supreme Court ruling affirmed that those laws were still in effect.[78] Before the Civil War, public schools in Washington, DC, were open to White students only. During the war, a separate school system for Black children was established, and Washington schools remained officially segregated until the Supreme Court ruled against "separate but equal" in Washington's schools in 1954.[79]

The United States military was segregated until President Harry Truman ordered integration in 1948.[80] Before that, facilities for non-White servicemen were generally inferior to those for Whites. At Naval Air Station Pensacola, for example, it was announced in the base newspaper on June 23, 1944, that funds had been released for "colored recreation buildings" at the base. Existing recreation facilities were open to Whites only, and the hotly contested inter-base baseball games, with major league players such as Ted Williams participating, were White-only affairs.[81] Truman's decision was sparked, at least in part, by the blinding of a Black World War II veteran who was beaten by local police after he had the audacity to insist to a bus driver while on the way home from his discharge that he allow him to use the bathroom during a brief stop.[82]

Federal policy in other areas helped perpetuate private and governmental racial segregation in the North.[83] The federal government, through the Federal Housing Authority (FHA), began subsidizing and guaranteeing home mortgages in 1934, but in a practice that became known as "redlining," these programs were open only to White homeowners in White neighborhoods until 1968. This contributed greatly to segregated housing patterns throughout the country and allowed Northern cities to unofficially segregate their schools simply by following the racial boundaries that defined neighborhoods. Historian Beryl Satter has documented how this phenomenon affected housing patterns and the wealth of Black families in Chicago, Illinois.[84] As law professor Sarah Shindler explains, the FHA actually refused to approve lending in racially mixed neighborhoods, leading one White developer in Detroit, Michigan, to build a concrete wall, known as the Eight Mile Wall, between his development and a neighborhood occupied by Black residents so that his development would not be considered to be in an area that the federal government termed racially "inharmonious."[85] In many northern city neighborhoods, racial housing patterns still follow the lending maps drawn up by the FHA pursuant to its "Whites only" policy. The legacy of *Plessy v. Ferguson* and the Supreme Court's embrace of Jim Crow lives on.

———————

A broad coalition of groups exerted a wide range of social forces to continue slavery's legacy of the subordination of people of color across the United States, most visibly in the South, where segregation and exclusion remained the norm until quite recently. Although *Plessy v. Ferguson* is the most well-known landmark in this odyssey, *Hall v. Decuir* played a significant, if largely forgotten, role in established the legal system's attitude toward segregation and the restoration of White supremacy after the Civil War.

A great deal has changed in the more than one hundred and forty years since the Supreme Court rejected Madame Decuir's plea for full recognition as a citizen of the United States. Although the quest for dignity and equality for people of color in the United States is far from complete, the actions of two women in the century following Madame Decuir's journey helped spark movement in that direction. The efforts of these two women of color seeking to preserve their dignity in a society dedicated to denying it helped begin a movement in law and society that has not yet reached its terminus.

Irene Amos Morgan was a descendant of generations of slaves who worked on farms in rural Gloucester County, Virginia. She grew up and lived in modest circumstances, with a father who was a day laborer and house painter. As far as we know, she did not speak French and was never treated like a White lady in Paris, but she did receive a bachelor of arts degree at the age of sixty-eight, long after her Supreme Court case. During World War II, she worked building B-26 Marauders for a defense contractor in her adopted hometown of Baltimore, Maryland, where she lived with her husband. Although we have no details concerning her work, her employment in a defense-related industry may have been made possible by President Franklin Delano Roosevelt's 1941 executive order prohibiting discrimination on the basis of "race, creed, color or national origin" in defense-related industries.[1] In 1944, Morgan suffered a miscarriage and traveled to her ancestral home in rural Virginia to recuperate with family. In July, she purchased a ticket for a Greyhound Bus in Hayes Store, Gloucester County, Virginia, to Baltimore, Maryland, to go home to her husband and for a doctor's appointment that she hoped would result in a clean bill of health so she could return to work.[2]

Virginia law required racial segregation on the bus. The bus was very crowded, and Morgan had to share a seat with another Black woman. When some White passengers departed in Saluda, twenty-six miles into the approximately 210-mile trip to Baltimore, Morgan moved to their vacated seats, which, contrary to law and custom, placed her in front of a White couple. When more White passengers boarded, the driver instructed Morgan to move further back, into the Black crowd at the back of the bus, and Morgan refused. The driver summoned the police, and Morgan was arrested, but not before she resisted by kicking and clawing at the deputy. She said she had planned on biting him but he was too dirty, so she punched and kicked him instead. She pleaded guilty to resisting arrest, and after trial she was convicted for violating Virginia's segregation requirement, but she refused to pay the ten dollar fine on the ground that Virginia's law violated the Interstate Commerce Clause as applied to interstate travelers like her. The state courts rejected this argument, and as Captain John Benson had done seventy years earlier, she took her case to the Supreme Court of the United States.[3]

At the Supreme Court, Morgan was represented by pioneering civil rights lawyers William Hastie, Leon Ransom, Spotswood Robinson III, and Thurgood Marshall. At the time, they, along with Charles Hamilton Houston and others, were engaged in the long-term plan of the National Association for the Advancement of Colored People (NAACP) to overturn *Plessy v. Ferguson*.[4] Their initial strategy was not to directly attack *Plessy*'s reading of the Equal Protection Clause immediately. Rather, they would claim that governments were violating *Plessy*'s condition that separate facilities be equal; for example, by paying teachers in schools for Black children less than those in White schools or by confining Black law students to a one-room unaccredited law school with four part-time teachers, rather than providing them with an education equivalent to that available to White students at the flagship state university.[5]

Morgan's case provided these lawyers with another opportunity to attack segregation without attacking *Plessy* directly. They renewed Morgan's argument that it was unconstitutional to apply Virginia's Jim Crow law to Morgan because she was traveling interstate. The first sentence in the substantive section of their brief cited the one case that most strongly supported their argument, that Virginia's Jim Crow law could not be applied to an interstate traveler like her: "That a state statute seeking to impose a local policy concerning racial segregation upon the interstate transportation of passengers on public carriers contravenes the commerce clause was clearly and decisively established by this Court in *Hall v. Decuir*."[6] They continued their argument by pointing out that, just as in *Hall*, different states might have different rules, which would burden interstate travel: "The very fact that one state may attempt to segregate interstate passengers in some fashion while an adjoining state may prohibit such segregation . . . compelled the Court to declare this entire subject matter beyond the reach of local law."[7] The Supreme Court ruled in Morgan's favor, echoing the opinion in *Hall v. Decuir*, that "the transportation difficulties arising from a statute that requires commingling of the races, as in the De Cuir case, are increased by one that requires separation, as here."[8]

The culmination of the NAACP Legal Defense Fund's decades-long battle to attack segregation was the Supreme Court's 1954 decision in *Brown v. Board of Education*, that "in the field of public education, the doctrine of 'separate but equal' has no place [because s]eparate educational facilities are inherently unequal."[9] While *Brown*'s rejection of separate but equal reverberated throughout the United States and paved the way for further advances beyond public education, including the passage of landmark civil rights legislation such as the Civil Rights Act of 1964 and the Voting Rights Act of 1965, change came slowly and painfully.[10] The reaction of White Southerners was perhaps best illustrated by the March 1956 "Manifesto," signed by one hundred Southern members of Congress and placed in the *Congressional Record*, declaring *Brown* "a clear abuse of judicial power," and that the doctrine of separate but equal was founded on "elemental humanity and commonsense."[11] Writing in a sort of reply soon after, essayist and author E. B. White wrote that "the sense that is common to one generation is uncommon to the next. Probably the first slave ship, with Negroes lying in chains on its decks, seemed commonsensical to the owners who operated it and to the planters who patronized it." White recounted the reaction of his cook, a White woman from Finland, to his reminder to "sit in one of the front seats" when she got on the bus in Florida: "A look of great weariness came into her face . . . and she replied 'Oh, I know—isn't it silly!'"[12]

Support throughout the South for the twin customs of segregation and exclusion did not wither away upon the Court's announcement of its decision in *Brown* or Congress's actions in the 1960s. In the most well-known episode of resistance to racial segregation post-*Brown*, in 1955, another Southern woman of color, Rosa Parks, was arrested for refusing to yield her seat on a city bus in Montgomery, Alabama, to a White passenger.[13] Parks, the daughter of a teacher and a carpenter, was the descendant of slaves, and could also document two White great-grandparents in her ancestry. She was also a civil rights activist, and had served as the secretary of the Montgomery chapter of the NAACP. As she explained, her refusal to yield her seat was an effort to preserve her dignity as a human being and assert her right to equal treatment as such: "People always say that I didn't give up my seat because I was tired, but that isn't true. I was not tired physically, or no more tired than I usually was at the end of a working day. I was not old, although some people have an image of me as being old then. I was 42. No, the only tired I was, was tired of giving in."[14] She was later found guilty of violating city law and fined ten dollars. On the day of her trial, supporters called for people of color to boycott the bus system, and a 381-day boycott of the Montgomery bus system followed, echoing the efforts of Louisiana's people of color to abolish the star car system nearly one hundred years earlier. Although the boycott was financially crippling, the system was integrated only after the local federal court and the US Supreme Court ruled that the city law requiring segregation violated the Equal Protection Clause of the Fourteenth Amendment.[15]

Irene Morgan and Rosa Parks found success where Madame Decuir suffered defeat. The unanswerable question is what would have happened if the Supreme Court had taken a stand against race discrimination in Madame Decuir's case and the others that reached the Court in the late nineteenth century. Undoubtedly, immediate unrest would have occurred, and sectional conflict between North and South may have flared up again, but perhaps after a difficult decade or two, segregation and exclusion would have disappeared long before the late twentieth century when the Civil Rights Act of 1964 came into full effect. As it is, the race problem remains a festering sore that has never been allowed to fully heal. US society is embedded in the legacy of slavery and Jim Crow, and millions of US citizens continue to live with it as part of their daily experience. National reconciliation at the expense of Black people was doomed to failure, and fail it has.

While it may be well known among legal historians whose work focuses on racial issues in the wake of the Civil War, Madame Decuir's journey is not widely known in the legal community. *Hall v. Decuir* does not appear in any major constitutional law textbook or even in books on race and the law, except for a brief mention in a leading casebook on race.[16] There has been some attention to her case in recent years but not commensurate with the importance of the case to the history of Louisiana and the United States.

———

Ninety years after the decision in *Hall v. Decuir*, in a report on race relations in the United States, the Kerner Commission proclaimed, "Our Nation is moving toward two societies, one black, one white—separate and unequal."[17] By failing to recognize the dignitary, citizenship, and related emotional grounding of Madame Decuir's claims and the post–Civil War claims of all people of color to be treated with the respect entailed by US citizenship and membership in the human race, the Supreme Court became an active participant in dividing the nation in two, between White society whose vision of a social order founded upon White supremacy would prevail, whatever the cost to the economic, spiritual, emotional, and physical well-being of those unfortunate enough to be considered members of the other, Black, US society. *Hall v. Decuir* was the Supreme Court's first step in that direction. What is perhaps most surprising is that today, almost one hundred and fifty years after Madame Decuir set out to accompany her new lawyer on the sixteen-hour boat ride from New Orleans to Point Coupée Parish, and after the enactment of numerous state and federal statutes outlawing racial discrimination, the race question still occupies a central place in national discourse of the United States.

The Commerce Clause

Origins of the Commerce Power

To understand the Supreme Court's Dormant Commerce Clause jurisprudence, it is first necessary to uncover the background of Congress's power over interstate commerce. At the founding, there was great disagreement and ambivalence among US political elites over how much power the central government should have and to what degree the separate states should retain the powers over trade and commerce usually exercised by sovereign nations. In the 1780s, US luminaries, including James Madison, lamented the national government's inability under the Articles of Confederation to do anything about state laws that obstructed the free flow of interstate commerce. Madison suggested that Virginia's delegates to the Continental Congress under the Articles of Confederation propose granting the central government power to regulate interstate commerce for twenty-five years. The Virginia legislature agreed, but only to a shorter thirteen-year-period. After these efforts failed to gain sufficient support in the national Congress, where unanimity was required for virtually all-important actions, a constitutional convention was called, charged with, inter alia, amending the Articles of Confederation to grant the central government power over interstate commerce.[1]

One of the first proposals to emerge from the constitutional convention's "Grand Committee" was to amend the Articles of Confederation to grant the Continental Congress the "sole and exclusive power of regulating the trade of the states." This proposal undoubtedly enjoyed widespread support at the convention.[2] The lack of centralized regulation of commercial activity was recognized as a major shortcoming of the government under the Articles of Confederation for at least two reasons; first, because state protectionist legislation impeded economic progress, and second, because it caused embarrassment in foreign relations. Foreign trading partners might be courted by the central government, which collected duties on imports, only to find that goods exported to one of the united states could not be sold due to local restrictions. This at a time when duties on foreign commerce were an important, and favored, source of federal government revenue. However, when the convention abandoned its mission of amending the articles and turned to the task of drafting an entirely new constitution, the words "sole and exclusive" no longer appeared in language granting the national government the power to regulate interstate commerce. The constitution that emerged granted Congress perpetual power "to regulate commerce with foreign nations, and among the several states, and with the Indian tribes" but said nothing about whether this power was exclusive or shared with the states. It was recognized in the period in which *Hall v. Decuir* was decided, however, that the purposes of the Commerce Clause included ensuring that Congress had the power to prevent states from imposing tariffs on goods imported from other states and preventing states from discriminating against commerce from other states.[3]

Regardless of the presence or absence of the word "exclusive" in the Commerce Clause, the scope of the federal government's commerce power, and its relation to traditional state powers, has been one of the more vexing legal issues to arise under the Constitution. The problems have involved both the reach of federal power and in discerning a boundary, if there is one, between federal power to regulate commerce and the states' traditional power over all manner of regulation directed at the health, safety, and welfare of the people, generally referred to as the "police power."

Fundamental principles of US federalism dictate that the states retain general regulatory power subject only to those powers explicitly delegated to the federal government in the Constitution. The problem is that many exercises of the state police power affect interstate commerce. State health and safety laws, when applied to goods produced out of state can reduce the volume and change the character of interstate commerce. Examples are simple to imagine: a state law that prohibits the sale of food products containing certain ingredients, for example, will have easily traceable effects on the fortunes of companies in other states involved in producing and selling food containing the disfavored ingredients. State laws like this may also affect the availability of goods and services in still more states as producers adjust their practices to meet regulatory burdens imposed by a few important states. If a product is banned in one state, producers may find it uneconomical to produce that product for sale, even in states where it is not banned.

Preserving state police power thus requires accepting a degree of interstate effects caused by state law. Because there is no question that a valid act of Congress, pursuant to its power to regulate interstate commerce, preempts any inconsistent state law, the desire to preserve traditional state powers is an important consideration in deciding the scope of federal power, whether the line is drawn by Congress itself in a federal statute or by the federal courts. In modern times, both Congress and the federal courts have read Congress's Commerce Power very broadly, allowing federal regulation of virtually all economic activity in the United States. The exceptions recognized in recent years, prohibiting state regulation of noncommercial activity traditionally regulated under state criminal law and prohibiting federal commandeering of state regulatory authorities, although lamented by some who favor expansive federal power, are minor when compared with the broad scope of federal power over interstate commerce.[4]

Dormant Commerce Clause Origins

Dormant Commerce Clause doctrine is a different matter. Because the Dormant Commerce Clause cases do not involve actual exercises of Congress's power, the question raised by those cases is whether the federal courts should play a role in determining how much state regulation to tolerate. The possibility that a state law might violate the Commerce Clause even in the absence of an act of Congress, was raised long before the Court actually struck down any state laws on such grounds. In the most widely cited early exposition of Congress's commerce power, 1824's *Gibbons v. Ogden*, the Court, in an opinion by Chief Justice John Marshall, held that a New York law purporting to grant Aaron Ogden a monopoly over steamboat ferry service between New York City and New Jersey could not prevent Thomas Gibbons from operating a competing federally authorized steamboat ferry service on the same route. The basic rule of *Gibbons* is that federal regulation of interstate commerce supersedes inconsistent state law even within the territory of the state. Marshall found this fundamental to a properly functioning national government. He observed that accepting the arguments for a narrower reach of federal power under which states would retain unlimited regulatory authority within their borders would make the Constitution "a magnificent structure . . . to look at, but totally unfit for use."[5]

In a concurring opinion, Justice William Johnson raised the possibility of a Dormant Commerce Clause, arguing that Congress's power over interstate commerce was exclusive so that any state attempt to regulate interstate commerce would be unconstitutional, even in the absence of federal legislation. Justice Johnson thought that exclusivity was inherent in Congress's power to regulate commerce:

The power of a sovereign state over commerce, therefore, amounts to nothing more than a power to limit and restrain it at pleasure. And since the power to prescribe the limits to its freedom, necessarily implies the power to determine what shall remain unrestrained, it follows, that the power must be exclusive; it can reside but in one potentate; and hence, the grant of this power carries with it the whole subject, leaving nothing for the State to act upon.[6]

Chief Justice Marshall also hinted that Congress's Commerce power might be exclusive, but because the case before the Court involved action by Congress, he did not find it necessary to opine on the question. And Johnson acknowledged that even if Congress's power is exclusive, difficult boundary questions would arise when states exercised their traditional police powers over goods or activities connected to interstate commerce.[7]

Five years later, Chief Justice Marshall made a more direct reference to a "Dormant" Commerce Clause. A Delaware law authorized the Black Creek Marsh Company to construct a dam across Black Bird Creek, a waterway running through marshland that connected to the Delaware River. The dam was part of a land reclamation project. The case arose when the operators of a boat dismantled part of the dam to allow their boat to pass through. In defense of a suit for damages under state law brought by the Black Creek Marsh Company, the defendants argued that the dam was an illegal obstruction of a navigable water of the United States that they had a federal right to remove. In particular, they argued that state law could not authorize the construction of a dam on a navigable water. Chief Justice Marshall's opinion rejecting the defense and upholding the construction of the dam was, by and large, a straightforward application of the principle that unless and until Congress acts, the states have power to enact laws like the one authorizing the construction of the dam. He did, however, raise the possibility that state laws interfering with interstate commerce might violate the Constitution, even in the absence of congressional action: "We do not think that the act empowering the Black Bird Creek Marsh Company to place a dam across the creek, can, under all the circumstances of the case, be considered as repugnant to the power to regulate commerce in its dormant state, or as being in conflict with any law passed on the subject." The Court cited no authority for its reference to "the power to regulate commerce in its dormant state" and did not elaborate on when a state law might be void even in the absence of congressional action.[8]

Later in the nineteenth century, three Dormant Commerce Clause theories emerged. The first was that some matters were of national importance and thus could be regulated only by the federal government and not by the states. The second was that state law could not discriminate against out-of-state businesses or in favor of in-state business interests. The third was the one that prevailed in *Hall v. Decuir*, that state laws are void if they unduly burden interstate commerce, even if they concerned local matters and were nondiscriminatory. Because all regulation and taxation burdens commerce to some degree, applying this third basis for invalidating state law under the Commerce Clause was, and remains, highly discretionary.

Before *Hall v. Decuir*, the Court's decisions applying Dormant Commerce Clause principles were relatively straightforward. A classic controversy implicating Dormant Commerce Clause doctrine arrived at the US Supreme Court in 1851. An 1803 Pennsylvania law required the hiring of a local pilot (or payment of a fine for the benefit of retired local pilots) for any ship arriving at or departing from port in Philadelphia. This is an exercise of traditional state police powers. While the state legislature might justify the law on safety grounds, to outsiders it looks like economic protectionism at best or interference with interstate commerce and transportation at worst. When the Board of Wardens for the Port of Philadelphia sued Aaron Cooley and other ship owners to recover fines assessed for failing to hire local pilots, the ship owners argued that they could not be regulated by the state of Pennsylvania because they were engaged in interstate commerce and because they traveled under federal license.[9]

In *Cooley v. Board of Wardens*, the Supreme Court rejected the shipowners' claims on the ground that the first Congress, in a statute passed in 1789, had legislatively consented to state regulation of harbor pilots.[10] The Court recognized that in the absence of specific federal legislation, the argument for finding a violation of the Dormant Commerce Clause amounted to an argument that the federal power over interstate commerce was, at least to an extent, exclusive. But in this case, the Court found that the existence of the federal statute made the exclusivity inquiry unnecessary. To the Court, the 1789 federal statute "manifest[ed] the understanding of Congress, at the outset of the government, that the nature of this subject is not such as to require its exclusive legislation." While the Court recognized that some subjects of national concern required exclusive federal control and uniform regulation, the Court was persuaded that variations in local conditions amply supported Congress's determination that local regulation of harbor pilots was appropriate. In short, the Court upheld Congress's determination that harbor pilotage was a matter of local concern.[11]

The opinion in *Cooley* offered a framework for evaluating Dormant Commerce Clause claims, under which the federal government would have exclusive power over matters of national concern, leaving state and local governments to deal with matters of local concern. However, when the Court actually got around to invalidating state legislation based on Dormant Commerce Clause doctrine, it did so on two different grounds: first, that state regulation could not impose an undue burden on interstate commerce, and second, that state law could not discriminate against interstate business in favor of local business.

The first case actually striking down a state law for interfering with Congress's power over interstate commerce in the absence of federal legislation was decided in 1872, right around the time that Madame Decuir's case arose. In the *Case of the State Freight Tax*, the Court invalidated a Pennsylvania tax on all freight carried by railroads in the state, including freight that was only passing through the state on the way to another state, on the ground that only Congress had the power to tax freight that was involved in interstate commerce.[12] This tax appeared to be aimed directly at interstate commerce, which the Court would not tolerate.

The antidiscrimination basis for Commerce Clause invalidation emerged slowly. In 1870, when confronted with a Maryland law that required nonresident merchants to procure a $300 license to sell goods in the state, while imposing much lower license fees ranging from twelve dollars to $150 on resident merchants, the Court invalidated the law as a violation of the Privileges and Immunities Clause of the Constitution, not the Commerce Clause.[13] Only Justice Joseph Bradley, in a concurring opinion, addressed whether the law also violated the Commerce Clause. While he agreed that discriminatory laws violate the Privileges and Immunities Clause, he would also have held that the $300 fee was an unconstitutional burden on interstate commerce even if resident merchants were required to pay the same fee. In other words, he would have found a violation based solely on the burden even in the absence of discrimination. To him, states should not be allowed to impose a steep license fee on interstate traders regardless of whether in-state traders are treated the same.[14]

In 1875, while Madame Decuir's case was pending, the Court finally struck down a state statute under the Commerce Clause for discriminating against out-of-state businesses. A Missouri law imposed a licensing requirement (and fee) on all "peddlers" of out-of-state goods. State law did not require licenses for peddlers of in-state goods. M. M. Welton, a salesman, was indicted for selling sewing machines made outside of Missouri without the required license, and after his conviction was upheld by the Missouri Supreme Court, Welton brought his case to the US Supreme Court. Viewing the licensing requirement as a form of taxation, the Court struck it down for discriminating against goods produced out of state. Referring to the Commerce Clause as a "protection" of interstate commercial dealings, the Court stated that "the commercial power continues until the commodity has ceased to be the subject of discriminating legislation by reason of its foreign character. That power protects it, even after it has entered the State, from any burdens imposed by reason of its foreign origin. The act of Missouri encroaches upon this power in this respect, and is therefore, in our judgment, unconstitutional and void." Although the Court mentioned "any privilege or immunity," the decision clearly rested on the Commerce Clause, with no explanation as to why the Privileges or Immunities Clause was not the proper location of the ban on discrimination against interstate commerce, as it had been in the Maryland case.[15]

The Court also clarified that discriminatory state laws violate the Commerce Clause, not only because of discrimination but because they burden interstate commerce by giving an advantage to in-state businesses. This makes sense because short of prohibiting the importation of out-of-state goods, which states clearly lack the power to do, the simplest way to reduce the volume of interstate commerce is through discriminatory taxation or regulation. If in-state goods are cheaper, the market for out-of-state goods will certainly suffer. And if other states respond in kind, the volume of interstate trade will decline even further.

The Court also explained why it felt that it was proper for it to act in the absence of congressional exercise of its power to regulate interstate commerce:

The fact that Congress has not seen fit to prescribe any specific rules to govern inter-State commerce does not affect the question. Its inaction on this subject . . . is equivalent to a declaration that inter-State commerce shall be free and untrammeled. As the main object of that commerce is the sale and exchange of commodities, the policy thus established would be defeated by discriminating legislation like that of Missouri.[16]

It cannot really be the case that that whenever it does not act, Congress intends to prohibit all state regulation affecting interstate commercial activity. Numerous state laws that are squarely within traditional state authority have effects that could be characterized as burdens on interstate commerce. Rather, the Court was applying an unstated standard that separates appropriate from inappropriate burdens on commerce. Despite its logical flaws, this reasoning paved the way for later decisions striking down state regulation purely on the basis of an undue burden on interstate commerce without any indication of discrimination against out-of-state business.

The Court's motivation for expanding its Dormant Commerce Clause jurisprudence to cover Madame Decuir's case may have involved an increased perceived need for national uniformity in the aftermath of the Civil War. In later cases, when the Court struck down state laws directed at interstate commerce, it stressed the uniformity factor, and it cited *Hall v. Decuir* as an example of a case in which the threat of disuniformity was intolerable.[17] Interestingly, while praising the general rule prohibiting states from interfering with interstate commerce, one nineteenth-century Commerce Clause scholar criticized *Hall v. Decuir* as misapplying the Dormant Commerce Clause because Madame Decuir's journey began and ended within the same state, a point that was echoed more recently by author Richard Kluger.[18] What the Court has never successfully explained is why it, rather than Congress, is the appropriate institution for determining when the need for uniformity is strong enough to preclude state regulation. And the Court has never successfully drawn a discernible line between appropriate exercises of state police power and inappropriate state interference with interstate commerce.

Regardless of what one thinks about the wisdom of the Court's Dormant or Negative Commerce Clause jurisprudence, for better or for worse, the creation and application of this legal doctrine is a textbook example of judicial activism of the nontextualist sort. The Commerce Clause appears in the list of Congress's powers, not among the Constitution's provisions limiting state power.[19] The text of the Constitution contains no provision limiting state power over interstate commerce or expressly granting Congress exclusive power to regulate interstate commerce. Often, when the framers wanted to prohibit state regulation, they did so expressly, even over subjects where the Constitution granted Congress an enumerated power. For example, article 1, section 8, of the Constitution grants Congress the power to "coin Money, regulate the Value thereof, and of foreign Coin, and fix the Standard of Weights and Measures," while article 1, section 9, of the Constitution provides, inter alia, that "No State shall . . . coin Money." Obviously, if article 1, section 8, grants exclusive power to Congress, there would be no need for section 9's provision prohibiting states from coining money. It thus may be inappropriate to read the Commerce Clause as granting an exclusive power to Congress, which is perhaps why nineteenth-century commentators expressed doubts over whether the federal commerce power was exclusive.[20]

Without entering deeply into the near-endless debate over judicial activism, nontextualist implication of a significant limitation on state power meets any reasonable definition of the phenomenon. Not only does Dormant Commerce Clause jurisprudence read something into the Constitution that is not there, it enhances judicial power by granting courts the power to determine when, in the absence of an act of Congress, state regulation interferes "too much" with interstate commerce. As Supreme Court justice Clarence Thomas, a longtime critic of Dormant Commerce Clause jurisprudence, has stated, the doctrine gives the Court the power to "make policy-laden judgments that we are ill equipped and arguably unauthorized to make." If the rules governing the Dormant Commerce Clause were clear and easy to apply, Justice Thomas's criticism might not hold, but without a clear rule, courts are called upon to make highly discretionary judgments.[21]

The doctrine also has its supporters from across the political spectrum. For example, Professor Michael Greve, a conservative legal scholar, has argued that the Dormant Commerce Clause doctrine is necessary to maintain a functioning national market and thus it was appropriate for the Court to have created it even in the absence of textual support.[22] Supreme Court Justice Stephen Breyer also defends Dormant Commerce Clause doctrine as necessary to prevent parochial state laws from harming the national interest.[23] Supporters of the Dormant Commerce Clause observe that while in theory it might be better for the Court to wait for Congress to act against state laws that interfere with interstate commerce, in practice, it is impossible for Congress to anticipate and act against every conceivable way that states might endanger the national market. Dormant Commerce Clause doctrine, which continues to spawn a high volume of challenges to allegedly protectionist state laws, allows the federal courts to partner with Congress in the enterprise of creating and maintaining a unified national economy.

A recent controversy involving Dormant Commerce Clause doctrine illustrates the continuing controversy the doctrine spawns. In 1992, the US Supreme Court decided that the Commerce Clause prohibited states from forcing out-of-state retailers to collect state sales tax on transactions in which the retailers shipped goods across state lines to their residents. The Court found that forcing retailers with no physical presence in the state (such as a retail outlet or an office) to charge and collect state sales tax was an intolerable burden on interstate commerce. Ironically, the Court observed that "Congress may be better qualified to resolve" the issue, apparently oblivious to the fact that the entire doctrine depends on the Court's own determinations regarding the extent of permissible burdens on commerce.[24] In the age of online commerce, this limitation on collection of state sales taxes can have substantial effects on competition, giving out of state internet retailers a significant price advantage in states with high sales taxes. Not surprisingly, the Court reconsidered the "physical presence" doctrine and ruled, in 2018, that states may compel out-of-state retailers to collect state sales taxes. Noting that application of the physical-presence doctrine resulted in imposition of "arbitrary" and "formalistic" distinctions, the Court abandoned it as the test for whether an effort to collect sales tax from out-of-state businesses violates the Dormant Commerce Clause. In its place, the Court announced that states may collect taxes from businesses with a "substantial nexus" to the state, a vague standard that is certain to spawn additional litigation.[25] Recurring litigation in Dormant Commerce Clause cases begs the question of whether the Court should leave superintendence of the economy to Congress.

NOTES

INTRODUCTION

1. Plessy v. Ferguson, 163 U.S. 537 (1896).

2. Raymond O. Arsenault, *Freedom Riders* (Oxford: Oxford University Press, 2005), 16, discussing Hall v. Decuir, 95 U.S. 485 (1878). Many sources cite *Hall* as having been decided in 1877, but the decision was handed down in January 1878. At the time, the date of decision was not included in the *United States Reports*, and the 1877 date apparently comes from the fact that the decisions included in volume 95 of the *United States Reports* are from the Court's October term, 1877. However, the chief justice's notebook, and contemporaneous newspaper accounts, establish that the decision was issued on January 14, 1878.

3. See note, Joseph R. Palmore, "The Not-So-Strange Career of Interstate Jim Crow: Race, Transportation, and the Dormant Commerce Clause, 1878–1946," *Virginia Law Review* 83, no. 8 (November 1997): 1774.

4. Jessica Decuir-Gunby, a descendant of distant relatives of Madame Decuir's husband Antoine and a professor of educational psychology has, in a perceptive essay, identified and analyzed the connection between Madame Decuir's case and *Plessy v. Ferguson*. See Jessica T. Decuir-Gunby, "Proving Your Skin Is White, You Can Have Everything: Race, Racial Identity, and Property Rights in Whiteness in the Supreme Court Case of Josephine DeCuir," in *Critical Race Theory in Education: All God's Children Got A Song*, eds. Adrienne D. Dixson and Celia K. Rousseau (New York: Routledge, 2006), 98–100, 106–110.

5. Rebecca J. Scott, "Public Rights, Social Equality, and the Conceptual Roots of the Plessy Challenge," *Michigan Law Review* 106, no. 5 (2008): 777. The importance of dignity to understanding Madame Decuir's case is illustrated by the title of Tamla T. Lee's unpublished master's thesis on the case, "'A Gross Indignity to her Personally:' Madame Josephine Decuir and Reconstruction in Louisiana" (master's thesis, University of Louisiana at Lafayette, 2013), 1872–1878, which is a quotation from the opinion of the Louisiana Supreme Court.

6. Rebecca J. Scott, "Dignité/Dignidade: Organizing Against Threats to Dignity in Societies After Slavery," in *Understanding Human Dignity*, ed. C. McCrudden (Oxford: Oxford University Press, 2013), 192.

7. See Caryn C. Bell, *Revolution, Romanticism, and the Afro-Creole Protest Tradition in Louisiana 1718–1868* (Baton Rouge: Louisiana State University Press, 1997), 222–275 (cited in Scott, "Public Rights," 777).

8. See Scott, "Public Rights," 782–784.

9. For the striking down of state railroad taxes on interstate freight and interstate passengers as intrusions on interstate commerce, see *Case of the*

State Freight Tax, 82 U.S. 232 (1872). The second such decision was apparently Welton v. Missouri, 91 U.S. 275 (1875).

10. See Eric Foner, *The Second Founding: How the Civil War and Reconstruction Remade the Constitution* (New York: W. W. Norton, 2019).

11. See Barbara Y. Welke, "When All the Women Were White, and All the Blacks Were Men: Gender, Class, Race, and the Road to Plessy, 1855–1914," *Law and History Review* 13, no. 8 (1995): 274.

12. The Marigny section of New Orleans was the pre- and postwar home to many of the more prosperous free people of color. See Shirley Elizabeth Thompson, *Exiles at Home: The Struggle to Become American in Creole New Orleans* (Cambridge, MA: Harvard University Press, 2009), 129–130.

13. *Civil Rights Cases*, 109 U.S. 3 (1883).

14. See Sarah M. Lemmon, "Transportation Segregation in the Federal Courts Since 1865," *Journal of Negro History* 38, no. 2 (April 1953): 174.

15. See Bob-Lo Excursion Co. v. Michigan, 333 U.S. 28, 29 (1947); Colorado Anti-Discrimination Comm'n v. Continental Air Lines, Inc., 372 U.S. 714, 720–22 (1963).

16. Lemmon, "Transportation Segregation," 192.

17. Blair L. M. Kelley, *The Right to Ride: Streetcar Boycotts and African American Citizenship in the Era of Plessy v. Ferguson* (Chapel Hill: University of North Carolina Press, 2010); Barbara Y. Welke, *Recasting American Liberty: Gender, Race, Law and the Railroad Revolution, 1865–1920* (Cambridge: Cambridge University Press, 2001); Lemmon, "Transportation Segregation."

18. Welke, *Recasting American Liberty*, 323–375.

19. Welke, *Recasting American Liberty*.

20. Rebecca J. Scott, "Discerning a Dignitary Offense: The Concept of Equal 'Public Rights' during Reconstruction," *Law and History Review* 38, no. 3 (2020): 519.

21. See, generally, Isabel Wilkerson, *Caste: The Origins of Our Discontents* (New York: Random House, 2020).

22. For an interesting discussion of the evolution of the term *Creole*, see Decuir-Gunby, "Proving Your Skin Is White," 98–100. See also James H. Dorman, "Louisiana's 'Creoles of Color': Ethnicity, Marginality, and Identity," *Social Science Quarterly* 73, no. 3 (September 1992): 616.

CHAPTER 1. LOUISIANA'S *GENS DE COULEUR* AND THE
DECUIR AND DUBUCLET FAMILIES

1. Justin A. Nystrom, *New Orleans after the Civil War: Race, Politics, and a New Birth of Freedom* (Baltimore, MD: Johns Hopkins University Press, 2010), 307. See also Transcript of Testimony of Plaintiff Charles Sauvinet, Sauvinet v. Walker, 27 La. Ann. 14 (1875), *aff'd*, 92 U.S. 90 at 34–35, 41, 43 (1875) [hereafter Sauvinet Transcript]. The record referred to is the handwritten transcription of lower court filings prepared for the Louisiana Supreme Court's consideration of the case. The case number in that court was 3513. The factual background of the case is summarized in Nystrom,

New Orleans, 96–98. See also Roger A. Fischer, *The Segregation Struggle in Louisiana, 1862–1877* (Champaign: University of Illinois Press, 1974), 69, 70.

2. Sauvinet Transcript, 42; Nystrom, *New Orleans*, 97.

3. Sauvinet Transcript, 35–36, 38, 39; Nystrom, *New Orleans*, 96.

4. For descriptions of the litigation, see Frank J. Wetta, *The Louisiana Scalawags: Politics, Race, and Terrorism During the Civil War and Reconstruction* (Baton Rouge: Louisiana State University Press, 2012), 176–77; Sauvinet Transcript, 39; Nystrom, *New Orleans*, 97.

5. Act No. 40, passed "to provide for carrying into effect the one hundred and thirty second article of the constitution of the State" required that licenses provide for no discrimination on account of race or color, stating that all licensed establishments "shall be open to the accommodation and patronage of all persons without distinction or discrimination on account of race or color." 1869 La. Acts 38; La. Rev. Stat. § 458 (1870); Transcript of Record at 49, Hall v. Decuir, 94 U.S. 485 (1877) [hereafter Decuir Transcript], quoting Civil Rights Stat., § 458. The process that led to the 1868 Louisiana Constitution's equal rights provisions is discussed in detail in Rebecca J. Scott, "Public Rights, Social Equality, and the Conceptual Roots of the Plessy Challenge," *Michigan Law Review* 106, no. 5 (2008): 777.

6. Sauvinet Transcript, 12–14.

7. Sauvinet Transcript, 56, 58–59.

8. Act No. 23 of January 2, 1871, 1871 La. Acts 57–58. In Sauvinet's case, the jury voted 11–1 in favor of the defendant. The defense attempted to strike a colored juror "on the ground that he was interested and prejudiced in this case on account of his color." Sauvinet Transcript, 94. This motion was denied as was a motion to strike, as incompetent, a juror who would not take the complete juror's oath because he was an atheist. Sauvinet Transcript, 95–96.

9. Although Sauvinet's complaint alleged that he "sustained damages to the amount of $10,000" which implies a claim for actual damages, the trial judge, in the judgment, characterized his $1,000 award as representing "exemplary" or punitive damages "to sanctify the principle involved and deter others from inflicting the same injury" (Sauvinet Transcript, 4 and 104–106); Sauvinet had abandoned his request that Walker's license to operate be revoked, so the Court did not rule on that issue (Sauvinet Transcript, 113).

10. See Sauvinet v. Walker, 27 La. Ann. 14 (1875); Sauvinet v. Walker, 4 (Howe and Wyly, J. J. dissenting).

11. See Walker v. Sauvinet, 92 U.S. 90 (1875).

12. See Scott, "Public Rights," 785–89. A volume produced by the Louisiana Historical Society in 1938 explained the conservative point of view: "The situation became intolerable. Negroes were holding political office from the highest to the lowest. The school system had been debased, disgraced and despoiled. Taxes were levied by the Federal maintained governments of the State and squandered. The rights of the citizens were trampled upon." See James A. Fortier, *Louisiana Historical Society, Carpet-Bag Misrule in Louisiana: The Tragedy of the Reconstruction Era Following the War*

between the States (New Orleans: T.J. Moran's Sons, 1938), 19. See also Fischer, *Segregation Struggle*, 61, 69; Geraldine M. McTigue, "Forms of Racial Interaction in Louisiana, 1860–1880" (unpublished PhD diss., Yale University, New Haven, CT, 1975). As Nystrom put it, "The old three-tiered racial caste system that had ordered New Orleans society since its founding now faced obsolescence." Nystrom, *New Orleans*, 60.

13. Gwendolyn Midlo Hall, "African Women in French and Spanish Louisiana: Origins, Roles, Family, Work, Treatment," in *The Devils Lane: Sex and Race in the Early South*, eds. Catherine Clinton and Michele Gillespie (New York: Oxford University Press, 1997), 258–259.

14. See Shirley Elizabeth Thompson, *Exiles at Home: The Struggle to Become American in Creole New Orleans* (Cambridge, MA: Harvard University Press, 2009), 111–163; McTigue, "Racial Interaction," 27, discussing arguments for "restoration of those rights stripped from the gens de couleur after the American cession," including the right to vote; Laura Foner, "The Free People of Color in Louisiana and St. Domingue; A Comparative Portrait of Two Three-Caste Slave Societies," *Journal of Social History* 3, no. 4 (Summer 1970): 406, 406–430; Paul F. LaChance, "The Formation of a Three-Caste Society: Evidence from Wills in Antebellum New Orleans," *Social Science History* 18, no. 2 (Summer 1994): 213–214; L. Foner, "Free People of Color," 416; Ted Tunnell, *Crucible of Reconstruction: War, Radicalism, and Race in Louisiana 1862–1877* (Baton Rouge: Louisiana State University Press, 1984), 67–68; Rodolphe L. Desdunes, *Our People and Our History* (Baton Rouge: Louisiana State University Press, 1973).

15. Kenneth R. Aslakson, *Making Race in the Courtroom: The Legal Consequences of Three Races in Early New Orleans* (New York: New York University Press, 2014); Tunnell, *Crucible of Reconstruction*, 67.

16. See Gwendolyn M. Hall, *Africans in Colonial Louisiana: The Development of Afro-Creole Culture in the Eighteenth-Century* (Baton Rouge: Louisiana State University Press, 1992), 60.

17. See Vernon V. Palmer, *Through the Codes Darkly: Slave Law and Civil Law in Louisiana* (Clark, NJ: Lawbook Exchange, 2012), 52; Code Noir art. 50 (1685). The Louisiana Code Noir, promulgated for Louisiana in 1724, required Supreme Court permission to free slaves "when the motives for setting free of said slaves . . . shall appear legitimate to the tribunal." The original French Code Noir of 1685, article 55, allowed masters to free their slaves "without their having to give just cause for their actions"; Code Noir art. 54 (1724).

18. Code Noir art. 19 (1724). See also Palmer, "Through the Codes Darkly," 71–78.

19. See Rebecca J. Scott, "Paper Thin: Freedom and Re-Enslavement in the Diaspora of the Haitian Revolution," *Law and History Review* 29, no. 4 (2011): 1061–1063. As Scott points out, more than three thousand people who had been slaves in St. Domingue, where slavery had been abolished, were essentially re-enslaved upon their arrival in New Orleans and Cuba, including some who arrived after 1808 when the importation of slaves became illegal in the United States (Scott, "Paper Thin," 1064, 1072). For details on the status of former slaves arriving in Louisiana from

Cuba, see also Rebecca J. Scott, "She Refuses to Deliver Herself as the Slave of Your Petition: Emigres, Enslavement and the 1808 Louisiana Digest of the Civil Laws," *Tulane European and Civil Law Forum* 24, (2009): 118–121. Rebecca Scott reports that in 1860, there were nearly nineteen thousand free people of color in Louisiana. See Rebecca J. Scott, *Degrees of Freedom: Louisiana and Cuba after Slavery* (Cambridge, MA: Harvard University Press, 1999), 14.

20. See Julie Eshelman-Lee, *The Decuir Family of Pointe Coupée Parish: As Told by Antoine Decuir* (Fort Collins, CO: Creole West Productions, 2002); Randy DeCuir, *Albert deCuire Arrives in Louisiana: 275th Anniversary 1720–1995* (Marksville, LA: Randy DeCuir, 1995); Marcel Giraud, *A History of French Louisiana: The Company of the Indies 1723–1731*, vol. 5 (Baton Rouge: Louisiana State University Press, 1991), 397–410; James F. Barnett, *The Natchez Indians: A History to 1735* (Jackson: University Press of Mississippi, 2007), 103–105; Julie Lee, pers. com. with author, July 2020.

21. Giraud, *History of French Louisiana*, 178; Brian J. Costello, *A History of Pointe Coupée Parish, Louisiana* (New Orleans: Margaret Media, 2010), 13–14.

22. Costello, *History of Pointe Coupée*, 38, 63.

23. See Kimberly S. Hanger, "Coping in a Complex World: Free Black Women in Colonial New Orleans," in *The Devil's Lane: Sex and Race in the Early South*, eds. Catherine Clinton and Michele Gillespie (New York: Oxford University Press, 1997), 218, 220.

24. See L. Foner, "Free People of Color," 408–409; Loren Schweninger, "Free Persons of Color in Postbellum Louisiana," *Journal of the Louisiana Historical Association* 30, no. 4 (Fall 1989): 346–347; Joan M. Martin, "Plaçage and the Louisiana Gens de Couleur Libre: How Race and Sex Defined the Lifestyles of Free Women of Color," in *Creole: The History and Legacy of Louisiana's Free People of Color*, ed. Sybil Kein (Baton Rouge: Louisiana State University Press, 2000), 57.

25. Hanger, "Coping in a Complex World," 218–231.

26. See Martin, "Louisiana Gens de Couleur," 58, 69. The term *quadroon* was also used more loosely to refer to mixed-race people with relatively light skin.

27. Mary Gehman, *The Free People of Color of New Orleans: An Introduction* (New Orleans: Margaret Media, 1994), 60–63; Thompson, *Exiles at Home*, 170–176.

28. See Martin, "Louisiana Gens de Couleur," 67. See also Gehman, *Free People*, 36–39; Fischer, *Segregation Struggle*, 16. Contrary to most accounts, Kenneth Aslakson states that "no evidence exists that the quadroon balls functioned as a form of debutante ball for young women of color to be introduced to wealthy white men." See Aslakson, *Making Race*, 108.

29. See Martin, "Louisiana Gens de Couleur," 65, 67.

30. See Ellen Holmes Pearson, "Imperfect Equality: The Legal Status of Free People of Color in New Orleans, 1803–1860," in *A Law Unto Itself? Essays in the New Louisiana Legal History*, eds. Warren M. Billings and Mark F. Fernandez (Baton Rouge: Louisiana State University Press, 2001), 197; Thompson, *Exiles at Home*, 111–163. See also Martin, "Louisiana Gens de Couleur," 69–71.

31. Eshelman-Lee, *Told by Antoine Decuir*, 9.

32. Eshelman-Lee, 10.

33. Eshelman-Lee, 10.

34. Eshelman-Lee, 10–11. The term *natural children* denoted something different from *illegitimate*. The designation indicated an intermediate space, similar to the intermediate racial space occupied by the French-speaking free people of color of Louisiana. These children were often the product of socially accepted (if not strictly socially acceptable) relationships with fathers who acknowledged and supported them. See Thompson, *Exiles at Home*, 167.

35. Eshelman-Lee, *Told by Antoine Decuir*, 11; Julie Lee, pers. com. with author, July 2020.

36. Eshelman-Lee, 13.

37. Charles Vincent, "Aspects of the Family and Public Life of Antoine Dubuclet: Louisiana's Black State Treasurer," *Journal of Negro History* 66 (Spring 1981): 26–36.

38. Ulysses R. Ricard Jr., "Pierre Belly and Rose: More Forgotten People," *Chicory Review* 1, no. 1 (Fall 1988): 13, 16. Identification as a member of the Nago tribe means that she or her ancestors would have been from the area around Africa's Bight of Benin, near present-day Ghana, Togo, Benin, and Nigeria along the West African coast. The French Code Noir punished "free men" who fathered children with slaves, except if the free man was unmarried at the time of the relationship, the punishment did not apply, and the free man was expected to marry the slave. Code Noir art. 9 (1685). Under the Louisiana Code Noir, only free Black people (and other slaves) were allowed to have sexual relations with and marry slaves. Code Noir art. 6 (1724).

39. Gwendolyn M. Hall, "African Women in French and Spanish Louisiana: Origins, Roles, Family, Work, Treatment," in *The Devils Lane: Sex and Race in the Early South*, eds. Catherine Clinton and Michele Gillespie (New York: Oxford University Press, 1997), 256.

40. Ricard, "Pierre Belly," 13, 14; Hall, "African Women," 256.

41. Vincent, "Aspects," 27.

42. Vincent, 27; Ricard, "Pierre Belly," 16 (see figure 2, family tree).

43. Mrs. Antoine Decuir, certificate of death, Ancestry.com, February 25, 1891.

44. Vincent, "Aspects," 27.

45. Vincent, 27 (quoting H. E. Sterkx, *The Free Negro in Ante-bellum Louisiana* [Rutherford, NJ: Fairleigh Dickinson University Press, 1972], 208).

46. Eric Foner, *Freedom's Lawmakers: A Directory of Black Officeholders During Reconstruction* (Baton Rouge: Louisiana State University Press, 1993), 65.

47. Schweninger, "Free Persons," 352.

48. See Vincent, "Aspects," 28; Tunnell, *Crucible of Reconstruction*, 136–150.

49. Vincent, "Aspects," 30.

50. Vincent, "Aspects," 32; James F. Vivian, "Major E. A. Burke: The Honduras Exile, 1889–1928," *Louisiana History: The Journal of the Louisiana Historical Association* 15, no. 2 (Spring 1974): 175–194.

51. Schweninger, "Free Persons," 345.

52. The census of 1880 records show Rosa and Joseph Antoine living with

Josephine in New Orleans at 145 Marigny Street. Rosa's age is listed at thirty-one, Joseph Antoine's is twenty-seven, and Josephine's is fifty-five. See US Census Bureau, "Joseph Antoine," Ancestry.com, 1880, https://www.ancestry.com/imageviewer/col lections/6742/images/4241378-00500?treeid=&personid=&hintid=&queryId=2600 eac5146ddcdfd9a9243e00c2e9af&usePUB=true&_phsrc=vEk6&_phstart=suc cessSource&usePUBJs=true&_ga=2.228167837.1895476323.1599680889-2093347846 .1599680889&pId=6210998.

53. See Joseph Logsdon and Caryn Cosse Bell, "The Americanization of Black New Orleans, 1850–1900," in *Creole New Orleans: Race and Americanization*, eds. Arnold R. Hirsch and Joseph Logsdon (Baton Rouge: Louisiana State University Press, 1992), 208–209; Julie Lee, pers. com. with author, January 2014; Tamala T. Lee, "'A Gross Indignity to her Personally': Madame Josephine Decuir and Reconstruction in Louisiana, 1872–1878" (unpublished master's thesis, University of Louisiana at Lafayette, 2013), 6–7. Madame Decuir's brother also sent his children to France to be educated. See Vincent, "Aspects," 28. Rodolphe Desdunes's book is replete with examples of people of color who were sent to France for their education. See Desdunes, *Our People*.

54. See Loren Schweninger, "Prosperous Blacks in the South, 1790–1880," *American History Review* 95, no. 1 (February 1990): 31–56; Alice Moore Dunbar-Nelson, "People of Color in Louisiana," in *Creole: The History and Legacy of Louisiana's Free People of Color*, ed. Sybil Klein (Baton Rouge: Louisiana State University Press, 2000), 26, 57; Robert J. Cottrol, *The Long Lingering Shadow: Slavery, Race, and Law in the American Hemisphere* (Athens: University of Georgia Press, 2013), 187–188; Jack D. L. Holmes, "The Abortive Slave Revolt at Pointe Coupée, Louisiana, 1795," *Louisiana History: The Journal of the Louisiana Historical Association* 11, no. 4 (Fall 1970): 341–362. One article on the 1795 slave revolt identifies Antoine and Joseph Decuir as witnesses in the proceedings regarding the revolt, but based on the date and the identification of Joseph Decuir as an "officer in militia," the identity of the particular members of the family to which the report refers is unclear. See Ulysses S. Ricard Jr., "The Pointe Coupée Slave Conspiracy of 1791," *Proceedings of the Meeting of the French Colonial Historical Society* 15 (1992): 129. On the 1811 revolt, see Daniel Rasmussen, *American Uprising: The Untold Story of America's Largest Slave Revolt* (New York: HarperCollins, 2011).

55. Schweninger, "Free Persons," 353; Dunbar-Nelson, "People of Color," 32.

56. Scott, *Degrees of Freedom*, 15. See also Laura Foner, "Free People of Color," 406–430.

57. See Desdunes, *Our People*, 35.

58. See Vincent, "Aspects," 28; Scott, *Degrees of Freedom*, 16.

59. Brief for Respondent at 19, 20, Hall v. Decuir, 95 U.S. 485 (1877).

CHAPTER 2. MADAME DECUIR RETURNS FROM FRANCE
AND HIRES NEW LAWYERS

1. Loren Schweninger, *Black Property Owners in the South 1790–1915* (Champaign: University of Illinois Press, 1990), 191–213; Charles Vincent, "Aspects of the Family

and Public Life of Antoine Dubuclet: Louisiana's Black State Treasurer," *Journal of Negro History* 66, (Spring 1981): 28; Loren Schweninger, "Prosperous Blacks in the South, 1790–1880," *American History Review* 95, no. 1 (February 1990): 47.

2. Succession of Antoine Decuir, July 24, 1865, Parish of Pointe Coupée District Courthouse.

3. See, e.g., N. Bank of Ky. v. Police Jury of Pointe Coupée, 25 La. Ann. 185 (1873); Levy v. Police Jury of Pointe Coupée, 24 La. Ann. 292 (1872).

4. Brian Costello, e-mail message to author, September 15, 2016.

5. Wink Dameron, *Conversations with My Grandfather* (Bloomington, IN: Xlibris, 2011), 27.

6. Decuir v. Benker, 33 La. Ann. 320 (1881); Labat v. Decuir, 33 La. Ann. 350 (1881).

7. See Succession of Decuir, 23 La. Ann. 166 (1871). On December 17, 1870, Antoine Dubuclet reiterated his claim that his net assets equaled $75,000.

8. See Letter from the Assistant Clerk of the Court of Claims Transmitting a Copy of the Findings of the Court in the Case of Antoine Decuir, Joseph Auguste Decuir and Rosa Decuir Macias, Heirs of Antoine Decuir, Deceased, against the United States, Senate Doc. No. 482, 59th Cong., 1st Sess. (June 9, 1906); An Act Making appropriation for payment of certain claims in accordance with findings of the Court of Claims, reported under the provisions of the Acts approved March third, eighteen hundred and eighty-three, and March third, eighteen hundred and eighty-seven, and commonly known as the Bowman and the Tucker Acts, and under the provisions of section numbered one hundred and fifty-one of the Act approved March third nineteen hundred and eleven, commonly known as the Judicial Code, 63rd Cong., 3rd Sess., 38 Stat. 972 (March 4, 1915). For a discussion of federal troops' actions in Pointe Coupée Parish during the Civil War, see Brian J. Costello, *A History of Pointe Coupée Parish, Louisiana* (New Orleans: Margaret Media, 2010), 116–118.

9. Loren Schweninger, "Free Persons of Color in Postbellum Louisiana," *Journal of the Louisiana Historical Association* 30, no. 4 (Fall 1989): 345; Succession of Decuir v. Ferrier, 26 La. Ann. 222 (1874) (Ludeling, J.).

10. Transcript of Record at 69, Hall v. Decuir, 94 U.S. 485 (1877) [hereafter Decuir Transcript].

11. Decuir Transcript, 69.

12. See Succession of Decuir, 26 La. Ann. 222 (1874).

13. See Cady v. Washington, no. 1813 (La. Ann. January 19, 1870).

14. New Orleans Justices of the Peace, "Index to Marriage Records, 1846–1880," Nutrias.org, http://nutrias.org/inv/jpmarrindex/bca_cam.htm; National Park Service, "Soldiers and Sailors Database," NPS.gov, 2007, https://www.nps.gov/civilwar/soldiers-and-sailors-database.htm. E. K. Washington is listed as having served in the Confederate army as a lieutenant in the 3rd Regiment, 3rd Brigade, 1st Division, Louisiana Militia.

15. The Slaughter-House Cases, 83 U.S. 36 (1872). In Berthin v. Crescent City Live-Stock Landing & Slaughter-House Co., 8 La. Ann. 210 (1876), Washington and Simeon Belden represented parties seeking to enforce restrictions on the location

of slaughterhouses in New Orleans. See also Crescent City Live Stock Landing & Slaughter-House Co. v. City of New Orleans, 33 La. Ann. 934 (1881), in which Washington represented Martin Wolf, a butcher seeking to preserve his business from the consequences of the monopoly on the slaughtering of animals in New Orleans granted by a state statute to the Crescent City Live Stock Landing & Slaughter-House Company.

16. Decuir Transcript, 30.

17. E. K. Washington, *Echoes of Europe; or, Word Pictures of Travel* (James Challen & Son, 1860).

18. "New Books," *New Orleans Republican* (New Orleans), July 17, 1870 (identifying poet E. K. Washington as the author of *Echoes of Europe*); *Daily Picayune* (New Orleans), Oct. 6, 1867, 4.

19. Washington, *Echoes of Europe*.

20. See David H. Donald, *Abraham Lincoln* (New York: Simon & Schuster, 1995), 576. One of Abraham Lincoln's stories, which he told to Admiral David D. Porter upon entering Richmond, Virginia, at the end of the Civil War, concludes with a disappointed office-seeker asking the president for "an old pair of trousers."

21. Washington, *Echoes of Europe*, 17–18. In the opening of the book, the author makes much of the fact that he will remain anonymous, not revealing any personal details about himself or the identity of his traveling companion. Washington, *Echoes of Europe*, 13.

22. Washington, *Echoes of Europe*, 209–215.

23. See David H. Donald, *Charles Sumner* (New York: De Capo Press, 1996), 49, 294–296 (at part 1); Stephen Puleo, *The Caning: The Assault That Drove America to Civil War* (Yardley, PA: Westholme, 2012), 19–22.

24. Washington, *Echoes of Europe*, 211, 638.

25. Note from J. Washington, stepfather to Mary Cady, granting Mary Cady permission to marry E. K. Washington, October 11, 1864 (on file with author).

26. Cady sued Washington for divorce in Louisiana in 1866. The record in that case is available at The University of New Orleans, "Mary A. Cady, Wife, v. E. K. Washington, Husband," Earl K. Long Library, New Orleans, LA, http://dspace.uno .edu:8080/xmlui/handle/123456789/38582. After that was unsuccessful, she traveled to Chicago and obtained a divorce there. See *New Orleans Republican*, June 9, 1870, 4 (reporting that her Louisiana petition for divorce alleging impotence had been denied previously). His filing against her is E. K. Washington v. Mary A. Cady, 22 La. Ann. (1867), http://dspace.uno.edu:8080/xmlui/handle/123456789/40552.

27. Information about the divorce case brought by Mary Cady against E. K. Washington is derived from the case file in Cady v. Washington, no. 1813 (La. Ann. January 19, 1870) (reviewing the judgment in Cady v. Washington, no. 18246 [Sixth District Court New Orleans, November 1, 1866]). Mary Cady filed a supplemental petition against "Eugene Keepers, alias E.K. Washington" claiming that she had learned "in the last few days" that E. K. Washington's real name was Keepers and that he had falsely represented himself as a member of the family of George Washington. See

Supplemental Petition, Cady v. Keepers, aka Washington, no. 18246 (6th Dist. Ct. for the Parish of Orleans, November 1, 1866), http://dspace.uno.edu:8080/xmlui/han dle/123456789/38582. I was unable to locate any information on "Eugene Keepers" or anyone with a similar name during that time period.

28. Michael Cercere, "How Lund Washington Saved Mount Vernon," *Journal of the American Revolution*, April 18, 2014, https://allthingsliberty.com/2014/04 /how-lund-washington-saved-mount-vernon/.

29. Answers to Interrogatories by Louisa Washington Robb at 303, Cady v. Washington, no. 1813, 22 (La. Ann. 1867), http://dspace.uno.edu:8080/xmlui/han dle/123456789/38582; Answers to Interrogatories by Thomas R. Davidson, Cady v. Washington, no. 1812, 22 (La. Ann. 1866) at 268, http://dspace.uno.edu:8080/xmlui /handle/123456789/38582.

30. Cady v. Washington, no. 1813 (La. Ann. 1870); See also *Daily Picayune* (New Orleans), January 17, 1870, 1.

31. See Washington v. Cady, no. 1581 (6th Dist. Ct. for the Parish of Orleans, June 26, 1871).

32. See Judgment in Washington v. Cady, no. 1581 (6th Dist. Ct. for the Parish of Orleans, June 26, 1871).

33. "An Unfounded Charge," *Daily Picayune* (New Orleans), September 18, 1870, 2, and "Not a True Bill," *Daily Picayune* (New Orleans), September 30, 1870, 2.

34. State *ex rel.* E. K. Washington v. the Clerk of the Sixth District Court, 23 La. Ann. 762 (1871).

35. See Petition for Writ of Mandamus, State *ex rel.* E. K. Washington v. Clerk of the Sixth District Court of the Parish of Orleans, No. 3499 (La. Ann. November 2, 1871), http://dspace.uno.edu:8080/xmlui/handle/123456789/40434web.uno.edu/jspui /handle/123456789/19083?mode=full&submit_simple=Show+full+item+record.

36. See Response to Petition for Writ of Mandamus in State *ex rel.* E. K. Washington v. Clerk of the Sixth District Court of the Parish of Orleans, no. 3499 (La. Ann. November 2, 1871), http://dspace.uno.edu:8080/xmlui/handle/123456789/40434.

37. Crescent City Live-Stock & Slaughter-House Co. v. Larrieux, 30 La. Ann. 798 (1878); Crescent City Live-Stock Landing & Slaughter-House Co. v. City of New Orleans, 33 La. Ann. 934 (1881); State v. Bayonne, 23 La. Ann. 7 (1871); Cottam v. Smith, 27 La. Ann. 128 (1875).

38. Act No. 55 of March 21, 1873, 1873, La. Acts 193 (located in Acts Passed by the General Assembly of the State of Louisiana at the Second Session of the Second Legislature).

39. "That the said Charles Swayne . . . did maliciously and unlawfully adjudge guilty of contempt of court and impose a fine of $100 upon and commit to prison for a period of ten days Simeon Belden, an attorney and counsel of law, for an alleged contempt of the circuit court of the United States." See U.S. Cong., *The Impeachment and Trial of Charles Swayne*, 58th Cong., 2d Sess., art. 10 (1904).

40. See "The Courts, Fourth District Court," *Times Picayune* (New Orleans), May 10, 1874, 2, discussing Peter Joseph v. David Bidwell.

41. *Daily Picayune* (New Orleans), January 29, 1882, 4; *Daily Picayune* (New Orleans), March 19, 1882,15. See Succession of Washington, no. 5188, Civ. Dist. Ct., Parish of Orleans, filed January 31, 1882.

42. He was also listed as five years old in the 1850 census. See United States Bureau of the Census, population schedule, 5th Ward, Municipality of New Orleans, Orleans Parish, LA, Seymour Snaer, Ancestry.com, 1850, https://www.ancestry.com/interactive/8054/4198709_00075?pid=2812971&backurl=https://search.ancestry.com/cgi-bin/sse.dll?db%3D1850usfedcenancestry%26h%3D2812971%26indiv%3Dtry%260_vc%3DRecord:OtherRecord%26rhSource%3D6587&treeid=&personid=&hintid=&usePUB=true&usePUBJs=true#?imageId=4198709_00075.

43. See Mary F. Berry, *We Are Who We Say We Are: A Black Family's Search for Home Across the Atlantic World* (Oxford: Oxford University Press, 2015), 33–34.

44. Succession of Boutte, 30 La. Ann. 128 (1878).

45. Berry, *We Are.*

46. Berry, 43–66.

47. See Joseph Logsdon and Caryn Cosse Bell, "The Americanization of Black New Orleans, 1850–1900," in *Creole New Orleans: Race and Americanization*, eds. Arnold R. Hirsch and Joseph Logsdon (Baton Rouge: Louisiana State University Press, 1992), 218–221.

48. See Eric Foner, *Freedom's Lawmakers: A Directory of Black Officeholders During Reconstruction* (Baton Rouge: Louisiana State University Press, 1993), 200.

49. Berry, *We Are*, 121–22.

50. U.S. Cong., Rep. of the Select Comm. on the New Orleans Riots, 171–172 (1867).

51. "The New Orleans Massacre," *Harper's Weekly* (New York), March 30, 1867, 202.

52. *Weekly Louisianian* (New Orleans), May 1, 1875, 3, a reprinted report from the *Terrebone Republican* that Snaer "read law with our former Learned Attorney General Simeon Belden Esq. and was admitted to the bar in 1873". The *Opelousas Journal* (New Orleans), June 24, 1871, 2, reported that "S. R. Snaer, who was examined before the Supreme Court here last week, and admitted to the Bar, is said to be the first colored man who ever became a lawyer in this State. We are informed he passed a first rate examination," quoted in Geraldine M. McTigue, "Forms of Racial Interaction in Louisiana, 1860–1880" (unpublished PhD diss., Yale University, New Haven, 1975), 107. Perhaps the 1873 date is a typo.

53. See J. Clay Smith, *Emancipation: The Making of the Black Lawyer, 1844–1944* (Philadelphia: University of Pennsylvania Press, 1993), 282; Rachel L. Emanuel, "History: Black Lawyers in Louisiana Prior to 1950," *Louisiana Bar Journal* 53, no. 2 (2005).

54. *Weekly Louisianian*, October 25, 1879, 3.

55. Because the address numbers in New Orleans have changed, it is sometimes difficult to determine exactly where a building stood in the nineteenth century.

56. *Weekly Louisianian*, October 25, 1879, 2, stating Snaer had been "renominated for the position by the Republican district convention".

57. "The New Iberia Murderers," *Donaldsonville Chief* (Donaldsonville, LA), July 5, 1873, 1; "From Iberia," *Lafayette Advertiser* (Vermilionville, LA), June 21, 1873, 2.

58. "Judge Lynch, Three Negro Murderers Hanged by a Mob," *Chicago Daily Tribune*, June 18, 1873, 1; "A Horse-Thief Lynched," *Chicago Daily Tribune*, June 18, 1873, 1; "Three Men in Louisiana and Another in Missouri Hung by Mobs," *Jackson City Patriot*, June 19, 1873.

59. Decuir Transcript, 72.

60. Berry, *We Are*, 106–107. The date of the marriage in the book is January 18, but the New Orleans marriage records, accessed through Ancestry.com, show a date of January 16.

61. Berry, 111–115.

62. Decuir Transcript, 69.

CHAPTER 3. MADAME DECUIR'S JOURNEY AND
RECONSTRUCTION

1. "Monthly Report of Barometer and Thermometer," *New Orleans Republican*, August 2, 1872, 5.

2. Transcript of Record at 69, Hall v. Decuir, 94 U.S. 485 (1877) [hereafter Decuir Transcript], 69.

3. Decuir Transcript, 69; describing two rooms in the White cabin on the *Bart Able* set aside for high-status people of color; they were provided with these sleeping quarters but were not allowed to enter the common area reserved for Whites. See Testimony of Captain V. B. Baranco, Decuir Transcript, 33.

4. Decuir Transcript, 69, 73.

5. Madame Decuir violated the prohibition on entering the cabin and was instructed by the captain of that boat, V. B. Baranco, to return to her room. See Decuir Transcript, 35, 37.

6. Blair L. M. Kelley, *The Right to Ride: Streetcar Boycotts and African American Citizenship in the Era of Plessy v. Ferguson* (Chapel Hill: University of North Carolina Press, 2010), 15–16.

7. See Roger A. Fischer, *The Segregation Struggle in Louisiana, 1862–1877* (Champaign: University of Illinois Press, 1974), 5–6.

8. See Keith W. Medley, *We As Freemen: The Fight Against Legal Segregation* (Gretna, LA: Pelican, 2003), 80–81.

9. See Barbara Y. Welke, *Recasting American Liberty: Gender, Race, Law and the Railroad Revolution, 1865–1920* (Cambridge: Cambridge University Press, 2001), 283–284.

10. Decuir Transcript, 33.

11. Decuir Transcript, 35.

12. Decuir Transcript, 37.

13. Decuir Transcript, 9.

14. Decuir Transcript, 69.

15. Decuir Transcript, 69–70.

16. Decuir Transcript, 9–11, 46, 50–51.

17. Decuir Transcript, 43, 70, 139.

18. Decuir Transcript, 51.

19. Decuir Transcript, 41, 48.

20. Decuir Transcript, 70.

21. Decuir Transcript, 46, 17,

22. Decuir Transcript, 44, 48.

23. Decuir Transcript, 48–49.

24. Welke, *Recasting American Liberty*, 303.

25. Decuir Transcript, 61–62.

26. Julie Eshelman-Lee, *The Decuir Family of Pointe Coupée Parish: As Told by Antoine Decuir* (Fort Collins, CO: Creole West Productions, 2002), 16; Charles Vincent, *Black Legislators in Louisiana During Reconstruction* (Baton Rouge: Louisiana State University Press, 1976), 52, 226, 228.

27. Decuir Transcript, 65; Rebecca J. Scott, "Public Rights, Social Equality, and the Conceptual Roots of the Plessy Challenge," *Michigan Law Review* 106, no. 5 (2008): 784n26; Decuir Transcript, 62.

28. Decuir Transcript, 66.

29. Decuir Transcript, 99.

30. Decuir Transcript, 66.

31. Rebecca J. Scott, "Discerning a Dignitary Offense: The Concept of Equal Public Rights during Reconstruction," *Law and History* Review 38, no. 3 (2020): 520.

32. Decuir Transcript, 56, 58–60.

33. Welke, *Recasting American Liberty*, 289, 304–305. See also Barbara Y. Welke, "When All the Women Were White, and All the Blacks Were Men: Gender, Class, Race, and the Road to Plessy, 1855–1914," *Law and History Review* 13, no. 8 (1995): 274.

34. Complaint of Madame Decuir, Decuir Transcript, 2.

35. As shown on the receipt included in the litigation record, she was charged five dollars for passage and one dollar for freight.

36. Decuir Transcript, 69.

37. See Laura F. Edwards, *A Legal History of the Civil War and Reconstruction: A Nation of Rights* (Cambridge: Cambridge University Press, 2015), 19, 94; *Official Journal of the Proceedings of the Convention of the State of Louisiana* (New Orleans: J. O. Nixon, 1861); *Official Journal of the Proceedings of the Convention for the Revision and Amendment of the Constitution of the State of Louisiana* (New Orleans: W. R. Fish, 1864), 183. The legislature never actually granted voting rights to any people of color under this constitution, and established schools for White children only. See Fischer, *Segregation Struggle*, 26–29; and James M. McPherson, *Battle Cry of Freedom: The Civil War Era* (Oxford: Oxford University Press, 1988), 418–421.

38. See, generally, Eric Foner, *Reconstruction: America's Unfinished Revolution 1863–1877* (New York: HarperCollins, 1988), 176–216.

39. Foner, *Reconstruction*, 197, quoting Richard L. Zuber, *Jonathan Worth: A Biography of a Southern Unionist* (Chapel Hill: University of North Carolina Press, 1965), 78.

40. See Fischer, *Segregation Struggle*, 26–27; Ted Tunnell, *Crucible of Reconstruction:*

War, Radicalism, and Race in Louisiana 1862–1877 (Baton Rouge: Louisiana State University Press, 1984), 96–97.

41. See Foner, *Reconstruction*, 55, 121, 206.

42. Foner, *Reconstruction*, 128–142. See generally Edwards, *Legal History*.

43. Foner, *Reconstruction*, 220.

44. See Eric Foner, "Rights and the Constitution in Black Life during the Civil War and Reconstruction," *Journal of American History* 74, no. 3 (December 1987): 863.

45. See Eric Foner, *The Second Founding: How the Civil War and Reconstruction Remade the Constitution* (New York: W. W. Norton, 2019); Foner, *Reconstruction*, 228–280.

46. Civil Rights Act of 1866, 14 Stat. 27-30 (1866).

47. See Foner, *The Second Founding*, 61.

48. U.S. Const. amend. XIV.

49. U.S. Const. amend. XV.

50. 42 U.S.C. § 1983. For a section-1983 case establishing the standard for evaluating whether excessive force was used in the course of an arrest, see Graham v. Connor, 490 U.S. 386 (1989).

51. Louisiana Const. of 1868, art. XIII.

52. See Fischer, *Segregation Struggle*, 57; Eric Foner, *Freedom's Lawmakers: A Directory of Black Officeholders During Reconstruction* (Baton Rouge: Louisiana State University Press, 1993), 67.

53. See *Acts Passed by the General Assembly of the State of Louisiana at the Second Session of the First Legislature*, Act No. 38 (New Orleans: A. L. Lee, 1869), 37.

54. *Acts Passed by the General Assembly of the State of Louisiana at the Second Session of the First Legislature*, Act No. 38 (New Orleans: A. L. Lee, 1869), 37.

55. Franklin Johnson, The Development of State Legislation Concerning the Free Negro (New York: Arbor Press 1919), 29

56. See Michael A. Ross, "Justice Miller's Reconstruction: The Slaughter-House Cases, Health Codes, and Civil Rights in New Orleans, 1861–1873," *The Journal of Southern History* 64, no. 4 (November 1998): 663, first quoting *Daily Picayune* (New Orleans), September 22, 1868; and then quoting *New Orleans Bee*, February 7, 1869.

57. See *Acts Passed by the General Assembly of the State of Louisiana at the Session of the Legislature*, Act No. 93, extra session (New Orleans: A. L. Lee, 1870).

58. See *Acts Passed by the General Assembly of the State of Louisiana at the First Session of the Second Legislature*, Act No. 23 (New Orleans: 1871), 56–57.

CHAPTER 4. MADAME DECUIR'S SUIT AGAINST CAPTAIN BENSON

1. *The Evening Picayune* (New Orleans), July 30, 1872, 2.

2. Transcript of Record at 1–2, Hall v. Decuir, 94 U.S. 485 (1877) [hereafter Decuir Transcript].

3. Decuir Transcript, 1–2; Barbara Y. Welke, *Recasting American Liberty: Gender,*

Race, Law and the Railroad Revolution, 1865–1920 (Cambridge: Cambridge University Press, 2001), 328.

4. Decuir Transcript, 1–2.

5. Decuir Transcript, 1–2.

6. This attachment, Antoine Dubuclet's guarantee, is not transcribed into the copied versions of the case file, handwritten or printed. However, it is attached to the complaint in the original state district court file. The word *trust* is behind the glue that attaches this document to the complaint, so it is uncertain if that is what it actually says.

7. Julie Lee, pers. com. with author, January 2014.

8. Charles McClain, "California Carpetbagger: The Career of Hendry Dibble," *Quinnipiac Law Review* 28, no. 4 (November 2010): 885–886, 899.

9. 1860 U.S. Census, Orleans Parish, Louisiana, population schedule, 4th Ward, Municipality of New Orleans, Bentinck Egan, available on Ancestry.com.

10. *Inscriptions on Egan Family Tomb*, Lake Lawn Metairie Cemetery, New Orleans, LA.

11. "The Late Bentinck Egan," *Daily Picayune* (New Orleans), January 5, 1882, 2.

12. "The Late Bentinck Egan."

13. See Mahood v. Tealza, 26 La. Ann. 108 (1874). Sometime soon after these events, Ms. Mahood died, leaving an estate valued at $13,123.71, or equivalent to approximately $298,000 in 2020 dollars. Succession of Lizzie Dean (Mrs. Eliza V. Mahood), 33 La. Ann. 867 (1881).

14. See Hubbard v. Moore, 24 La. Ann. 591 (1872); see also Sampson Brothers v. Townsend, 25 La. Ann. 78 (1873).

15. 26 La. Ann at 111 (Morgan, J. dissenting).

16. "The Late Bentinck Egan," 2, col. 3.

17. Decuir Transcript, 3–4.

18. Decuir Transcript, 5.

19. See Records of the Superior District Court (Orleans Parish), 1872–1877, City Archives, New Orleans Public Library, http://nutrias.org/~nopl/inv/vss.htm.

20. "Extra Edition," *Times-Picayune* (New Orleans), November 21, 1872.

21. Claude F. Oubre and Keith P. Fontenot, "Liber Vel Non: Selected Freedom Cases in Antebellum St. Landry Parish," *Louisiana History: The Journal of the Louisiana Historical Association* 39, no. 4 (Fall 1998): 325–331.

22. "Morning Edition," *New Orleans Crescent*, September 29, 1868, 1.

23. *New Orleans Democrat*, August 24, 1876, 1.

24. See Citizens and Taxpayers of Natchitoches Parish v. Board of Supervisors, 49 La. Ann. 641 (1897) (reviewing decision by Judge Collum).

25. Decuir Transcript, 6.

26. Decuir Transcript, 6.

27. Decuir Transcript, 6.

28. See State ex rel. Belden v. Fagan, 22 La. Ann. 545 (1870), *aff'd* Slaughter-House Cases, 83 U.S. 36 (1872). The *Lochner* era refers to the period of the late nineteenth

and early twentieth centuries during which the Supreme Court invalidated federal and state economic regulation as violating libertarian principles it found embodied in the Due Process Clauses of the Constitution. See Lochner v. New York, 198 U.S. 45 (1905); Allgeyer v. Louisiana, 165 U.S. 578 (1897); Howard Gilman, *The Constitution Besieged: The Rise & Demise of Lochner Era Police Powers Jurisprudence* (Durham, NC: Duke University Press, 1993).

29. See "The Civil Rights Suits," *Times-Picayune* (New Orleans), May 10, 1874, 4.

30. See Dan Abrams and David Fisher, *Lincoln's Last Trial: The Murder Case That Propelled Him to the Presidency* (New York: Hanover Square Press, 2018).

31. Decuir Transcript, 69–70, 45.

32. Decuir Transcript, 70.

33. Decuir Transcript, 61.

34. Decuir Transcript, 65–69.

35. Decuir Transcript, 56.

36. Decuir Transcript, 29.

37. Decuir Transcript, 16.

38. Decuir Transcript, 8, 23 (Mossop's name in the printed transcript is misspelled as "Mossoss").

39. Decuir Transcript, 48.

40. See Benton R. Patterson, *The Great American Steamboat Race: The Natchez and the Robert E. Lee and the Climax of an Era* (Jefferson, NC: McFarland, 2009).

41. *Waterways Journal*, July 4, 1908, reprinted in Benjamin G. Humphreys, *The Famous Race Between the "Lee" and the "Natchez": Extension of Remarks of Hon. Benjamin G. Humphreys of Mississippi in the United States House of Representatives, October 22, 1914* (Washington, DC: US Government Publishing Office, 1914).

42. See *Biographical and Historical Memoirs of Louisiana*, vol. 2 (Chicago: Goodspeed, 1892), 486; "Woman Steamboat Captain," *Times-Picayune* (New Orleans), May 22, 1927, 79; "First Woman Packet Pilot Keeps Renewing License," *Times-Picayune* (New Orleans), November 12, 1939, 29; Blanche Leathers (steamboat captain, Packet Natchez), interview by William G. Nott, February 13, 1927, transcript, 4, http://louisianadigitallibrary.org/islandora/object/state-lwp%3A8272.

43. Decuir Transcript, 43.

44. Decuir Transcript, 24, 49.

45. Decuir Transcript, 42.

46. In Bells v. Leathers, Captain Leathers was sued in state court for violating the same Louisiana Statute relied upon by Madame Decuir in her suit against Captain Benson. Although I have been unable to locate any published material on that case, it is referred to by the Court in its memorandum, explaining the judgment in Madame Decuir's case. See Decuir Transcript, 80. Captain Leathers also had a case in the Supreme Court of the United States in the 1870s. In Work v. Leathers, 97 U.S. 379 (1878), a libel in admiralty was filed against Captain Leathers in federal court. Captain Leathers had leased a riverboat from Work, promising to pay a monthly rental and to return it in the same condition in which it was provided to him, excepting ordinary

wear and tear. In the second month of the lease, it suffered a catastrophic engine failure requiring $5,000 to fix. Leathers paid rent up to the date of the breakdown and refused to repair the boat. The Supreme Court of the United States affirmed a circuit court decision for Leathers, holding that under admiralty law, the owner of a ship is responsible for ensuring that the boat is seaworthy and in proper repair. See Work v. Leathers, 97 U.S. 379 (1878).

47. Decuir Transcript, 29.

48. Decuir Transcript, 29–30.

49. Decuir Transcript, 33.

50. Decuir Transcript, 17–18.

51. Carolina Landing is upriver from Vicksburg near present-day Valewood, Mississippi.

52. Decuir Transcript, 41.

53. Decuir Transcript, 43.

54. Decuir Transcript, 33, 35–36.

55. See Barbara Y. Welke, "Beyond Plessy: Space, Status, and Race in the Era of Jim Crow," *Utah Law Review* 2000 (2001): 288; C. Vann Woodward, *The Strange Career of Jim Crow* (Oxford: Oxford University Press, 2002), 31.

56. Decuir Transcript, 71–72.

57. Decuir Transcript, 70.

58. See Ariela J. Gross, *What Blood Won't Tell: A History of Race on Trial in America* (Cambridge, MA: Harvard University Press, 2008), 9, 48–72. The "performance of race" refers to ways in which a person's actions and behavior imply their racial identity.

59. Decuir Transcript, 56.

60. Decuir Transcript, 58.

61. Decuir Transcript, 55–59.

62. Decuir Transcript, 59–60.

63. See Gross, *What Blood Won't Tell*, 44.

64. Decuir Transcript, 68–69.

65. Decuir Transcript, 37.

66. Decuir Transcript, 40–41. Snaer was referring to Orleans Parish Sheriff Charles Sauvinet who won his case challenging his exclusion from the Bank Coffeehouse.

67. See Peggy Pascoe, *What Comes Naturally: Miscegenation Law and the Making of Race in America* (New York: Oxford University Press, 2009), 115–119.

68. Decuir Transcript, 56.

CHAPTER 5. JUDGE COLLUM DECIDES

1. Transcript of Record at 74, Hall v. Decuir, 94 U.S. 485 (1877) [hereafter Decuir Transcript].

2. Decuir Transcript, 74. This statement by Judge Collum is not strictly accurate. As noted, Madame Decuir's grandmother Rose Belly was a slave, freed by her owner/husband. Further, it is a virtual certainty that anyone in North America with

Black African ancestry would be descended from slaves, although it appears that Madame Decuir's ancestors, other than her grandmother Rose, were freed before living memory.

3. Decuir Transcript, 75.

4. Decuir Transcript, 75.

5. Decuir Transcript, 75. This characterization of her request for damages is not completely accurate. In her complaint, Madame Decuir asked for "the full sum of seventy-five thousand dollars for actual and exemplary damages." Decuir Transcript, note 10, 2.

6. Decuir Transcript, 75.

7. Keene v. Lizardi, 5 La. 431 (1833).

8. Decuir Transcript, 75.

9. Decuir Transcript, 75–76, 79.

10. Decuir Transcript, 79

11. See Herbert Hovenkamp, "Social Science and Segregation Before Brown," *Duke Law Journal* (1985): 641.

12. Decuir Transcript, 76–77.

13. Decuir Transcript, 76.

14. Decuir Transcript, 77, 79.

15. Decuir Transcript, 76–77.

16. Civil Rights Act of 1871, 17 Stat. 13 (1871).

17. Jencks v. Coleman, 2 Sumn. 221, 13 F. Cas. 442 (C.C.R.I. 1835). Daniel Webster was the plaintiff's lawyer in this case.

18. Decuir Transcript, 77.

19. See Eric Foner, *Reconstruction: America's Unfinished Revolution, 1863–1877* (New York: HarperCollins, 2014), 118–119, 454–459, 553–556.

20. Decuir Transcript, 77.

21. Decuir Transcript, 78, quoting James Kent, *Commentaries on American Law*, vol. 1: *Of Constitutional Restrictions on the Powers of Several States*, lect. 19 (Livonia, MI: Lonang Institute, 2006), 1826–1830. Judge Collum did not quote Kent's next sentence: "The power of Congress on this subject comprehended navigation within the limits of every state, and it might pass the jurisdictional line of a state, and be exercised within its territory, so far as the navigation was connected with foreign commerce, or with commerce among the several states. This power, like all the other powers of congress, was plenary and absolute."

22. Decuir Transcript, 78.

23. Decuir Transcript, 78.

24. Decuir Transcript, 79.

25. Decuir Transcript, 79.

26. Decuir Transcript, 80.

27. Decuir Transcript, 80.

28. Decuir Transcript, 80.

29. Decuir Transcript, 81.

CHAPTER 6. THE LOUISIANA SUPREME COURT AFFIRMS

1. Transcript of Record at 81, Hall v. Decuir, 94 U.S. 485 (1877) [hereafter Decuir Transcript].

2. Decuir Transcript, 81.

3. Decuir Transcript, 83.

4. See Evelyn L. Wilson, *The Justices of the Supreme Court of Louisiana, 1865–1880* (Lake Mary, FL: Vandeplas Publishing, 2015), 65–67.

5. See Richard N. Current, *Three Carpetbag Governors* (Baton Rouge: Louisiana State University Press, 1967), 55; Eric Foner, *Reconstruction: America's Unfinished Revolution, 1863–1877* (New York: HarperCollins, 2014), 354; Joseph Logsdon and Caryn Cosse Bell, "The Americanization of Black New Orleans, 1850–1900," in *Creole New Orleans: Race and Americanization*, eds. Arnold R. Hirsch and Joseph Logsdon, (Baton Rouge: Louisiana State University Press, 1992), 252–254.

6. See Decuir v. Benson, 27 La. Ann. 1 (1874). The official report in the case includes a date of January 1875, but the opinion in the record is dated April 6, 1874, and the US Supreme Court took jurisdiction over the case on April 22, 1874.

7. *National Cyclopedia of American Biography*, vol. 13: *Ludeling, John Theodore* (New York: James T. White, 1906), 592; Wilson, *The Justices*, 70.

8. See Frank J. Wetta, *The Louisiana Scalawags: Politics, Race, and Terrorism During the Civil War and Reconstruction*, (Baton Rouge: Louisiana State University Press, 2012); Ted Tunnell, *Crucible of Reconstruction: War, Radicalism, and Race in Louisiana 1862–1877* (Baton Rouge: Louisiana State University Press, 1984), 123.

9. Wilson, *The Justices*, 72.

10. Tunnell, *Crucible of Reconstruction*, 123, 124; Rebecca J. Scott, "Discerning a Dignitary Offense: The Concept of Equal Public Rights during Reconstruction," *Law and History Review* v. 38, no. 3 (2020): 520.

11. See Wilson, *The Justices*, 72–73. The justices appointed by Nicholls then ruled that Nicholls was governor; State ex rel. Mercier v. Judge of Superior District Court, 29 La. Ann. 223 (1877).

12. For details on how the White League violently prevented Ludeling from campaigning, see "Fighting for Louisiana," *New York Times*, November 17, 1879, 1.

13. "The Killing of Young Ludeling," *New York Times*, March 1, 1881, 1, col. 4.; reporting that alleged killers were found not guilty by a jury in Louisiana, see "Ludeling's Murderers Acquitted," *New York Times*, April 29, 1881, 1.

14. Sauvinet v. Walker, 27 La. Ann. 1, 1 (1875).

15. *Sauvinet*, 27 La. Ann., 2–3.

16. *Sauvinet*, 2.

17. See the *Case of the State Freight Tax*, 82 U.S. 232 (1872).

18. *Sauvinet*, 4.

19. *Sauvinet*, 5.

20. *Sauvinet*, 5, quoting Keene v. Lizardi, 5 La. 431, 433 (1833).

21. *Sauvinet*, 6.

22. *Sauvinet*, 6.

23. Wilson, *The Justices*, 87–88.

24. *Sauvinet*, 8.

25. The boundary between legitimate exercises of the state police power and Congress's authority to regulate interstate commerce has always been very difficult to discern. For a discussion of this in the context of federal review of nineteenth-century state laws imposing fees on transportation of immigrant workers into the United States, see Tony Allan Freyer, *The Passenger Cases and the Commerce Clause: Immigrants, Blacks, and States' Rights in Antebellum America* (Lawrence: University Press of Kansas, 2014), 106–107.

26. *Sauvinet*, 13.

27. *Sauvinet*, 6–13.

28. *Sauvinet*, 13.

29. The *Civil Rights Cases*, 109 U.S. 3 (1883).

30. See Wilson, *The Justices*, 232.

31. Decuir Transcript, 95.

CHAPTER 7. CAPTAIN BENSON TAKES HIS CASE TO THE US SUPREME COURT

1. See Transcript of Record at 96–98, Hall v. Decuir, 94 U.S. 485 (1877) [hereafter Decuir Transcript].

2. See Rebecca J. Scott, "Discerning a Dignitary Offense: The Concept of Equal Public Rights during Reconstruction," *Law and History* Review v. 38 No. 3 (2020): 546–547.

3. See Doris Kent, "Certain R.H. Marr is Winner," *Times-Picayune* (New Orleans), August 1, 1920, 1. The article, which refers to his selection as the Democratic nomination for district attorney, describes the younger Marr as "the kind of man children 'take to,' dogs follow and negroes 'borrow from.'" His daughter Katherine is quoted as describing him as a "sure winner." He was sworn in as Orleans Parish district attorney on December 6, 1920. See "Luzenberg Drops Mantle on Marr," *Times-Picayune* (New Orleans), December 7, 1920, 4.

4. Rev. Dr. Palmer, "Robert H. Marr: An Eloquent Tribute to his Memory," *Times Picayune* (New Orleans), September 25, 1892, 11; Charles Lane, *The Day Freedom Died: The Colfax Massacre, the Supreme Court, and the Betrayal of Reconstruction* (New York: Henry Holt, 2008), 155–157.

5. Ex parte Garland, 71 U.S. 333 (1866).

6. Lane, *The Day Freedom Died*, 156.

7. Justin A. Nystrom, *New Orleans After the Civil War: Race, Politics, and a New Birth of Freedom* (Baltimore, MD: Johns Hopkins University Press, 2010), 119, 153.

8. United States v. Cruikshank, 92 U.S. 542 (1876); Lane, *The Day Freedom Died*; Nystrom, *New Orleans*, 158; on R. H. Marr as one of the lawyers for the *Cruikshank* defendants, see James K. Hogue, *Uncivil War: Five New Orleans Street Battles and the Rise and Fall of Radical Reconstruction* (Baton Rouge: Louisiana State University Press, 2006), 124.

9. Eric Foner, *Reconstruction: America's Unfinished Revolution 1863–1877* (New York: HarperCollins, 1988), 237.

10. Nystrom, *New Orleans,* 171, 175; James A. Fortier, *Carpet-Bag Misrule in Louisiana: The Tragedy of the Reconstruction Era Following the War Between the States* (New Orleans: Press of T. J. Moran's Sons, 1938), 42; Stuart O. Landry, *The Battle of Liberty Place* (Gretna, LA: Firebird Press, 2000), 92.

11. "Proceedings Before the Congressional Committee," *New York Times,* February 4, 1875, 5.

12. "Proceedings Before the Congressional Committee," *New York Times,* February 4, 1875, 5.

13. Handwritten Record in Hall v. Decuir, Order on Remand, Decuir Transcript.

14. Evelyn L. Wilson, *The Justices of the Supreme Court of Louisiana, 1865–1880* (Vandeplas Publishing, 2015), 171.

15. See Saloy v. City of New Orleans, 33 La. Ann. 79 (1881), citing Shields v. Pipes, 31 La. Ann. 765 (1879). This was an interesting case. In *Saloy,* the Louisiana Supreme Court held that a new constitutional limit on city taxation could not be applied to prevent New Orleans from imposing sufficient taxation to pay its pre-existing debts.

16. City of New Orleans v. Vergnole, 33 La. Ann. 35 (1881).

17. City of New Orleans v. Jackson, 33 La. Ann. 1038, 1040, 1043 (1881).

18. "Judge Robert H. Marr Is Missing," *New York Times,* April 21, 1892, 1. Deschamps and Baker had been convicted of separate murders and they were scheduled to be hanged on April 22, 1892, two days after Marr disappeared. Baker, convicted of murdering his boss's wife, claimed to have evidence that the husband was the actual murderer. Deschamps, an elderly French doctor described as "magnetic," was convicted of assaulting and chloroforming a thirteen year old. The question in his case was not guilt but insanity. There was time pressure to resolve the matter in time for the April hanging while Nicholls was still governor. See "Trying to Cheat the Gallows," *New York Times,* April 13, 1892, 2. See also "Disappearance of Judge Marr," *Times-Picayune* (New Orleans), April 20, 1892, 2.

19. See "Say They Have Judge Marr," *New York Times,* August 1, 1892, 1.

20. Palmer, "Robert H. Marr," 11.

21. Christopher M. Duncan, "Benjamin Morgan Palmer: Southern Presbyterian Divine" (unpublished PhD diss., Auburn University, 2008), 192.

22. Duncan, "Benjamin Morgan Palmer," 4.

23. Duncan, 132–136.

24. Duncan, 141.

25. See generally Duncan, 4, 132–136, 141, 181.

26. Obituary from the *Interior,* June 5, 1902, 734. http://www.pcahistory.org/HCLibrary/periodicals/spr/bios/palmer.html.

27. "Confirmations of the Senate," *Daily Picayune* (New Orleans), July 1, 1892, 10.

28. *Daily Picayune* (New Orleans), November 14, 1875, 3.

29. Copy of Marriage Certificate in numbered and separated file, State of

Louisiana, Secretary of State, Division of Archives, Records Management, and History, Vital Records Indices, Baton Rouge, LA, vol. 5, p. 396

30. These documents, and all correspondence regarding the case, are located in the US Supreme Court's file in Hall v. Decuir, accessible via case name and docket number, 17 in the October 1877 term of the Court, housed in the National Archives in Washington, DC.

31. Motion to Substitute Eliza Jane Hall as plaintiff-in-error, Hall v. Decuir, 95 U.S. 485 (1877).

32. The defense lawyers in the Supreme Court in *Cruikshank* consisted of the distinguished group of Reverdy Johnson, David Dudley Field, and R. H. Marr. The decision in *Cruikshank* limited the effect of the Bill of Rights on states, holding basically that the First Amendment right to assembly did not limit the powers of states with regard to their own citizens, and that the Second Amendment right to bear arms did not apply against the states. See United States v. Cruikshank, 92 U.S. 542 (1876).

33. Brief and Argument for Plaintiff in Error, Hall v. Decuir, 95 U.S. 485 (1878) [hereafter Hall Brief] at 1–2.

34. Marr argued that while the Civil Rights Act of 1875 might prohibit segregation, "it cannot affect the rights of defendant in error; because it was passed nearly three years after the cause of action propounded by her arose." Marr also argued that the Reconstruction-era amendments to the US Constitution could not support the judgment in Madame Decuir's favor because they protect only against state action, and even if they did apply to Benson's conduct, "*equality* does not mean *identity*." This last argument hinted at what later would become the argument for "separate but equal" as the proper understanding of equal protection.

35. Hall Brief, 11.

36. Hall Brief, 12.

37. For example, Marr cited West Chester & P. R. Co. v. Miles, 55 Pa. 209 (1867), which appealed to divine law requiring separation of the races as justification for allowing a railroad to separate passengers by race:

Why the Creator made one black and the other white, we know not; but the fact is apparent, and the races distinct, each producing its own kind, and following the peculiar law of its constitution. Conceding equality, with natures as perfect and rights as sacred, yet God has made them dissimilar, with those natural instincts and feelings which He always imparts to His creatures when He intends that they shall not overstep the natural boundaries He has assigned to them. The natural law which forbids their intermarriage and that social amalgamation which leads to a corruption of races, is as clearly divine as that which imparted to them different natures. The tendency of intimate social intermixture is to amalgamation, contrary to the law of races. The separation of the white and black races upon the surface of the globe is a fact equally apparent. Why this is so it is not necessary to speculate; but the fact of a distribution of men by race and color is as visible in the providential arrangement of the earth as that of heat and cold. The natural separation of the races is therefore an undeniable fact, and all social organizations which lead to their amalgamation are repugnant to the law of nature. From social amalgamation it is but a step to illicit intercourse, and but another to intermarriage. But to assert separateness is not to declare inferiority in either; it is not to declare one a slave and the other a freeman—that would be to draw the illogical sequence of inferiority from difference only. It is simply to say that following the order of Divine Providence, human authority ought not to compel these widely separated races to intermix. The right of such to be free from social contact is as clear as to be free from intermarriage. The former may be less repulsive as a condition, but not less entitled to protection as a right. When, therefore, we declare a right to maintain separate relations, as far as is reasonably practicable, but in a spirit of kindness and charity, and with due regard to equality of rights, it is not prejudice, nor caste, nor injustice of any kind, but simply to suffer men to follow the law of races established by the Creator himself, and not to compel them to intermix contrary to their instincts.

Hall Brief, 23–24.

38. State v. Cincinnati, 19 Ohio 178 (1850); State v. McCann, 21 Ohio St. 198 (1871). The brief cites to Howard's Practice Reports 49, page 249, for a decision that allowed Buffalo, New York, to maintain separate schools, but there is no such case in that volume. The only case that is remotely relevant to the question in Howard's reports is one involving the status of teachers at New York City's "colored schools" after that city abolished public school segregation. See People ex rel. Ray v. Davenport, 2 How. Pr. N.S. 17 (N.Y. Sup. Court 1885). See also Roberts v. City of Boston, 59 Mass. 198 (1850); State vs. Duffy, 7 Nev. 342 (1872); People ex rel. Workman v. Board of Education, 18 Mich. 400 (1869).

39. Roberts v. City of Boston, 59 Mass. 198 (1850).

40. State v. Gibson, 36 Ind. 389 (1871).

41. Hall Brief, 31, 32-33.

42. Hall Brief, 22.

43. Hall Brief, 37–38.

44. Hall Brief, 8–9.

45. Hall Brief, 54. See also Roth v. Board of Regents, 408 U.S. 564 (1972), creating the "entitlement theory" of property.

46. U.S. Const., art. 1 § 8.

47. See the *Passenger Cases*, 48 U.S. 283 (1849); and *Case of the State Freight Tax*, 82 U.S. 232 (1872).

48. Hall Brief, 44.

49. Plessy v. Ferguson, 163 U.S. 537 (1896).

50. Hall Brief, 47–48.

51. Hall Brief, 48–49, citing the act of February 28, 1871, ch. 41, 41st Cong., 3d Sess.

52. Hall Brief, 50–51.

53. Hall Brief, 53–54.

54. Brief and Argument for Defendant in Error at 1, Hall v. Decuir, 95 U.S. 485 (1878) [hereafter Decuir Brief].

55. Decuir Brief, 2.

56. Decuir Brief, 2.

57. Decuir Brief, 4–5.

58. Decuir Brief, 8.

59. Decuir Brief, 7–8, 10.

60. Decuir Brief, 14–15. There is a Latin maxim, derived from the poetry of Ovid: *non bene junctarum discordia semina rerum*, which translates to "the discordant seeds of things ill joined."

61. Decuir Brief, 11, 13, 15. I have been unable to locate a source in US Supreme Court opinions for the first quote. The second quote is from Justice Washington's opinion for himself only in Ogden v. Saunders, 25 U.S. 213, 270 (1827).

62. Washington, A. & G.R. Co. v. Brown, 84 U.S. 445, 560, 567–568 (1873).

63. Decuir Brief, 18.

64. Decuir Brief, 21.

65. Decuir Brief, 22.

CHAPTER 8. LOUISIANA (AND THE ENTIRE SOUTH) REDEEMED

1. See Michael Ross, *The Great New Orleans Kidnapping Case: Race, Law, and Justice in the Reconstruction Era* (Oxford: Oxford University Press, 2014), 111.

2. Geraldine M. McTigue, "Forms of Racial Interaction in Louisiana, 1860–1880" (unpublished PhD diss., Yale University, 1975).

3. La. Const. of 1879, arts. 188, 208. On devices to prevent Blacks from voting more generally, see Michael J. Klarman, *From Jim Crow to Civil Rights: The Supreme Court and the Struggle for Racial Equality* (Oxford: Oxford University Press, 2004), 28, 39.

4. See Nicholas Lemann, *Redemption: The Last Battle of the Civil War* (New York: Farrar, Strauss & Giroux, 2006).

5. James A. Fortier, *Carpet-Bag Misrule in Louisiana: The Tragedy of the Reconstruction Era Following the War Between the States* (New Orleans: Press of T. J. Moran's Sons, 1938), 72.

6. Carolyn E. DeLatte, "The St. Landry Riot: A Forgotten Incident of Reconstruction Violence," *Louisiana History: The Journal of the Louisiana Historical Association* 17, no. 1 (Winter 1976): 41–49; for a discussion of efforts by Democrats to woo Black voters in 1877,

see Roger A. Fischer, *The Segregation Struggle in Louisiana, 1862–1877* (Champaign: University of Illinois Press, 1974), 134.

7. Cong. Globe, 42d Cong., 1st Sess., 458 (1871).

8. Daniel J. Sharfstein, *The Invisible Line: A Secret History of Race in America* (London: Penguin, 2011), 173.

9. *Slaughter-House Cases*, 83 U.S. 36 (1873).

10. *Slaughter-House Cases*, 83 U.S. at 60.

11. *Slaughter-House Cases*, 83 U.S. at 61.

12. Testimony of Dr. E. S. Lewis before the Louisiana House of Representatives

Special Committee on the Removal of the Slaughter Houses in 1867, as quoted and cited in Michael A. Ross, "Justice Miller's Reconstruction: The Slaughter-House Cases, Health Codes, and Civil Rights in New Orleans, 1861–1873," *Journal of Southern History* 64, no. 4 (November 1998): 654, quoted in Paul Kens, *Justice Stephen Field: Shaping Liberty from the Gold Rush to the Gilded Age* (Lawrence: University of Kansas Press, 1997), 118; State v. Fagan, 83 U.S. 553; Ronald M. Labbe, "New Light on the Slaughterhouse Monopoly Act of 1869," in *Louisiana's Legal Heritage*, ed. Edward F. Haas (Pensacola, FL: Perdido Bay Press, 1983), 150.

13. *Slaughter-House Cases*, 83 U.S. at 71–72, 78.

14. See Lochner v. New York, 198 U.S. 45 (1905).

15. Ross, "Miller's Reconstruction," 649–676. See also Erwin Chemerinsky, *Constitutional Law: Principles and Policies*, 5th ed. (Philadelphia, PA: Wolters Kluwer, 2015), 502: "the Supreme Court interpreted the clause in an extremely narrow manner and thus precluded its use as a vehicle for applying the Bill of Rights to the states."

16. Washington, A. & G. R. Co. v. Brown, 84 U.S. 445, 452–453 (1873).

17. Walker v. Sauvinet, 92 U.S. at 90 (1875).

18. Walker v. Sauvinet, 92 U.S. at 92–93. This is no longer the prevailing understanding of due-process clause. See Frank Easterbrook, "Substance and Due Process," *Supreme Court Review* 1982, (1982): 82.

19. United States v. Reese, 92 U.S. at 214, 215 (1875).

20. The Enforcement Act of 1870, 16 Stat. 140–146; United States v. Reese, 92 U.S. at 216–217.

21. United States v. Reese, 92 U.S. at 221.

22. Lemann, *Redemption*, provides a comprehensive view of the era. See also Frances Fox Piven and Richard Cloward, *Why Americans Don't Vote* (New York: Pantheon, 1988), 78–95.

23. Lemann, *Redemption*, 11.

24. See Eric Foner, *Reconstruction: America's Unfinished Revolution 1863–1877* (New York: HarperCollins, 1988), 437; Charles Lane, *The Day Freedom Died: The Colfax Massacre, the Supreme Court, and the Betrayal of Reconstruction* (New York: Henry Holt, 2008).

25. See Lane, *Day Freedom Died*, 133–134, 259; Lemann, *Redemption*, 6. The number killed is uncertain, with estimates ranging from around sixty-two to as high as four hundred, with the lower number likely closer to correct; Lane, *Day Freedom Died*, 265–266.

26. See Richard Rubin, "The Colfax Riot: Stumbling on a forgotten Reconstruction Tragedy, in a Forgotten Corner of Louisiana," *Atlantic*, July/August 2003.

27. United States v. Cruikshank, 92 U.S. 542 (1876).

28. *Cruikshank*, 92 U.S. 542.

29. *Cruikshank*, 92 U.S. at 554.

30. *Cruikshank*, 92 U.S. at 553–554.

31. *Cruikshank*, 92 U.S. at 552.

32. *Cruikshank*, 92 U.S. at 554.

33. *Cruikshank,* 92 U.S. at 552.

34. McDonald v. Chicago, 561 U.S. 742 (2010).

35. *Cruikshank,* 92 U.S. at 565 (opinion of Clifford, J.)

36. See Fortier, *Carpet-Bag Misrule,* 40–41, 49.

37. See Lehmann, *Redemption,* 77. For many years, a monument erected to commemorate this battle contained an inscription lauding the uprising and endorsing of White supremacy. This was followed by decades of conflict over the message and placement of the marker. See Fortier, *Carpet-Bag Misrule,* 48;

38. Foner, *Reconstruction,* 575–580. See also C. Vann Woodward, *Reunion and Reaction: The Compromise of 1877 and the End of Reconstruction* (Oxford: Oxford University Press, 1966).

CHAPTER 9. THE SUPREME COURT DECIDES

1. Donald G. Stephenson, *The Waite Court: Justices, Rulings and Legacy* (Santa Barbara, CA: ABC-CLIO, 2003), 3.

2. C. Peter Magrath, *Morrison R. Waite: The Triumph of Character* (New York: Macmillan, 1963), 18.

3. Magrath, *Morrison R. Waite,* 18–19; David H. Donald, *Charles Sumner and the Rights of Man* (Cambridge, MA: Da Capo Press, 1996), 581.

4. Correspondence concerning the case and its procedural history are drawn from documents contained in the Supreme Court's official case file in *Hall v. Decuir,* housed at the National Archives in Washington, DC, and accessible by case name and docket number 17 in the court's October 1877 term.

5. The 5–3 vote is reflected in the chief justice's official docket book contained in his papers at the Library of Congress, container number 31, Morrison R. Waite Papers, Manuscript Division, Library of Congress, Washington, DC. Those papers are the source of a number of the historical references in this chapter.

6. See Tinsley E. Yarbrough, *Judicial Enigma: The First Justice Harlan* (Oxford: Oxford University Press, 1995), 55–56.

7. See Stephenson, *The Waite Court,* 12. Waite's correspondence with Harlan is contained in Waite's papers in the Library of Congress, container number 11, Morrison R. Waite Papers, Manuscript Division, Library of Congress, Washington, DC.

8. Yarbrough, *Judicial Enigma,* 46–55, 141, 164–169.

9. See Magrath, *Morrison R. Waite,* 263–266; Stephenson, *The Waite Court,* 238.

10. Divergence between the vote tally at conference and the actual publication of dissenting views was apparently common during this period, and perhaps it is simply attributable to the Court's high caseload, which led justices to abandon planned dissents. A norm favoring the appearance of consensus may also have contributed to the common practice of justices failing to file dissents in cases in which they voted against the majority. See Stephenson, *The Waite Court,* 50–51.

11. Hall v. Decuir, 95 U.S. 485 (1878).

12. The only hint that race was a social issue was contained in the opinion's comment that the law would require "[a] passenger in the cabin set apart for the use of

whites without the State must, when the boat comes within, share the accommodations of that cabin with such colored persons as may come on board afterwards[.]" Hall v. Decuir, 95 U.S. 489.

13. See John T. Noonan, *Persons and Masks of the Law: Cardozo, Holmes, Jefferson, and Wythe as Makers of the Masks* (Berkeley: University of California Press, 2002).

14. Hall v. Decuir, 95 U.S. at 487.

15. *Hall*, 95 U.S. at 477–488.

16. *Hall*, 95 U.S. at 488–89.

17. *Hall*, 95 U.S. at 489.

18. See Robert Cover, "Violence and the Word," *Yale Law Journal* 95 (1986): 1603.

19. Hall v. Decuir, 95 U.S. 489.

20. According to Professor Larry Lessig, the first direct reference to a Negative, or Dormant, Commerce Clause appeared in Willson v. Black Bird Creek Marsh Co., 27 U.S. 245, 252 (1829). See Lawrence Lessig, "Translating Federalism: United States v. Lopez," *Supreme Court Review* 1995 (1995): 156. In Willson, the Court upheld Delaware's construction of a dam on a navigable water, but Chief Justice Marshall noted that a law could be struck down if it was "repugnant to the power to regulate commerce in its dormant state." Thus, although the Dormant Commerce Clause idea had long been expressed in Court opinions, the first case actually striking down a state law for interfering with Congress's power in the absence of federal legislation appears to have been in the *Case of the State Freight Tax*, 82 U.S. 232 (1872). In that decision, the Court invalidated a Pennsylvania tax on all freight carried by railroads in the state, including freight that was passing through the state on the way to another state, on the ground that only Congress had the power to tax freight that was involved in interstate commerce. Earlier, in the *Passenger Cases*, 48 U.S. (7 How.) 283 (1849), the Court struck down state fees on the landing of passengers from overseas as encroaching on Congress's exclusive authority to regulate commerce with foreign nations. See Julian M. Eule, "Laying the Dormant Commerce Clause to Rest," *Yale Law Journal* 91 (1982): 429n29, citing the *Passenger Cases* as the "first case to hold state's action violative of commerce clause in absence of controlling federal enactment."

21. The Tenth Amendment provides that "the powers not delegated to the United States by the Constitution, nor prohibited by it to the States, are reserved to the States respectively, or to the people." This provision significantly undercuts the argument that the Commerce Clause, or any other provision of the Constitution, implicitly grants Congress an exclusive power. Rather, the Tenth Amendment strongly implies that exclusivity should be recognized only when it is explicit in the text of the Constitution. See also John J. Greffet Jr., Comment, "Factoring in Tradition: The Proper Role of the Traditional Governmental Function Test," *St. Louis University Law Journal* 53 (2009): 895: "a state law challenged as violative of the Dormant Commerce Clause should be accorded a presumption that the state legislature did not act outside of those powers reserved to it by the Tenth Amendment and structural principles of federalism." It has also been argued that Dormant Commerce Clause jurisprudence is inconsistent with the Ninth Amendment. See

Kurt Lash, *The Lost History of the Ninth Amendment* (Oxford: Oxford University Press, 2009), 172–177.

22. Hall v. Decuir, 95 U.S. at 490.

23. See Swift v. Tyson, 41 U.S. 1 (1842), *overruled by* Erie Railroad Co. v. Tompkins, 304 U.S. 64 (1938).

24. Hall v. Decuir, 95 U.S. at 490–491.

25. Railroad Co. v. Fuller, 84 U.S. 560 (1873).

26. 84 U.S. at 567.

27. Brief and Argument for Defendant in Error at 1, Hall v. Decuir, 95 U.S. 485 (1878), 18 [hereinafter Decuir Brief].

28. Stephenson, *The Waite Court*, 59.

29. Magrath, *Morrison R. Waite*, 101, 104, 260.

30. Hall v. Decuir, 95 U.S. at 492–494, 498 (Clifford, J. concurring in the judgment).

31. Hall v. Decuir, 95 U.S. at 497, 507 (Clifford, J. concurring in the judgment).

32. Hall v. Decuir, 95 U.S. at 499 (Clifford, J. concurring in the judgment).

33. Stephenson, *The Waite Court*, 62; Hall v. Decuir, 95 U.S. at 503–504.

34. See Nicholas R. Parrillo, *Against the Profit Motive: The Salary Revolution in American Government, 1780–1940* (New Haven, CT: Yale University Press, 2013).

35. See *Yorkville Enquirer* (York, South Carolina), January 17, 1878, 2; see also *New York Herald*, January 14, 1878; and *Chicago Tribune*, January 15, 7.

36. Brothers of Liberty, *Justice and Jurisprudence: An Inquiry Concerning the Constitutional Limitations of the Thirteenth, Fourteenth, and Fifteenth Amendments* (Philadelphia, PA: Lippincott, 1889) reprint (New York, Negro Universities Press, 1969), 240.

37. See Brothers of Liberty, *Justice and Jurisprudence*, 35, 37, 240, 394.

38. See *The Sue*, 22 F. 843, 844–45 (D. Md. 1885), citing Hall v. Decuir for the proposition that operators on boats on navigable waters are free to make reasonable rules, including separating the sleeping quarters of passengers by race. In *The Sue*, the court found in favor of the plaintiffs (known as libelants because the case was an action in admiralty), because the accommodations reserved for colored people were dirty, the mattresses were in poor condition, washing facilities were not provided, and the passageway to the cabin was obstructed by cattle, making them far from equal to those accommodations provided for Whites. See also Williams v. Carolina Coach Co., 111 F. Supp. 329 (D. Va. 1952): "It is foreclosed by binding decisions of the Supreme Court which hold that an interstate carrier has a right to establish rules and regulations which require white and colored passengers to occupy separate accommodations provided there is no discrimination in the arrangement. See Hall v. Decuir, 95 U.S. 485."

CHAPTER 10. THE COMPLETION OF THE LAW'S JOURNEY
TO "EQUAL, BUT SEPARATE"

1. United States v. Harris, 106 U.S. 629 (1883).

2. This was part of section 2 of the Civil Rights Act (Ku Klux Klan Act) of 1871, 17 Stat. 13–14, codified later at Revised Statutes § 5519.

3. United States v. Harris, 106 U.S. at 639–632.

4. See Ron Chernow, *Grant* (New York: Penguin, 2017), 708.

5. United States v. Harris, 106 U.S. at 638, 640.

6. United States v. Harris, 106 U.S. at 641.

7. United States v. Harris, 106 U.S. at 641–642.

8. United States v. Harris, 106 U.S. at 643.

9. See Bray v. Alexandria Women's Health Clinic, 506 U.S. 263 (1993). For a history of the dormancy of 42 U.S.C. § 1985(3) and its revival, see Jack M. Beermann, "The Supreme Court's Narrow View on Civil Rights," *Supreme Court Review* 1993 (1993): 212–232.

10. Civil Rights Cases, 109 U.S. 3 (1883).

11. See "An Act to protect all citizens in their civil and legal rights," also known as the Civil Rights Act of 1875, 18 Stat. 335 (1875).

12. See History, Art & Archives, "Langston, John Mercer," (biography), United States House of Representatives, accessed September 15, 2020, http://history.house.gov/People/Detail/16682?ret=True#biography; Tinsley E. Yarbrough, *Judicial Enigma: The First Justice Harlan* (Oxford: Oxford University Press, 199), 15.

13. See Eric Foner, *Freedom's Lawmakers: A Directory of Black Officeholders During Reconstruction* (Baton Rouge: Louisiana State University Press, 1993), 128.

14. See Frederick J. Blue, *Charles Sumner and the Conscience of the North* (Arlington Heights, IL: Harlan Davidson, 1994), 202–203; George Rutherglen, *Civil Rights in the Shadow of Slavery: The Constitution, Common Law, and the Civil Rights Act of 1866* (Oxford: Oxford University Press, 2013), 88.

15. See Stephen Puleo, *The Caning: The Assault that Drove America to Civil War* (Yardley, PA: Westholme, 2012).

16. David H. Donald, *Charles Sumner and the Rights of Man* (Cambridge, MA: Da Capo Press, 1996), 586–587.

17. Civil Rights Cases, 109 U.S. at 9–10.

18. Civil Rights Cases, 109 U.S. at 8.

19. Civil Rights Cases, 109 U.S. at 10. Section 2 of the Thirteenth Amendment and section 5 of the Fourteenth Amendment granted Congress power to enforce the provisions of the respective amendments "by appropriate legislation."

20. Civil Rights Cases, 109 U.S. at 13.

21. Civil Rights Cases, 109 U.S. at 14, 15.

22. Civil Rights Cases, 109 U.S. at 20 (emphasis supplied).

23. Civil Rights Cases, 109 U.S. at 20.

24. Civil Rights Cases, 109 U.S. at 22.

25. Civil Rights Cases, 109 U.S. at 24–25.

26. Plessy v. Ferguson, 109 U.S. at 25. This understanding of state law may have been true at one time, but it was soon replaced with an understanding that businesses that had traditionally been required to accept all paying customers were free to separate based on race. See Joseph William Singer, "No Right to Exclude: Public Accommodations Law and Private Property," *Northwestern University Law Review* 90 (1996): 1287–1301.

27. See Henry M. Turner, *The Barbarous Decision of the United States Supreme Court Declaring the Civil Rights Act Unconstitutional and Disrobing the Colored Race of All Civil Protection. The Most Cruel and Inhuman Verdict against a Loyal People in the History of the World Also the Powerful Speeches of Hon. Frederick Douglass and Colonel Robert G. Ingersoll, Jurist and Famous Orator* (Atlanta, GA: n.p., 1893).

28. J. Clay Smith Jr., "Justice and Jurisprudence and the Black Lawyer," *Notre Dame Law Review* 69, no. 5 (March 2014): 1099.

29. Civil Rights Cases, 109 U.S. at 35, 41. The argument that licensed businesses are state actors by virtue of their licenses was rejected by the US Supreme Court in Moose Lodge v. Irvis, 407 U.S. 163 (1972). Harlan's argument here is also a good example of the operation of the canon of construction under which statutes are construed to be constitutional whenever possible. Harlan's limitation to licensed places of public amusement does not appear in the text of the Civil Rights Act of 1875, but Harlan construed it that way in his attempt to rescue it from invalidation.

30. Paul Kens, *The Supreme Court under Morrison R. Waite, 1874–1888* (Columbia: University of South Carolina Press, 2010), 43, 60; C. Peter Magrath, *Morrison R. Waite: The Triumph of Character* (New York: Macmillan, 1963), 315.

31. See Singer, "No Right," 1354–1357; C. Vann Woodward, *The Strange Career of Jim Crow* (Oxford: Oxford University Press, 2001), 73–82.

32. See Louisville, N.O. & T. Ry. Co. v. State of Mississippi, 133 U.S. 587 (1890); Louisville, N. O. & T. Ry. Co. v. State, 6 So. 203, 203 (Miss. 1889).

33. *Louisville*, 6 So. at 204.

34. *Louisville*, 133 U.S. at 590.

35. Hall v. Decuir, 95 U.S. at 489.

36. *Louisville*, 133 U.S. at 591.

37. Plessy v. Ferguson, 163 U.S. 537 (1896).

38. Civil Rights Cases, 109 U.S. at 11.

39. Charles A. Lofgren, *The Plessy Case: A Legal-Historical Interpretation* (New York: Oxford University Press, 1987), 28.

40. See Lofgren, *The Plessy Case*, 29.

41. Rodolphe L. Desdunes, *Our People and Our History* (Baton Rouge: Louisiana State Univeristy Press, 1973), 142–143, translation of *Non Hommes et Notre Histoire*, published in 1911, Montreal, Arbour & DuPont, translated by Sister Dorothea Olga McCants.

42. See Joseph Logsdon and Caryn Cosse Bell, "The Americanization of Black New Orleans, 1850–1900," in *Creole New Orleans: Race and Americanization*, eds. Arnold R. Hirsch and Joseph Logsdon (Baton Rouge: Louisiana State University Press, 1992), 201–204; Robert J. Cottrol, *The Long Lingering Shadow: Slavery, Race, and Law in the American Hemisphere* (Athens: University of Georgia Press, 2013), 188.

43. Lofgren, *The Plessy Case*, 30.

44. Lofgren, 33, 39.

45. See Keith Weldon Medley, *We as Freemen: Plessy v. Ferguson* (Gretna, LA: Pelican, 39–49).

46. See Lofgren, *The Plessy Case*, 40; State ex rel. Abbott v. Hicks, 44 La. Ann. 770, 775 (1892).

47. Lofrgen, *The Plessy Case*, 41, 42; *Ex Parte Plessy*, 45 La. Ann. 80 (1893).

48. See Medley, *We as Freemen*, 196–197,

49. Plessy v. Ferguson, 163 U.S. at 543–44.

50. Plessy v. Ferguson, 163 U.S. at 544. See Rebecca J. Scott, "Public Rights, Social Equality, and the Conceptual Roots of the Plessy Challenge," *Michigan Law Review* 106, (2008): 777

51. Plessy v. Ferguson, 163 U.S. at 544.

52. Plessy v. Ferguson, 163 U.S. at 551.

53. Blair L. M. Kelley, *The Right to Ride: Streetcar Boycotts and African American Citizenship in the Era of Plessy v. Ferguson* (Chapel Hill: University of North Carolina Press, 2010).

54. Plessy v. Ferguson, 163 U.S. at 544.

55. Gibson v. Mississippi, 162 U.S. 565 (1896).

56. Plessy v. Ferguson, 163 U.S. at 557 (Harlan, J. dissenting).

57. Plessy v. Ferguson, 163 U.S. at 559 (Harlan, J. dissenting).

58. Plessy v. Ferguson, 163 U.S. at 552 (Harlan, J. dissenting).

59. Plessy v. Ferguson, 163 U.S. at 540.

60. McCabe v. Atchison, T. & S.F. R. Co., 235 U.S. 151, 160 (1914).

61. Plessy v. Ferguson, 163 U.S. at 554–55 (Harlan, J dissenting).

62. Day v. Atlantic Greyhound Corp., 171 F.2d 59, 60 (4th Cir. 1948): "It is foreclosed by binding decisions of the Supreme Court which hold that an interstate carrier has a right to establish rules and regulations which require white and colored passengers to occupy separate accommodations provided there is no discrimination in the arrangement. See Hall v. DeCuir, 95 U.S. 485[.]" See also Boyer v. Garrett, 88 F. Supp. 353, 354, n. 1 (D. Md. 1949); Williams v. Carolina Coach Co., 111 F. Supp. 329, 332 (E.D. Va. 1952).

63. See Giles v. Harris, 189 U.S. 475 (1903) (Holmes, J.). See also Giles v. Teasley, 193 U.S. 146 (1904).

64. See Rebecca J. Scott, *Degrees of Freedom: Louisiana and Cuba after Slavery* (Cambridge, MA: Harvard University Press, 1999), 197, discussing the litigation in State ex rel. Ryanes v. Gleason, 112 La. 612 (1904).

65. See D. E. Tobias, *Freed But Not Free: The Grievances of the Afro-American* (pamphlet) (S. H. Burroughs, 1898).

66. Michael J. Klarman, *From Jim Crow to Civil Rights: The Supreme Court and the Struggle for Racial Equality* (New York: Oxford University Press, 2004), 10; Paul Finkelman, "Civil Rights in Historical Context: In Defense of Brown," *Harvard Law Review* 118 (2005): 980–990.

67. Chernow, *Grant*, 817.

68. See, generally, Ryan A. Swanson, *When Baseball Went White: Reconstruction, Reconciliation, and Dreams of a National Pastime* (Lincoln: University of Nebraska Press, 2014), 13.

69. Swanson, *When Baseball Went White*, 185–187.

70. See, generally, Vann Woodward, *Strange Career*, 31; Michael J. Klarman, *From Jim Crow to Civil Rights: The Supreme Court and the Struggle for Racial Equality* (New York: Oxford University Press, 2004).

71. Eric Foner, *The Second Founding: How the Civil War and Reconstruction Remade the Constitution* (New York: W. W. Norton, 2019), 60–62.

72. See Vann Woodward, *Strange Career*, 23–24; Kelley, *Right to Ride*, 15–32.

73. *The Sue*, 22 F. 843, 844 (D. Md. 1885).

74. McGuinn v. Forbes, 37 F. 639, 641 (D. Md. 1889).

75. See David Abshire, *The South Rejects a Prophet: The Life of David Key* (New York: F. A. Praeger, 1967), 30–59, 66–70, 73, 82–90, 154, 208; Eric Foner, *Reconstruction: America's Unfinished Revolution 1863–1877* (New York: HarperCollins, 1988), 580–581.

76. Murphy v. Western & A. R. R., 23 F. 637, 639 (E.D. Tenn, 1885).

77. *Murphy*, 23 F. at 640, 641.

78. District of Columbia v. John R. Thompson Co. Inc., 346 U.S. 100 (1953).

79. Bolling v. Sharpe, 347 U.S. 497 (1954).

80. See Executive Order 9981 of July 26, 1948, Establishing the President's Committee on Equality of Treatment and Opportunity in the Armed Services, 13 FR 4313 (July 26, 1948).

81. See "Bronson Repeats over NAS to Win 2nd Round Title," *Gosport Newspaper* (Pensacola Naval Air Station), June 30, 1944, 3; "Funds Released for Colored Recreation Buildings at Fields," *Gosport Newspaper* (Pensacola Naval Air Station), June 23, 1944, 8.

82. See Richard Gergel, *Unexampled Courage: The Blinding of Sgt. Isaac Woodard and the Awakening of President Harry S. Truman and Judge J. Waties Waring* (New York: Farrar, Straus & Giroux, 2019).

83. See Douglas A. Massey and Nancy A. Denton, *American Apartheid: Segregation and the Making of the Underclass* (Cambridge, MA: Harvard University Press, 1993); Richard Rothstein, *The Color of Law: A Forgotten History of How Our Government Segregated America* (New York: Liveright, 2017).

84. Beryl Satter, *Family Properties: Race, Real Estate, and the Exploitation of Black Urban America* (New York: Henry Holt, 2009), 42.

85. See Sarah Schindler, "Architectural Exclusion: Discrimination and Segregation through Physical Design of the Built Environment," *Yale Law Journal* 124, no. 6 (April 2015): 1955. See also Massey and Denton, *American Apartheid*, 54.

EPILOGUE

1. Executive Order 8802: Prohibition of Discrimination in the Defense Industry, 6 Fed. Reg. 3109 (1941).

2. Morgan v. Commonwealth, 184 Va. 24, 27 (1945), *reversed* 328 U.S. 373 (1946). Much of the detail about Mrs. Morgan is drawn from Raymond O. Arsenault, *Freedom Riders* (New York: Oxford University Press, 2005), 11–12.

3. Arsenault, *Freedom Riders*, 12–13.

4. See Mark Tushnet, *The NAACP's Legal Strategy against Segregated Education, 1925–1950* (Chapel Hill: University of North Carolina Press, 1987).

5. See Michael J. Klarman, *From Jim Crow to Civil Rights* (New York: Oxford University Press, 2006), 146–152, 204–212, 217–225.

6. Brief for Appellant at 8, Morgan v. Virginia, 328 U.S. 373 (1946).

7. Brief for Appellant at 8, Morgan v. Virginia, 328 U.S. 373 (1946).

8. Morgan v. Virginia, 328 U.S. 373, 384–385 (1946).

9. Brown v. Board of Education of Topeka, 347 U.S. 483, 495 (1954).

10. Civil Rights Act of 1964, Pub. L. 88–352, 78 Stat. 241, July 2, 1964; Voting Rights Act of 1965, Pub. L. 89–110, 79 Stat. 437, August 6, 1965.

11. 102 Cong. Rec. 4515–16 (1956).

12. E. B. White, "The Ring of Time," in *Essays of E. B. White* (New York: Harper & Row, 1977).

13. See Herbert Kohl, "Rosa Parks and the Montgomery Bus Boycott Revisited," in *Should We Burn Babar*, ed. Herbert Kohl (New York: New Press, 1995); Arsenault, *Freedom Riders*, 57–80.

14. Rosa Parks and Jim Haskins, *Rosa Parks: My Story* (London: Puffin Books, 1999).

15. Browder v. Gayle, 142 F. Supp. 717 (M.D. Ala. 1956), *affirmed* 352 U.S. 903 (1956).

16. See Derrick A. Bell, *Race, Racism, and American Law*, 5th ed. (New York: Aspen, 2004), 225n7.

17. National Advisory Commission on Civil Disorders, *The Kerner Report: The 1968 Report of the National Advisory Commission on Civil Disorders* (New York: Pantheon, 1988), 1.

APPENDIX: THE COMMERCE CLAUSE

1. Chris DeRose, *Founding Rivals: Madison vs. Monroe, The Bill of Rights, and The Election that Saved a Nation* (Washington, DC: Regnery History, 2013).

2. The proposal, submitted by a committee to the convention, was as follows:

Art. 14. The United States in Congress Assembled shall have the sole and exclusive power of regulating the trade of the States as well with foreign Nations as with each other and of laying such prohibitions and such Imposts and duties upon imports and exports as may be Necessary for the purpose; provided the Citizens of the States shall in no instance be subjected to pay higher duties and Imposts that those imposed on the subjects of foreign powers, provided also, that all such duties as may be imposed shall be collected under such regulations as the united States in Congress Assembled shall establish consistent with the Constitutions of the States Respectively and to accrue to the use of the State in which the same shall be payable; provided also, that the Legislative power of the several States shall not be restrained from laying embargoes in time of Scarcity and provided lastly that every Act of Congress for the above purpose shall have the assent of Nine States in Congress Assembled, and in that proportion when there shall be more than thirteen in the Union.

Journals of the Continental Congress, 1774–1789, ed. Worthington C. Ford et al., 34 vols. (Washington, DC: Government Printing Office, 1904–1937), 31:494–495. See also Michael J. Klarman, *The Framers' Coup: The Making of the United States Constitution* (New York: Oxford University Press, 2016), 151–152.

3. U.S. Const., art I, § 8. See also E. Parmalee Prentice and John G. Egan, *The Commerce Clause of the Federal Constitution* (Chicago: Gallaghan, 1898; reprinted by Fred Rothman, 1981), 2–9.

4. See United States v. Morrison, 529 U.S. 598 (2000); United States v. Lopez, 514 U.S. 549 (1995); Printz v. United States, 521 U.S. 898 (1997); New York v. United States, 505 U.S. 144 (1992).

5. Gibbons v. Ogden, 22 U.S. 1, 87 (1824).

6. Gibbons v. Ogden, 22 U.S. at 89 (Johnson, J. concurring).

7. See Herbert A. Johnson, *Gibbons v. Ogden: John Marshall, Steamboats and the Commerce Clause* (Lawrence, KS: University Press of Kansas, 2011), 118–120, 127–128.

8. See Willson v. Black Bird Creek Marsh Co., 27 U.S. 245, 252 (1829), discussed in Lawrence Lessig, "Translating Federalism: United States v. Lopez," *Supreme Court Review* 1995 (1995): 156.

9. See Cooley v. Board of Wardens, 53 U.S. 299 (1851).

10. *Cooley*, 53 U.S. at 299.

11. *Cooley*, 53 U.S. at 319, 320.

12. *Case of the State Freight Tax*, 82 U.S. 232 (1872). Earlier, in the *Passenger Cases*, 48 U.S. (7 How.) 283 (1849), the Court had struck down state fees on the landing of overseas passengers as encroaching on Congress's exclusive authority to regulate commerce with foreign nations. See Julian M. Eule, "Laying the Dormant Commerce Clause to Rest," *Yale Law Journal* 91, no. 3 (January 1982): 429n29, citing the *Passenger Cases* as the "first case to hold state's action violative of commerce clause in absence of controlling federal enactment."

13. See Ward v. State, 79 U.S. 418 (1870).

14. *Ward*, 79 U.S. at 432–444 (Bradley, J. concurring).

15. See Welton v. Missouri, 91 U.S. 275, 281, 282, 283 (1875).

16. Welton v. Missouri, 91 U.S. at 282.

17. E.g. Wabash, St. Louis & Pacific Ry. Co. v. Illinois, 118 U.S. 557, 585–89 (1886).

18. See Frederick Cooke, *The Commerce Clause of the Federal Constitution* (New York: Baker, 1908; reprinted by Fred Rothman, 1987), 231, n. 89; Richard Kluger, *Simple Justice: The History of Brown v. Board of Education and Black America's Struggle for Equality* (New York: Vantage Books, 1975), 73.

19. Compare U.S. Const. art. I § 8 with art. I § 9.

20. See Prentice and Egan, *The Commerce Clause*, 10–12; See Cooke, *The Commerce Clause*, 109–125.

21. Camps Newfound/Owatonna v. Town of Harrison, 520 U.S. 564, 619 (1997) (Thomas, J. dissenting). Justice Thomas also stated that "the negative Commerce Clause has no basis in the text of the Constitution, makes little sense, and has proved virtually unworkable in application." See *Camps Newfound* at 610. Justice Antonin

Scalia, also a critic of Dormant Commerce Clause doctrine, sounded many of the themes discussed here in his opinions. See, e.g., Tyler Pipe Indus. v. Washington State Dept. of Revenue, 483 U.S. 232, 260–265 (1987) (Scalia, J. dissenting).

22. See Michael Greve, *The Constitution: Understanding America's Founding Document* (Washington, DC: American Enterprise Institute, 2013).

23. See Stephen Breyer, *Making Our Democracy Work: A Judge's View* (New York: Vintage Books, 2010), 129–130.

24. Quill Corp. v. North Dakota, 504 U.S. 298, 318 (1992).

25. See South Dakota v. Wayfair, Inc., 138 S. Ct. 2080 (2018).